SUBURBAN BEIJING

SUBURBAN BEIJING

Housing and Consumption in
Contemporary China

FRIEDERIKE FLEISCHER

University of Minnesota Press
Minneapolis
London

Portions of this book were previously published as "'To Choose a House Means to Choose a Lifestyle': The Consumption of Housing and Class-Structuration in Urban China," *City and Society* 19, no. 2 (2007): 287–311; "Settling into Uncertainty: Migrants in Beijing's Suburban Transformations," Max Planck Institute for Social Anthropology Working Paper 96 (2007); and "Speaking Bitter-Sweetness: China's Urban Elderly in the Reform Period," *Asian Anthropology* 5 (2006): 31–55 (reprinted with permission of the editors of *Asian Anthropology,* Tan Chee-Beng and Gordon Mathews).

Photographs in the book were taken by the author; copyright Friederike Fleischer.

Published by the University of Minnesota Press
111 Third Avenue South, Suite 290
Minneapolis, MN 55401-2520
http://www.upress.umn.edu

Library of Congress Cataloging-in-Publication Data

Fleischer, Friederike.
   Suburban Beijing : housing and consumption in contemporary China / Friederike Fleischer.
       p. cm.
   Includes bibliographical references and index.
   ISBN 978-0-8166-4596-1 (hc : alk. paper) — ISBN 978-0-8166-6587-7 (pb : alk. paper)
   1. Suburban life—China—Beijing—Wangjing. 2. Wangjing (Beijing, China)—Social conditions. 3. Wangjing (Beijing, China)—Economic conditions. 4. Wangjing (Beijing, China)—History. I. Title.
   HT352.C552W364 2010
   307.740951'156—dc22

                                    2010032181

To my parents,
Rosemarie and Klaus (in memoriam)

CONTENTS

INTRODUCTION

Transforming Suburban Life in China

CLOUDS OF DUST HUNG IN THE STILL AUGUST AIR. A maze of cranes, towering over rows and rows of half-finished apartment complexes, swung ceaselessly back and forth, each like a conductor's wand over an orchestra. The music, however, was a cacophony of jack-hammering, screeching, drilling, and the monotonous grind of cement mixers, accompanied by the rumble of sand- and gravel-loaded trucks that thundered by on the newly paved, yet unmarked, four-lane road. Sweating under the blistering sun, a group of tanned construction workers, chatting in regional dialects, gathered around a small food stall propped up on the narrow strip of dirt beside the pavement. Behind it ran an open canal that, buried in garbage, suffocated the surroundings with its penetrating stench. On the other side of the road, a bulldozer was relentlessly knocking down one small house after the other, while a group of poorly dressed men and women picked up the bricks, cleaned them, and stacked them on horse carts that were waiting in a line. A few red-cheeked children stood by and stared. Not far behind rose the tall fence of a recently finished, expensive-looking residential neighborhood. The elegantly designed apartment towers, with lush and ample greenery surrounding a fountain and goldfish pond, were guarded by security staff that stopped cars and pedestrians at the entrance gate and inquired about the purpose of their visit.

This was the scene when I visited Wangjing, a new suburban de-velopment zone in Beijing's northeast, during the summer of 2000. Planted on practically empty fields, Wangjing lies adjacent to a devel-opment zone for electronics factories that was established in the 1950s in the rural hinterland of the Chinese capital. In the 1990s, the locale became one of Beijing's hotspots for new residential and commercial development. As an urban special economic zone and due to its close proximity to the capital's airport, the locale quickly attracted large foreign companies to set up shop; soon after, developers began constructing new housing complexes. The municipal government, in fact, envisions the roughly fourteen-square-kilometer Wangjing suburban zone to become the largest residential and commercial development area in all Asia, home to around 250,000 people by the end of this decade. While the suburb covers only about 3 percent of the city's total area, in 1999 it bustled with about 13 percent of that year's housing construction in the capital (*China Daily* 1999).

In recent years, Wangjing has become especially popular among young, affluent Chinese who cited, for example, the environment or the proximity and convenient traffic connections to the Central Business District (CBD) in Beijing's east as selling points. Most often, however, when I asked the affluent residents why they had chosen to move to Wangjing I received the answer: "The west is where the intellectuals live, the east is for the aristocrats, the south is where the poor live, but the wealthy live in the north." This was a liberal interpretation of the old saying about the capital's cosmologically inspired city structure in imperial times, *dong fu xi gui,* which means "the elite lives in the west, the wealthy in the east."[1] Affluent suburbanites adapted a proverb from imperial times to explain their reform-period residential choice. They connected today's economic boom and its social and spatial effects to the imperial past, but skipped the entire Maoist period in their subjective positioning. As members of the new middle class they claimed a "natural," that is, historically grown, right to the suburban space. In their imagery, no reference existed either to Wangjing's industrial antecedents or to the other people who lived by their side: residents of the remaining Soviet-style complexes built by state-owned factories and migrants from the countryside who try to get a share of Beijing's new wealth.

Thirty years of reforms have dramatically transformed Chinese people's lives. The privatization of collective resources, the opening of the country to foreign investments, and the availability of vast amounts of cheap labor have generated unprecedented economic growth with double-digit annual GDP growth rates over more than two decades. Political and legal reforms have changed administrative procedures, responsibilities, and lines of authority. The economic, political, and ideological changes have also affected social relationships and social hierarchies. Today, China's previously relatively homogeneous urban society is marked by growing socioeconomic stratification as well as residential differentiation. With its mix of residents and their diverging claims to space, suburban Wangjing epitomizes the contrasts and contradictions that arise from China's transformation process. The suburb highlights the effects of China's "marketization," its transformation from state socialism to a socialist market economy that is entangled in global processes. Chinese city centers are under the extreme scrutiny of the regime's official modernization effort that allows only for high-tech development intended to attract foreign investment and tourists and to project a representative image of China to the world (Zhang L. 2001). The expanding edges of the built-up space, in contrast, are dynamic zones where the reconfiguration of space with all its conflicting characteristics becomes apparent. It is here, in this vibrant suburban realm, where the emerging socioeconomic differentiations of reform-period China visibly play out, where the diverging interests of the various "players" who take part in the reconfiguration of space meet and, at times, clash. In fact, as I argue in this book, the suburban space underlines and enforces growing socioeconomic stratifications that mark reform-period Chinese society.

The Production of Space

This book is an ethnographic study of a suburb in the making. Drawing on scholarly debates among cultural geographers (e.g., Harvey 1989, 1990; Massey 1994; Soja 1989), and especially the work of Henri Lefebvre (1991), my premise here is that space comprises physical, mental, and social dimensions. Moreover, space is not a neutral background or empty "container," but is constituted through concrete human practices and power relations and, in turn, shapes social and political processes. Thus, tracing the social and spatial processes and transformations in Wangjing, in this study I explore how the suburban space is produced and examine people's role as social agents in the process. The analysis focuses on the experiences of three main groups of suburban residents—affluent professionals, residents of old state-owned complexes, and migrant entrepreneurs—to draw an intimate picture of how Chinese people deal with the social, economic, and spatial transformations of recent years, and what they think about them.

Looking at Wangjing's economic and social transformations on the basis of these three groups is unquestionably a simplification of matters; social differentiations among the population are certainly more complex. Nonetheless, presenting different age groups, educational backgrounds, and trajectories that connect personal pasts and futures, these people reflect the situation of many others in Beijing today. More generally, the three groups hold distinct social positions in today's society and embody larger realities about current urban transformation processes in China.[2] Neither residents of old state-owned complexes nor migrants, for example, are in the position to claim the suburban space in the same way the newly affluent do. State-factory workers are part of the static centralized distributional system that China aspires to leave behind; and migrants, with only temporary residence rights in the city, are considered a serious social problem by officials and urban residents alike. Nevertheless, as I will show in this study, both groups are importantly connected to the suburban space; both affect its constitution and are deeply involved in the realities of everyday suburban life. The disparate group of newly affluent, on the other hand, appears to increasingly shape its status around a new set of collective interests. Foremost among these are their modes of consumption and privileged access to resources, domains that overlap in the affluents' consumption of suburban housing. Yet, their privileged position in today's society, and their claim on and perceived entitlement to the suburban realm, can only be understood in relation to the other groups who live in the suburb and within the context of China's larger historical transformation process.

The comparison of the three groups thus dramatically highlights their growing differentiation and draws attention to the way China's urban population today is being socially, economically, and spatially stratified. Segments of society are differently affected by and involved in the socioeconomic changes. As a result, the suburban space is not only differently experienced by diverse groups but can take on different meanings for them. In addition, urban residents have developed distinguishing values and behaviors. Lifestyle and location of residence have become markers of social class and status but also reflect back on citizens' power in the negotiation of space—a phenomenon new to China. Both the market and the state are important forces behind this social and spatial structuration process, yet people's practices and subjective experiences, which are highlighted here, importantly impinge on it. Hence, by examining the three groups together, I draw attention to the interplay of the various agents who produce and negotiate the suburban space in everyday practices and discourses. As will become apparent, Wangjing is the result of the complicated and long-term negotiations between the state project of modernization,[3] the market, and people over space and social organization.

A Suburb in the Making

To get a better sense of the complex suburban makeup, let us return to Wangjing. In the summer of 2001 when I began my research, the suburb was bustling with massive construction. On some days one suffocated from the clouds of dust that hung over the ever new rising complexes. Wangjing seemed to be "alive" in that it constantly changed: a row of one-story shops disappeared from one day to the next, a market hall was razed overnight, and new fences were put up around yet another construction site. Throughout the fourteen months of my study, I experienced the destruction of five areas of small shops and brick houses, the razing of two outside markets, and the rise of about seven new apartment complexes, as well as two supermarkets, which, both in style and in price, clearly aimed at a wealthier clientele (Figures 1 and 2). The future dimension of the zone could be seen by the pattern of roads, half of which led only into

Figure 1. While I was conducting research in China in 2001, many new residential complexes rose throughout Wangjing.

Figure 2. The few new supermarkets in Wangjing were all targeted at affluent residents. [2001]

empty fields for the time being. At the very edge of this planned zone, however, the production facilities of several multinational companies had already been built, as well as the campus of an as yet uninaugurated gigantic new high school.

East of Wangjing, separated by the elevated six-lane Capital Airport Highway that traverses the suburban fringe diagonally, lies the older industrial zone Jiuxianqiao. At the time, the roads here were narrower and the built-up area denser. There existed still a number of old residential compounds, built after the 1950s and home to employees of state-owned companies in the area. Many of these compounds were dominated by a retired population since the younger generation chose, or was forced, to move into commercial housing. Nonetheless, depending on the commercial success of the company during the reform period, some of the state-owned compounds have been improved, and a number of new ones have been built.

On the western side of the Capital Airport Highway, in contrast, new development had started on practically empty land. A couple of dilapidated state-owned compounds were surrounded by generously wide roads, and gated apartment complexes with tight security invaded the fields. Some of the streets toward Jiuxianqiao were still lined by one-story makeshift buildings that had sprung up during the reform period and that housed venues of all sorts: occasional book and clothing stores, various bakeries, telecommunications offices, one or two banks, and a wide array of restaurants, from fast food to specialty locales. But these structures were disappearing one after another.

The new residential compounds that dominated Wangjing varied in quality and price, but were all in the upper-middle to higher price category and therefore out of reach for most Chinese people. The more expensive these complexes were, the more distinctive design features and extravagant names they had. One of the most upscale finished developments in the area at the time was Atlantic Place, where apartments had initially sold for a minimum of 5,500 yuan (US$733) per square meter.[4] By the end of my research, it was about to be superseded and overtaken in price by several projected new complexes that had set up sales offices in the Wangjing neighborhood. Residents of these new commercial compounds are mostly nuclear families, typically young couples with one or no child and sometimes retired parents. They generally belong to the new class of "chuppies"—Chinese urban professionals employed in skilled positions, in the public or private sector, and in international ventures.

Scattered throughout the area were leftover islands of the one-floor, brown brick *pingfang* (single-story) houses that had been typical of the countryside. These were usually composed of only one room and had outside kitchenettes and no private bathrooms. Huddled together, and accessible only through a labyrinth of small dirt paths, these used to be the houses of the agricultural population. Now migrants to the city found temporary accommodation in them. The areas were often in unsanitary conditions; as they were bound to be torn down in the near future, the city seemed to have given up on the provision of services such as garbage collection, for example. Around several of these islands of pingfang houses were in- and outside markets where the migrants and low-income urban residents bought and sold everything they needed for life: clothes, fresh produce, fruit, herbs, books, household wares, electrical appliances, and so forth. Products were generally cheap and low quality.

A bus ride on one of the diagonally outspreading roads, behind the recently finished northern part of the Fifth Ring Road, brings one to the countryside, where small villages were strewn along the route. This was where many of the workers—waitresses and cooks in restaurants, and the salespeople from the cheap markets who did not have a Beijing residence permit *(hukou)*—receded while the city grew. Here they found accommodation when the pingfang houses were razed. At the same time, the original population, who in the past used to be farmers, today usually commutes to work in the city.

Emerging from this description we can see various "players" or groups of people, institutions, and factors involved in the production of Wangjing suburban space: a younger, affluent, and generally well-educated generation who lives in new exclusive residential complexes; residents of old state-owned and new low-level compounds; and diverse groups of migrants who work or settle in the neighborhood. Significant influence on this space, however, is also exerted by the national and local government and by the market, which is represented in part by real estate companies and investors. Yet, in the analysis of the different factors that contribute to the weaving of the suburban fabric, one also has to take into account novel aspirations, as well as ideologies of consumption and modernity. In addition, the sociospatial transformation processes do not happen on "a blank sheet of paper" but are influenced by history, changing conceptions of city planning, and the politics of the prereform era. Thus, these are the layers we have to consider in the examination of present-day urban reconfigurations of space and society.

Social Stratification: Class, Culture, and Space

Examining social, economic, and spatial differentiation processes in urban China, this study must be situated within larger scholarly debates about social stratification or class "structuration" (Giddens 1973). Indeed, among the most conspicuous changes in China since the beginning of the reform period is the socioeconomic stratification of society. During the Maoist era, society was far from being the socialist ideal of equality; it was divided by rural or urban residence status, access to power, and *guanxi* (personal networks), among other things.[5] Today, however, it is economic disparities that gain ever more significance (see Bian et al. 2005; Feng W. 2003). Deng Xiaoping's 1979 plan to create a "well-off society" *(xiaokang shehui)*[6] by allowing some people to "get rich first" *(xian fuqilai)* did not so much accept emerging socioeconomic differentiations as an inevitable by-product of economic development as it endorsed them as a motor of transformation. Successive reform policies have exacerbated and engraved this calculated social revolution that is diametrically opposed to the Communist ideal of equality.[7] Yet, while there is little doubt that Chinese society is becoming socioeconomically stratified, social groups still appear somewhat amorphous and lacking the cohesiveness required by the traditional definitions of class. Thus arises the question of how to conceptualize the ongoing stratification process (e.g., Li, Yang, and Wang 1991; Yan Z. 2002).[8]

During the Mao period, class *(jieji)* was a highly politicized concept. Ideological categories such as "capitalists," "proletarians," or "the working class" were associated with the often-times atrocious class struggle that painfully affected many people.[9] It is therefore not surprising, as Zhang Li (2004) points out, that even today Chinese remain reluctant to talk about social stratification and inequality in terms of class. Instead, it is the less ideologically loaded term *jieceng,* stratum, that is used to speak about the complex and confusing socioeconomic differentiations that have emerged in the reform period. This Chinese distinction between class and stratum somewhat mirrors the apparently opposing conceptualizations of class long prevalent in scholarly debates. Marxist approaches consider class as economically grounded conflictual relations that determine everything else. The Weberian tradition, in contrast, distinguishes between class stratification and differentiations of culturally defined status groups. At the same time, both "traditions" have proponents who argue for either more objectively or more subjectively defined classes (Hanser 2008, 4–5).

More and more research, however, suggests that these contrasting conceptualizations are not as clearly distinguishable as suggested. E. P. Thompson's *The Making of the English Working Class* remains one of the most inspiring contributions to the study of class formation that bridges such divides. Thompson understands class not as a structure or category, but as a historical *process* that "happens (and can be shown to happen) in human relationships" (1966, 8). Sociologists Anthony Giddens (1973) and Pierre Bourdieu (1990) similarly draw attention to the processual and relational character of stratification. Recently, various studies (e.g., Hanser 2008; Liechty 2003; Patico 2008; Yanagisako 2002) have further supported the assertion that the economic and cultural dimensions of stratification processes cannot be meaningfully distinguished. It is suggested that economy and culture are not static or stable structures but *practices* carried out in everyday life. Moreover, Thompson (1966), Giddens (1973), Bourdieu (1990), and others (e.g., Zhang L. 2004) argue that class is a social and cultural formation that arises not only in and through relations of production, but equally in the spheres of community, family, and consumption. Thus, for Bourdieu (1990) class involves both objective and subjective factors and results from negotiations between economy and culture. Class identities and practices therefore emerge out of both economic resources and cultural orientations (Hanser 2008, 5).

The conception of class formation as a processual and relational process that is informed by both economy and culture is especially relevant for the analysis of socioeconomic differentiations in China with its mix of state and market economy where people work several jobs in different sectors. Here class is far from definite; instead stratification is an ongoing process of differentiation in and through various domains. Emphasizing the importance of community, for example, the above studies draw our attention to the spatial dimension of social stratification and class formation processes. As Lefebvre (1991) suggested, social relationships and people's conceptions of the world are shaped by and inscribed in spatial organization; space reflects or sustains inequalities of class.[10] Mike Davis (1990) applies this insight in his study of Los Angeles. He convincingly demonstrates how spatial organization is loaded with sociopolitical meanings and that it plays a prominent role in the structuring of class relations and class consciousness. In fact, architectural styles and the spatial layout of buildings, streets, and public spaces help maintain power relations and social domination.[11] Soja (1989), however, also points to the reverse effect, namely that space and the political organization of space not only express social relationships but in turn also shape them.

This interlinking of space with stratification processes highlights the continued importance of existing spatial distinctions, and the growing significance of new sociospatial stratifications in China. One of the most profound distinctions remains, after all, the one between urban and rural residents as realized through the household registration system *(hukou zhidu)*. While rural-to-urban migrants today can obtain temporary residence permits, and some of them have prospered in the city, they remain excluded from the privileged spaces of urban residency, be it equal access to housing, education, or job opportunities.[12] They are pushed out to the social and geographical fringes of city life. Zhang Li (2002, 313) accordingly speaks of urban citizenship as "the site of an enduring spatial politics whose terms have been set by the hukou system, which divides national space into two hierarchically ordered parts: the city and the countryside."

Yet, even among urban residents social and spatial stratification processes merge when the inner city is redeveloped and residents relocated to far out of the city locations. In a similar move, the former industrial zone Jiuxianqiao in Beijing's northeast is now transformed into the larger middle-class suburb Wangjing. How do these dislocations affect residents? What is the effect of growing "zones of affluence" (Hu and Kaplan 2001), of the new residential compounds in which people with similar economic means are grouped together? Will shared space and interaction affect residents' identifications? As we will see in this study, residential compounds in specific suburban locations have become important markers of status and a means of distinction. The emergence of Wangjing can thus only be understood as an *integral* aspect of ongoing stratification processes, that is, as a constituting element of the socioeconomic (re)structuration of urban society.

At the same time, however, the position that the built environment is a form of domination, that it contributes to the maintenance of power through the control of movement and surveillance of bodies in space, neglects the lived experience of the individual. It also ignores the resistance of individuals and groups to architectural forms of social control (see Low 1996).[13] Against this one-sided approach, de Certeau argues in *The Practice of Everyday Life* that people reappropriate space through their "ways of operating." These are practices of everyday life that involve clandestine "tactics" by groups or individuals who are "already caught in the nets of 'discipline'" (1984, xiv–xv). Tracing out the operations of walking, naming, narrating, and remembering the city, de Certeau develops a theory of lived space in which spatial practices escape the discipline of urban planning. Reminiscent of Walter Benjamin's flaneur, de Certeau suggests that through the act of walking the pedestrian acts out place; she creates and represents public space rather than being subjected to it. This, then, is the other side in the production of space that we have to take into account when examining suburban Wangjing: the way people use and appropriate the area, their practice of living the suburban space. Wangjing residents' subjective experiences might be structured and influenced by the space they live in, but at the same time the suburb is shaped—produced— by residents' everyday life practices.[14]

Social Stratification through Consumption

Besides relations of production and the community, both Thompson and Giddens highlighted the importance of consumption in social stratification processes. Indeed, various studies have shown how consumption—both as ideology and as practice—is a key domain through which status groups are delineated and negotiated (e.g., Bourdieu

1984; D. Davis 2000; Douglas and Isherwood 1979; Liechty 2003; Miller 1998; Patico 2008; Shevchenko 2002). Bourdieu (1984), for example, argues that a close study of domestic investments can identify social boundaries and hierarchies.[15] Shevchenko (2002), in turn, suggests that the field of consumption lies on the intersection between the personal (identity, conveniences, self-expression) and the political (market, production, price policy). It translates political and economic processes into immediately understandable and consequential trends experienced by every Chinese household. Consumption and consumer behavior are evidently important areas of investigation of socioeconomic differentiations.

In China, this appears especially relevant. The increase of consumer spending, after all, has been one of the key efforts of the regime since the 1990s. With the intention to both balance the country's export-oriented economy and to create a growing middle class that will guarantee political and social stability, salaries were raised and holidays extended so that people could spend on tourism, higher education, and cars, as well as on financial and insurance services. Consumption has in fact become a *telos,* an almost "moral imperative," in present-day China that is imbued with notions of modernity (see below).[16] A telling example of this development is the products a man is expected to offer a woman in a good marriage match: in the 1970s it was bicycles and sewing machines; in the 1980s and early 1990s it was a TV and a refrigerator that were perceived as status symbols. With the new millennium, however, these were replaced by a car and a home (Carmel 2001; Ye J. 2002a).

The reforms have brought Chinese citizens into close contact with transnational capitalist goods, ideas, and practices. These have triggered a consumerism that profoundly changes relationships and self-identities (Chen et al. 2001). "What comes into being," writes Mayfair Yang, "is a culture of desiring, consuming individuals yearning to be fulfilled" (1997, 303). Yet, evidently not everybody is able to engage in conspicuous consumption. Whereas newly wealthy Chinese travel and consume internationally, many other citizens suffer from the rising costs of living, including education and health care as well as the purchase of the most basic nationally produced goods. At the same time, at least for the older generation, the new consumer ideology is also a radical departure from the anticonsumption, antibourgeois socialist ideology of the Maoist period during which they grew up. For them the lived experience of daily life today is marked by what Bourdieu (1977) terms the "hysteresis of habitus," that is, the lack of fit between the social conditions for which an individual was socialized and the social conditions of the moment. Older Chinese thus have to somehow come to terms with the emerging market economy and reestablish their subjective identities. Yet, as Zhang Li demonstrates for the Wenzhou migrants she studies, consumption can also be a means to claim belonging. While they are denied formal urban citizenship, migrants "seek alternative ways of reinforcing their presence in the city by participating in urban social and economic life" (2001, 45). In Wangjing, in contrast, migrants from the countryside had the least financial means to participate in today's consumer culture. Instead, they commonly engaged in a kind of indirect spending, not on themselves but on their child. They deferred their own comfort and aspirations for the sake of their children on whom their hopes for the future were built.

As we can see, consumption power and practices have become crucial differentiating factors among China's population. Moreover, while many objects have a practical value, in many ways their significance is linked to the status they symbolize. Objects are not only consumed to satisfy simple needs, but also to gain status, which is possible because of their differential relationship with other objects. In a fully developed consumer society, objects become signs of status, while the aspect of necessity is secondary. Consumption thus does not homogenize, but, on the contrary, it differentiates through the "sign system of objects" (Kellner 1994, 92). Not only economic needs, but lifestyle and values are the basis of social life (Lechte 1994).

Nonetheless, consumption is often seen as a mere passive act, where agency and creativity are located only in the act of production: the consumer appears to be a "mindless creature" who follows the lure of the object, and consumption is merely the recognition or misrecognition of the aesthetic intention. From a different perspective, however, consumption can be understood as a symbolic act of creativity. As Storey (1993, 121) puts it, "Commercially provided culture . . . is redefined, reshaped and redirected in strategic acts of selective consumption and productive acts of reading and articulation, often in ways not intended or even foreseen by its producers."[17] Developing his theory of shopping, Miller (1998), on the other hand, suggests that consumption should be understood as a social process that is born from and relates to specific social relations and historical moments. Consumption is a social act and a meaningful practice.

These two positions are not necessarily mutually exclusive. On the contrary, in the context of China's urban transformations, status-producing, creative consumption practices are in fact a vital element of the ongoing stratification processes and, by extension, a crucial dimension of the production of space. After all, consumption is, as Sack (1992) has argued, a place-creating and place-altering act. Indeed, within the limited social, economic, and physical space that has emerged from the state withdrawal in everyday life affairs,[18] Chinese people have become not only discerning consumers, but agents who make deliberate choices. They design their own lives, carve out individual niches, and create new identities. Among their choices is where and how they want to live. These decisions transmit specific messages. As we will see in this study, especially for the newly affluent, residential compounds have become the basis for identity and lifestyle formation. They use these to distinguish themselves from others, thereby underlining and reinforcing the growing disparities in Chinese society. In effect, the consumption of suburban housing has turned into a marker of difference, an indicator of the new class "structuration" in reform-period China. Consumption behavior thus plays a crucial role in the reconfigurations of social space in present-day urban China.[19]

Discursive Politics

In the context of social stratification processes and more generally the production of space, discourses and ideologies propagated in the mass media also become important. Social inequalities in China, Hanser (2008) observes, are increasingly understood through a discourse that portrays the rise of the market and market value as both positive and inevitable. Wealth, consumer power, and monetary value are now translated into indicators of modernity. Similarly Jeffrey (2001, 25) comments: "Whereas Maoism equated capitalism with immorality, today we find a discourse (both official and popular) of the market as a civilizing practice that implies and confers proximity to the modern." Socialism, in contrast, is depicted as a tarnished element of the past. People and organizations associated with state socialism and the planned economy are considered as tainted, as lagging behind the nation's march to modernity. This applies to workers of old state factories as well as to peasants and the countryside. Their "backwardness" *(luohou),* that is, their perceived distance from the present, is translated into a lack of worth in the new market economy (Chen et al. 2001; Hanser 2008).

This backwardness is also commonly associated with incivility and low "quality" *(suzhi).* As Anagnost (1997) notes, the readying of the Chinese population for participation in global capitalism has taken place through a state-initiated civilizing process aimed at remaking subjectivities into those appropriate for a disciplined, efficient workforce. As a result, in official and urban residents' discourse migrants, for example, are presented as a homogeneous, inferior group that needs to be civilized and transformed by higher moral codes set by permanent urban residents (Cohen 1993; Hanser 2008; Zhang L. 2001). But questions of "civilization" also affect the registered urban population when municipal government campaigns target residents' public behavior with new rules and regulations. Men taking off their shirts in the blistering summer heat of the city, people strolling at night through the old narrow alleys in their pajamas, or elderly men taking ice baths in the city lakes—all of these are customs that have been criticized or even forbidden as "unmodern" behaviors. During the civilizing campaign that preceded the 2008 Olympic Games in Beijing, the drive to produce a modernist aesthetics intensified. "Modernity" thus has become the new government legitimation for public surveillance and control.

Feeding into the new ideology of modernity and the modernist aesthetics are environmental concerns for "green space" *(lüdi, lühua)* and "clean air" *(kongqi, qingkong).* Associated with a worldly, civilized lifestyle, these are increasingly important discursive keywords that in many ways influence new middle- and upper-class urban residents' residential choices. In turn, they are employed by real estate companies and advertising agencies to promote consumption of commercial housing. Intensifying this trend are public and indeed academic discussions of the appropriate lifestyle for the different, emerging socioeconomic groups. Especially since the late 1990s, the "middle class" has become the new normative model of citizenship; the emblem of modern Chineseness now is the person with high cultural capital ("good quality") and the power to consume. This is also a distinctly national project: for many Chinese it is the emergence of a middle class that signifies membership in the developed world. More importantly, however, as Anagnost (2008) concludes, the self-responsible, entrepreneurial, and consuming subject is also at the base of a new mode of govern-ment.[20] This is what I call the "citizenship of consumption."[21]

The discourse of migrants and the urban working class as back-ward, as less modern, indeed less "civilized," than the "modern middle class" shapes ongoing stratification processes in urban China. Besides the growing socioeconomic stratifications of society, discourses them-selves create new boundaries and enclosures that underline physical differentiations. This discourse, however, remains not uncontested. While socialism always appropriated language for the state project, because of this politicization of language both informal and nonverbal communications also become important forms of resistance (Kaneff 2002; Verdery 1991; see also Modan 2006). Indeed, as we will see, old suburban state employees discursively position themselves "outside" of today's consumer ideology and thus revalue their marginal social (and geographical) position. Migrants in the suburban markets, on the other hand, apparently accepted their alleged lower "quality" as rural citizens, yet countered this disparagement by emphasizing their hon-esty and moral integrity as salespeople.

In light of the power and importance of language, in both legitimiz-ing state discourse and forming a socialist subjectivity, and also as a form of resistance, it is thus pertinent to examine how Chinese people themselves reflect upon the changes. Analyzing the discourses and ideologies connected to and behind present-day urban transforma-tions, this book shows how newly produced (sub)urban space is differ-ently experienced and represented by diverging groups of people. As Flyvbjerg and Richardson (1998, 9–10; cited in Richardson and Jensen 2003, 7) conclude:

> Spaces, then, may be constructed in different ways by different people, through power struggles and conflicts of interest. This idea that spaces are socially constructed, and that many spaces may co-exist within the same physical space is an important one. It suggests the need to analyze how dis-courses and strategies of inclusion and exclusion are connected with partic-ular spaces.

Urban Transformations and Suburbanization

Before the Chinese government initiated its economic reform program, urban development was highly controlled by the central government and led by ideology rather than market forces. Socialist planning aspired to turn cities into productive entities and created industrial and agricultural zones inside urban areas. In addition, city districts were planned to be self-sufficient. The system of household registration kept people in their native places; migration was virtually non-existent.[22] In effect, cities and the countryside were divided "as clearly as a moated city wall" (D. Davis 1995, 2). Similarly, within cities, state-assigned work and housing more or less eradicated residential mobility. Most urban Chinese spent their lives within the gated compounds of state-run work-units *(danwei)* that provided the necessities of daily life. Working, shopping, dealing with social services and institutions, and taking care of children and elders—all this was organized within the limited spatial orbit of the danwei.

Since 1978, a significant departure has been made from the Maoist economic system toward a socialist market economy, or market economy with Chinese characteristics. The reforms have dramatically transformed urban areas. The number of cities in China multiplied from two hundred in the late 1970s to seven hundred today,[23] and the formally registered urban population increased from 191 million in 1980 to nearly 540 million in 2004 (ChinaToday.com 2007; Worldwatch Institute 2006).[24] Between 1990 and 1995, the growth rate of urban land area was more than four times faster than that of the urban population (Zhang T. 2000), and between 1980 and 2004, nearly 113,916 square kilometers of agricultural land were lost to development (Campanella 2008). At the same time, changes in the political economy have altered the lines of authority and the flow of resources between the central government and the municipalities. Cities have become more autonomous in terms of political economy, hierarchical structures, and authority over resource allocation, as well as more embedded in their immediate locale. Decentralization and greater reliance on market mechanisms have, in turn, decisively changed Chinese cities' environments. The uniform, gray horizons of the 1960s and 1970s have been taken over by signs of capitalist enterprises that color the cityscape today: the ubiquitous yellow arches of McDonald's fast-food restaurants compete with the red and white of *kekou kele* (Coca-Cola) advertisements and the bright yellow signs of the Kodak photo studios.

As part of the reform of the state sector, the regime encouraged people to leave their work units and to find jobs and housing on the free market. Market reforms thus broke the close connection between home and workplace, and residential differentiation began to appear on the intraurban scale. Land reforms in the late 1980s (re)introduced land prices, with the result that urban fringes, where the cost of land remains lower, experience sustained growth. Especially since the 1990s, a flurry of housing construction has been rapidly replacing the Soviet-inspired monotonous apartment blocks that characterized Chinese cities during Maoism. Chinese cities in the early 1990s grew around specialized centers of commerce, finance, and trade. Increased differentiation and specialization between cities on the national level has been paralleled by a high degree of specialization of commercial and industrial function that has developed or reemerged within urban centers.

China's urban transformations continue to generate a great deal of research interest. Deborah Davis's work on urban spaces (Davis et al. 1995) explored how the character of city life changed after political and economic restructuring intensified in 1984, and how this change affected the creation of new physical, economic, and cultural spaces in urban China. In *The Consumer Revolution* (2000), Davis in turn examined the interpersonal consequences of rapid commercialization of Chinese society. The book showed that capitalism has brought urban Chinese both a higher material standard of living and new freedoms to create a private life beyond the control of the state. Contributors to Nancy N. Chen, Constance D. Clark, Suzanne Z. Gottschang, and Lyn Jeffery's edited volume (2001), on the other hand, analyzed the place that urban space holds in China's imagination and challenged the reader to rethink the meaning of the "urban." Other recent anthropological studies of China have looked at changing social relations, processes of stratification, state power, gender relations, and cultural politics (e.g., Anagnost 1997; Brownell 1995; Hanser 2008; Hsu 2007; Ikels 1996; Yang 1994, 1999).

Besides this anthropological research of the reform period's effects on urban residents' lives, various studies examine the structures and mechanics of the restructuring process, for example the emergence of the urban land market (e.g., Li and Siu 2001; Ning 2000; Xie, Parsa, and Redding 2002) or the details of the housing reforms (e.g., Li B. 2002; Li Shouen 2003; Wang Y. 2001; Ye S. 1987; Zhong and Hays 1996; Zhu 2000). Generally, this research on the transformations of China's urban landscape has focused on structural changes and larger trends (e.g., Broudehoux 2004; Campanella 2008; Dutton, Lu, and Wu

2008; Friedmann 2005; Gaubatz 1995, 1999; Logan 2002; Lu D. 2006; Tang and Parish 2000). Among these latter studies, Broudehoux's stands out for its attention to the effect of spatial transformations on people's lives.

More recently, suburbanization has also received attention. Comparing the Chinese suburbanization process with that in the United States, studies find certain similarities in the factors that contribute to the development, such as improved transportation, rapid urban growth, inner city renovation, and rising incomes (Wang and Zhou 1999).[25] Yet, research also shows distinct local features. Li and Siu (2001), for example, highlight the continued importance of the work unit. Together with the municipal bureau they consider it to be the primary driving force behind suburbanization in China today. Yan et al. (2002), in turn, emphasize that suburbanization of Chinese metropolises is the result of the interaction of several elements, but that it depends mainly on the involvement of local government and city planning policies. The housing reforms and the emergence of a real estate market have provided a basis for peripheral development, while modern transportation and information techniques accelerate the process. Especially the spatial adjustment of the metropolitan industrial structure accelerates the gathering of industries and population in the periphery of cities. Similarly, Zhou and Logan (2005, 2008) highlight the *political* dimension of the process where "at every level the economic processes that facilitate and shape suburban growth are grounded in policy choices" (ibid. 2005). Zhou and Logan analyze three interrelated domains—the national economy and system of urban planning, the system of housing and real estate development, and the composition of neighborhoods—to show how policy shifts in these areas facilitated the suburbanization process. Feng et al.'s (2004) analysis of Chinese suburbanization, in turn, distinguishes processes "at the level of economy" from processes at "the level of society" (cited in Zhou and Logan 2005). In their analysis, both shifts in economic activity (industrial decentralization and development of large supermarkets, reflecting a wider shift in retail services) and changes in residential locations contribute to suburbanization. Other economic factors that influence the process include urban land-use transformation, renovation of the inner city, real estate investments (both domestic and foreign), and improvement of public transportation. But Feng et al. also note important social changes: growing socioeconomic differences are manifested in spatial inequalities. These are represented in both practical and symbolic terms by the increasing use of private automobiles. In addition, Feng et al. observe that residents' attitudes toward the use of space have changed.

Most of these and other studies on suburbanization (e.g., Gu and Liu 2002; Hu and Kaplan 2001; Li Si-ming 2003; Meng 2000; Wang and Zhou 1999; Wu and Liu 2000) draw on large data sets and focus on structural changes and larger trends. Few investigations, however, have combined the anthropological focus on daily lives and subjective experiences with an analysis of spatial transformations. Notable exceptions to this lacuna are Lisa Rofel's (1999) research on factory space and Zhang Li's (2001) investigation of Wenzhou migrants in Beijing.[26] With this ethnographic study, I hope to contribute to the burgeoning scholarship on suburbanization by adding a more person-centered perspective on the process.[27] Examining the everyday lives and practices of people, and presenting Wangjing residents' personal views, opinions, and feelings, my questions here are these: How do Chinese urbanites experience the transformation of the city; how are they subjectively affected by suburbanization and the privatization of housing? What are their views on issues connected to housing and location of residence? How do urbanites choose their homes today, and how much choice do they have in the process to start with? How are residents' lives affected by the breaking of the close connection between homes and workplaces? And how do they negotiate these changes? Finally, what is the effect of their actions on the suburban space?

Beijing and the Fieldsite Wangjing

In 1949, when the Communist regime made Beijing once again the capital of the newly established People's Republic of China,[28] the city looked back upon more than two thousand years of history. Originally designed to represent ideas combining the cosmological order with rules of government and spatial form, key elements of the city epitomized the traditional Confucian worldview.[29] Although Beijing was destroyed and rebuilt various times, despite wars, revolts, Western commercialization, and the industrialization of the previous century, in the early twentieth century its general layout still reflected the original plan.

Today, the municipality of Beijing comprises roughly 16,800 square kilometers. In the attempt to blur the distinctions between town and country, in 1949 the Communist government added a large rural adjunct to the city's jurisdiction; Beijing came to constitute nine urban districts *(qu)* plus nine adjacent rural counties *(xian)*[30] (L. Ma 1979; Sit 1995) (Map 1). The planned urban sector of 1,040 square kilometers is defined as extending from Dingfuzhuang in the east to Shijingshan in the west, and from the Qing River in the north to Nanyuan in the south (Map 2). The inner city is made up from the four old districts *(shixiaqu)* Dongcheng, Xicheng, Chongwen, and Xuanwu. Around these lie the "near suburbs" *(jinjiaoqu)*—Haidian, Chaoyang, Shijingshan, and Fengtai—that grew mainly after 1949 and cover 1,282.9 square kilometers. The "outer suburbs," in turn, used to be mainly rural in character but have experienced increased growth in recent years (Beijing tongjiju 2001; Li X. 2002; Sit 1995; Wang D. 2002a).

Map 1. The Beijing municipality.

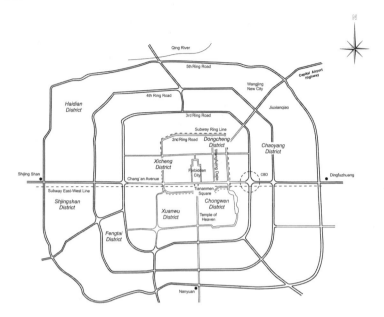

Map 2. The city of Beijing.

While Beijing possesses a distinctive history, the transformations it
has undergone over the last decades are generally comparable to those
in other large urban centers in China. Formerly relatively homogeneous and undifferentiated, cities in China today face growing economic
and social differences. In Beijing, the white-tiled commercial structures
built during the initial years of the reform already started to crumble
in the early 1990s and within a few years were followed by a new generation of green-glazed office towers. With the new millennium, more and
more of these are being replaced by "globalized" skyscrapers, designed
by internationally known architects (Lim 2004). At the same time, the
emerging stratification of the populace is increasingly reflected in the
city's changing structure and environment and influences residents'
daily lives in different ways. New apartment buildings offer previously
unknown luxuries in terms of standards and living space. But at the
same time, old houses are being torn down and people (forcefully)
evicted and resettled to areas far outside the city proper.

Sprawl, *tan da bing* (making a big pancake) in Chinese, has actually become one of the most visible effects of China's urban reforms.
Campanella (2008) claims that Beijing today is one of the fastest

sprawling cities in the world: its built-up area increased from 335 square kilometers in 1978 to 488 square kilometers in 1998, an increase of 45.6 percent (Gu and Shen 2003). Yet, between 1980 and 1990, 77 percent of all new housing was built in outlying suburban districts. Over the same time period, Beijing's central districts lost eighty-two thousand people while the inner and outer suburbs gained nearly 1.7 million new residents. Between 1990 and 2000 the trend increased: the city's core lost another 220,000 people while the suburbs gained nearly three million residents (Campanella 2008).[31]

Wangjing, the research locale, is one of such sprawling suburbs that have mushroomed around Beijing. It is part of Chaoyang District in Beijing's northeast (Map 3). Today, the district attracts not only the

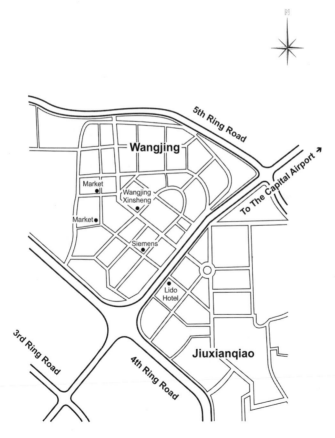

Map 3. The Wangjing suburban area.

greatest number of migrants ("temporary residents"),[32] but also the majority of the foreign investment in the city.[33] It is also the location of the new CBD where many of the affluent Wangjing residents work.

I discovered Wangjing accidentally. In 1999, I followed, together with a friend, an ad for "Ms. Shanan's Bagels," a café-cum-bagel factory, in a newly published English city magazine. The address vaguely pointed to a suburban area in the northeast of the city, where during bike rides on my previous visits to Beijing I had found nothing but fields, simple farm houses, and the occasional group of old state factories. Our taxi driver had never heard of the address, which, at a time when the city seemed to look different every day, was actually not surprising. Driving along one of the diagonally outspreading roads that led beyond the Third Ring Road, we passed some of the new office towers that at the time were springing up all over the city. Soon after, we came through a zone of shacks and garages with car and machinery repair shops. Beyond this point appeared the ghostly, because not yet inaugurated, loops, bridges, and lanes of the Fourth Ring Road. We continued to follow the narrowing road until we arrived in a small town–like area that appeared to be years behind the development of the city proper. The five-story apartment buildings lining the streets were still coated in the typical gray color-scheme of the Maoist period. Here and there, first signs of the private economy jumped brightly into sight: a red awning over a new store, a private fruit vendor who had propped up her produce on a horse cart, a commercial sign advertising Coca-Cola or Wall's ice cream. But there existed no skyscrapers with glass facades, no fast-food joints, and no new roads.

Beyond this point the taxi driver no longer knew where to go. He had never driven this far out of the city proper and was as bewildered by the environment as we were. Asking some pedestrians did not help; nobody had heard of "Ms. Shanan's Bagels." At last one man suggested continuing to drive to the Lido Hotel complex, because "there are lots of foreigners and new things." And so we did. Following a tree-lined road, crossing a smelly canal, we turned around a few corners and quite suddenly found ourselves amid a "brave new world": a four-lane, freshly paved, straight road led us by barely finished highrises, glitzy shops, and a supermarket that was just being opened. Balloons flew over the red roof, and young women in tidy uniforms stood in front of rows of flower baskets waiting to welcome customers, but the street was empty.

That day, by mere chance, we finally discovered the café we had been looking for in the backyard buildings of a small, closed-down factory. It turned out to be the attempt by a Chinese American to introduce bagels and bread to the Chinese market. Despite the novelty of something like that in Beijing at the time, I was, however, much more intrigued by the new neighborhood we had discovered. What was this incredibly spacious and modern new area? Did it belong to the city? When had it been built? What had spurred this outburst of growth on the urban fringe? Who lived in those expensive-looking new apartment buildings, and why had people moved to this location? None of my Chinese or Western friends knew the area. Most had heard of the Lido Hotel, but they were all surprised to learn about the neighborhood we had seen. A map of Beijing that I had bought indicated "Jiuxianqiao," the small town–like neighborhood we had driven through on our way. But beyond that, the map showed only empty fields. It took some more searching before I eventually found a city map that showed, instead of fields, a loop of streets marked by the name "Wangjing."

After that first encounter, I returned to Wangjing several times and walked along the ample streets. What stirred my curiosity ever more was the apparent contradiction between the sleek, expensive-looking residential complexes and the few remaining, dilapidated work-unit compounds and islands of farmers' houses that I discovered on these explorations. How and when had the people who lived in these latter places found their way to this distant location? What happened to them during the blitz of modernization, and how did they feel about the changes? What were their relations and interactions with the affluent living so close by, yet in status and style apparently so far away? My interest in these issues only increased when I realized that there existed no in-depth ethnographic research on the (sub)urban living experience. For this reason, I decided to study the production of the Wangjing suburban space. This book, then, is the result of my fourteen months of anthropological fieldwork in the markets, shops, and residential compounds of Wangjing from August 2001 to September 2002, and two short visits in the summer of 2000 and in January 2007.

My goal in this book is to show that present-day social, economic, and spatial stratifications are importantly connected to China's past. The chapters that follow are thus organized to reflect the historic trajectory of Wangjing and the differentiations among its residents. In fact, the majority of my older informants came to Beijing only after the 1949 Communist revolution. They vividly remembered the early years of the newly founded People's Republic and the revolutionary zeal of creating a "new society." Focusing on the emergence of Wangjing's antecedent Jiuxianqiao, chapter 1 portrays the socialist makeover of Beijing. We will see how the creation of such institutions as the hukou and the danwei socially and spatially positioned the population in ways that continue to affect peoples' lives today. By the late 1970s, this suburban industrial zone had become the social, political, and economic center of people's lives. Yet, the reforms that were launched in 1978 would completely transform my informants' lives. This process is examined in chapter 2 where I document how the reform of the state sector, the opening of the private sector, migration, as well as the land and housing reforms have affected the suburban living experience.

Chapter 3 zooms the ethnographic lens on the various housing options that exist in Wangjing and on their differences in design. Here I also portray Wangjing residents and their increasingly different styles of living. In chapter 4 I further analyze the growing socioeconomic differentiations in Chinese society. I show how these are connected to history, ideology, and emerging market forces and explore the interplay of these factors with the increasingly diverging values and behaviors of Wangjing residents. Chapter 5 focuses on the interconnections between the stratification processes and consumption. I argue that the consumption of space and housing has become one of the foremost arenas within and through which differentiations are realized by imbuing or denying residents status and prestige.

In the Conclusion I draw out more clearly the connections between space, consumption, and housing explored in the previous chapters. I explicate the dual role of the state in the transformation process, both vigorously pursuing modernization and promoting consumption as the engine of development. The result is the "citizenship of consumption" that increasingly differentiates society. At the same time, I highlight that suburban residents exert significant agency in the processes of social transformation of life in China. As will become apparent, suburbanization in China today is more than simply an economically and politically motivated process.

In sum, this is a book about the dramatic social, economic, and spatial transformations in urban China and their effects on the everyday lives of Beijing people. But above all, it is an account of the ways in which Wangjing residents reflect on and deal with the changes they have experienced over the course of their lifetimes.

1 A HISTORY OF WANGJING

Building the Suburban Industrial Zone

TODAY Wangjing's exclusive residential neighborhoods and shiny new apartment towers can be easily reached via a six-lane highway that connects the suburb with the inner city. Until the 1990s, however, this was the rural hinterland, an agricultural zone interspersed with a few industrial clusters of socialist planning. One such cluster, Jiuxianqiao, lies to the east of Wangjing. It was established in the 1950s as a development zone for electronics factories. With dirt roads and only one bus connection to the urban center, the small conglomeration of factories and residential quarters strewn among farmers' small houses resembled for many years more a village than a part of the capital or suburban area. Sixty-five-year-old Fang Hongzhu,[1] who was assigned to one of the electronics companies as a young man, described how he saw the neighborhood change:

> There was no paved road; only a dust road. Nothing but fields. Step by step, things are changing. Especially after the Cultural Revolution, it was different every year. Sometimes, we [feel like] we cannot recognize it anymore ourselves. We used to ride bikes downtown. Now we have buses that go everywhere in the city. We planted the trees ourselves when we were young. We helped the farmers during the harvest, since the fields were around us. Now we see no fields, only shops and skyscrapers.

The transformation of the urban built environment, however, did not begin with the reform period in 1978. After the Communist revolution, the regime had ambitious redevelopment plans for Chinese cities.[2] One of the central tenets of economic and urban planning after 1949 was, for example, to eradicate the contradiction between town and countryside.

Suburban residents were acutely aware of the tremendous changes that Beijing has undergone. They were both subjects and actors in this economic and political project. The majority of them had moved to the capital only after the Communist revolution when vast areas of the countryside were devastated after years of civil war and Japanese occupation. In fact, the 1950s industrialization drive drew hundreds of thousands of peasants to the cities in search of new employment opportunities and a better living situation, until new migration policies at the end of the decade curbed the flow. Jiuxianqiao, Wangjing's antecedent, emerged and grew exactly through these movements of people and the implementation of various state policies. It turned from the small conglomeration of factories set in the fields far out of the city proper into a consolidated, self-sufficient industrial cluster that became the all-encompassing social, political, and economic lifeworld of its residents. It is this formation process brought about by people and policies that I trace in this chapter.

Through the experiences of my informants, here I illustrate the Maoist transformation of Beijing and the antecedents of Wangjing. I show the dramatic scale of the social, economic, political, and spatial restructuring that people have experienced during their lifetime. My focus lies on the way urban residents were affected by the changes, and how people in my interviews commented on them. We will see how Maoist city planners transformed the imperial capital into a "productive city" where all other functions were subordinated to the aim of economic self-reliance. At the same time, Beijing became the showcase for new technologies of population control and work organization that radically broke with the historically grown city structure. These sociospatial transformations and new institutions generally improved workers' living standards, but they also fixed people in a specific status and place. The critical distinction into urban and rural residents in the late 1950s had further far-reaching structural and social effects. On the eve of the reforms in 1978, Beijing was marked by a chessboard pattern of residential-cum-workplace compounds and had little functional and residential segregation. Even more important, the socialist policies strongly influenced and formed the older generation's subjectivities and identities.

Poverty and Lack of Housing:
The Early Years of Restoration and Industrialization

Jiuxianqiao's first factories were set up in the 1950s. At the time, the First Five-Year Plan (1953–57) stipulated measures to turn Beijing into

into a "productive" city and a leading industrial base whose status was considered to befit a socialist national capital.

After the civil war and Japanese occupation, Beijing was in a state of decay when the new Communist regime took office. Inflation, unemployment, a breakdown of public services, crime, and social distress of all kinds dominated urban life. Beijing was filthy, with inadequate sewage facilities and water supplies, and little garbage collection. Moreover, there was not sufficient housing stock and two-thirds of all housing was dilapidated (Hu and Kaplan 2001; L. Ma 1979; Strand 1995). Reviving and rebuilding the capital was thus a paramount task. Yet, the makeover of Beijing—the capital and model for the country—became an ideologically inspired national project (Samuels and Samuels 1989).[3] It was a showcase for the new urban planning principles developed to realize the socialist transformation of the country. The central idea of the new stipulations was to achieve cities' independence; under socialism rural areas should no longer be exploited by urban centers. Parasitic "consumer cities" *(xiaofei chengshi)* should be turned into centers of production, or "producer cities" *(shengchan chengshi).*[4] The new centrally planned economic system, based on five-year plans, thus emphasized production activities, such as (heavy) industries, construction, transport, and communication. It was in the wake of these new policies that the Jiuxianqiao industrial zone with ten major electronics manufacturers was established in Beijing's northeast. Other industrial zones for mechanical engineering and textiles production grew in the east, west, and south of the city. In fact, the entire capital was subject to hectic, large-scale construction to turn it simultaneously into the administrative center of the country as well as into an industrial hub (Sit 1995).[5]

The new planning principles, however, considered activities that did not result in tangible products as secondary to the socialist transformation of cities. Thus, housing, categorized as nonproductive construction, had low priority with state investment.[6] Even though the new government had transferred existing private housing stock to government ownership and begun with the construction of new housing after the revolution, demand still could not be met. People who had flocked into the cities to escape the devastation in the countryside and find work in the newly established factories had to accept whatever kind of shelter could be found. Many lived in slum-like conditions. Luo Hongjie, a retired female factory worker in her fifties, for example, recounted how she grew up in a primitive little brick house without running water in the south of Beijing. Her parents had come to the city in 1950 to work in two of the newly established factories: her mother in a textile plant, and her father in a car parts factory. They were lucky to find a house in the vicinity. Other informants whose parents began to work in Jiuxianqiao recounted how they had to cramp in with relatives or acquaintances because of the lack of housing. As this woman recalled, "We lived in the house of my father's friend. . . . It was . . . very shabby and small."

This abysmal housing situation was further exacerbated in the late 1950s, when the factories in Jiuxianqiao hired more people to further expand their industrial production. At the time, Mao suggested that economic development could be accelerated through the mobilization of the people. They would be more effective than new technology and managerial innovations, and China—in a "Great Leap Forward"— could surpass major industrial countries within a short time.[7] In Beijing, coal fields were developed in the west of the city, and automaking and internal combustion engine–manufacturing plants were set up in the eastern suburbs. Large numbers of people—among them the majority of my older informants—followed the regime's mobilization calls and came to Beijing to work in the new and enlarged factories. The industrial drive actually resulted in a population rise from 2.09 million in 1949 to 7.87 million in 1965 (Beijing tongjiju 1999).[8] The number of employees in urban state and collective enterprises doubled.[9] Yet, as my informants vividly recalled, sufficient housing did not exist for all the new workers in the factories. While the total housing floor space increased from 13.54 to 30.52 million square meters between 1949 and 1965, this was not enough to accommodate the rapidly growing urban population. Moreover, the Great Leap Forward's emphasis on production further reduced the expenditure on housing construction. Instead of the previous 9 percent, now only 3 percent of basic construction funds were allocated to housing (Brugger and Reglar 1994). As a result, per capita housing floor space decreased from 4.75 square meters in 1949 to 3.68 in 1965 (Lu D. 2006).

Suburban areas were especially affected by the shortage of housing and facilities because construction concentrated on productive structures (Lu D. 2006). Informants who had begun to work in the factories of Jiuxianqiao had problems finding proximate accommodation. They often faced extremely long commutes to their places of work. Yang Guofen, a retired worker born in 1934, for example, continued to live with her parents even after she got married. Both she and her husband had to take care of their elderly parents, but they could not find a house that would accommodate them all. The parents' house, however, was far away from her workplace in Jiuxianqiao, "on the other side of the city," as Yang said. She described her daily commute: "I lived near Qianmen [south of Tiananmen Square]. I had to change buses three or four times to get to my workplace. The sun hadn't risen when I left home and it was already dark when I came back. It was very hard for me *(dui wo hen kunnan)*." Other informants lived in rooms or houses they rented from farmers in the factories' vicinity. This reduced their commute to work but offered little comfort. Mr. and Mrs. Wang's recollections of their living conditions at the time were exemplary for many other older informants: "We found a house in the countryside . . . which was about twenty square meters [big], including bedroom and kitchen. . . . [It was] a single story house without gas or heating. There were fields around, and we had to go outside to use the toilet." The general lack of urban housing and necessary facilities also affected regular daily concerns: informants reported how they had to walk, bike, or take long bus rides to buy groceries and bring their children to school. Days off from work were spent doing laundry or visiting the public bath house (see also Lu D. 2006).

A number of informants who worked in the factories at Jiuxianqiao continued to live in such poor conditions up into the reform period. But besides the destitute housing situation, what people remembered most vividly about this period was the extreme poverty. Indeed, after a few short years of general life improvements, and despite the efforts in industrialization and housing construction, the result of the Great Leap Forward was quite contrary to its intention. China's investment in heavy industry rose to 43.4 percent of the national income in 1959. At the same time, however, grain exports to the Soviet Union were increased to pay for more heavy machinery. In consequence, the average amount of grain available to each person in China's countryside dropped from 205 kilograms in 1957 to 183 kilograms in 1959 and to 156 kilograms in 1960. The result was famine on a gigantic scale, which claimed more than thirty million lives between 1959 and 1962.[10] While the countryside bore the worst of the effects, even urban areas suffered from food shortages, as recalled here by fifty-two-year-old Hu Lanfu:

My childhood was during the time of the Three Years Calamity *(san nian zainan)*. Our food was rationed; an adult received 14.25 kilograms per month. We had ration cards for soy oil, meat, and clothes. Food other than staples was completely lacking. We could only have meat or fish on holidays. We ate steamed buns and corn flour; we didn't have as much different food as today. Every time my mother cooked, she used the scale to measure the food. Otherwise we would be starving at the end of the month. Life was hard *(shenghuo hen kunnan)*.

Despite these difficulties, urban residents retained a definite advantage over China's rural population due to their access to various subsidized benefits. Take-home salaries effectively doubled through these privileges and created an "urban labor aristocracy" (Tang and Parish 2000, 24). Long Fengzhan, a sixty-four-year-old retired worker, explained: "Our salary was low but we had free housing, free health care, free education; so 120 yuan per month was enough for a family [of four]." Not surprisingly, the advantages of urban living and working only increased the flow of peasants into the cities (Logan 2002). Yet the national government was unable to sustain an unlimited number of urban residents. By the mid-1950s, voluntary labor migration to the cities was considered a serious problem. To regulate rural–urban migration, the regime thus decided new measures to stop the unregulated flow of peasants and to sustain social stability (see Zhang L. 2001).

Becoming Urban Residents: Hukou and Danwei

In 1958, the system of household registration (hukou) was reinforced.[11] Since then, hukou has been the most important base of social stratification and segregation in socialist China.[12] Indeed, the introduction of hukou registration was a decisive watershed in the development and transformation of Chinese cities and society; it proved crucial for the lives of my informants. It was the hukou that turned them into "urban residents," with all the connected rights and benefits, and with the corresponding self-identification.

About 90 percent of my older informants had come to the capital in the ten-year period between the revolution and the late 1950s. They left their homes to find work, education, and an improved living situation elsewhere. Often families moved a couple of times in search of better conditions; they went to Shanghai, to Tianjin, before they eventually made their way to Beijing. In other cases, one or several family members worked in the city while their spouses, children, or parents stayed behind in the village. Now, however, the hukou system effectively divided the population into those with agricultural status *(nongye hukou)* and nonagricultural status *(feinongye hukou),* establishing what has been called a "bamboo wall" (Tang and Parish 2000, 24) between them.[13] Born into the privileged nonagricultural status, one was eligible for various urban entitlements. In the countryside, in contrast, peasants received some social benefits through the communes; these, however, were never as extensive as in the city.[14]

During the initial years of the hukou system the new residential restrictions were not so strongly enforced, and my informants reported about a certain scramble to acquire the privileged status. Some men who already worked in the city, for example, urged their families to follow them in order to eventually receive urban residence status for the entire family. Wen Hong, a technical worker and cadre in his late fifties who grew up in Tianjin, explained: "I lived in the countryside until I was ten years old. In 1956, my father asked my mother to come with him to Tianjin because the government was going to give out hukou to inhabitants of cities; so my mother was able to become an urban resident too." After 1960, however, the government made a concerted effort to enforce the law. Now migration from rural to urban areas and from small towns to cities was prohibited, and every person needed police approval to change residence. It was usually only labor demand that enabled the transfer from one place to another. Such reassignments, however, were not necessarily permanent, and a number of workers in the factories of Jiuxianqiao were sent back to the countryside at the end of the Great Leap Forward movement.[15] Only a few were as lucky as this woman: "My hukou was moved to the city in 1958, as was my husband's. In 1962, all the people coming from the countryside were sent to the countryside to do farm work *(pai dao noncun gonzuo).* We were among the ones on the list, but my husband was the best worker in the factory and so the leaders decided to let my husband stay."[16]

But even for those who had received a treasured urban hukou, the new regulations could significantly complicate their lives, for example, when spouses were assigned to work in different cities. In order to be able to live together in one place, one spouse had to obtain the permission to transfer, which usually meant trading workplaces with another person from that city. Several of my informants thus lived apart from their spouses for many years. After finishing university, Zhu Laoning, a retired radio technology engineer in her early sixties, for example, was assigned to work in Nanjing while her husband worked in Jiuxianqiao. The couple remained separated for ten years, seeing each other barely every couple of months. Only after she had her second child was Zhu finally able to receive a transfer.

> I came back [to Beijing] after 1973. Every year there were several positions available to be transferred to in different places. I made a request and waited in line. It was the end of the movement [the Cultural Revolution]. My leader told his supervisor about my situation, being separated from my husband, and it was reported to the National Defense Ministry. After their investigation, and my waiting, I was finally transferred to Beijing. I had an advantage: it was that I had a university degree. It made it easier. Although the political situation had changed, there were still a lot of people who were not allowed to go back to Beijing for four or five more years.

Evidently such separations had far-reaching effects on people's lives that shaped their experiences and identities.

Despite these difficulties, the fortuitous and quite arbitrary urban residence status that the new hukou system granted the migrants who had come to the city after the revolution or during the Great Leap Forward was a fortunate and decisive turn. Importantly, until today the institution serves as a basis for urbanites' self-identification, setting them off, especially, from the current migration of rural population to the cities. Although many of my older informants had come to Beijing (or other cities) only shortly before the hukou system was rigorously enforced, ever since receiving urban residence status they considered themselves an integral part of the urban population. Not a few of them expressed dislike or disregard for present-day peasant migration to the city. The segregation of China's population into rural and urban residents thus imparted my informants with a new status and a (real and perceived) right to the privileged urban realm.

It was, however, through another distinct socialist institution that the specific Maoist urban reorganization of people and space, and thus the Jiuxianqiao suburban cluster, was realized: the danwei.[17] An extension of the state apparatus, as Tang and Parish (2000, 29) explain, the danwei functioned as a form of social organization based on the workplace. Since most adults in China worked during the Maoist era, work units became an all-encompassing institution affecting practically all aspects of life. As an independent unit, the danwei provided medical insurance, labor protection, pensions, direct subsidies, and employment for offspring under the replacement system *(dingti)*.[18] But the work unit also acted "as parent, caretaker, mediator, and even matchmaker" (Tang and Parish 2000, 29). It supplied employees with basic provisions (such as clothing items and food stuffs), and it granted permission to get married or divorced and to have a child. In addition, the work unit was a "political unit where government policies were implemented, loyalty to the party was promoted, political mobilization carried out, public opinion was collected, and where voting took place" (ibid.). Indeed, the danwei became so central to Chinese urban residents' lives that when meeting someone for the first time, people asked each other to which danwei they belonged. A popular saying stated that one could be without a job but not without danwei (He 1998; Lü and Perry 1997).[19]

One of the most important functions of the work unit became the construction and distribution of housing. In the socialist system, all land belonged to "the people" represented by the government. Housing, in turn, was built, owned, and distributed by employers—usually state-owned enterprises. It was considered a welfare benefit for which both employer and state were responsible.[20] While employers (danwei) paid low wages to the employees, they had to provide subsidized housing. The allocation of housing was based on job rank and seniority: the higher the job and the more work years, the more likely one was to access public housing.[21] Newly constructed danwei compounds ideally integrated work and residential functions. While this principle was not realized in Jiuxianqiao, over the years the factories built close-by living quarters that followed the typical multifunctional danwei style. The compounds were highly controlled environments with utilitarian and regimented architecture. Behind walls and guarded gates stretched orderly rows of three- to five-story-high brick or cement buildings. Inside, several separate stairwells led to the two to four dwellings and one communal bathroom on each landing. Units included both apartments, often shared by several families, and dormitories for single workers. Between the buildings, the common areas served as bicycle parking lots, children's play areas, and recreational and green space. Other facilities within the compound varied but ideally included dining halls, provision shops, medical facilities, meeting rooms, and administrative offices. In sum, danwei compounds were miniature walled cities that offered a wide range of services for their employees, fostering home and neighborhood life, and leaving little reason to go outside (D. Bray 2005; Gaubatz 1995).[22]

For a long time, however, many workers of the factories in Jiuxian-qiao could not obtain such newly constructed work-unit apartments. The danwei were notoriously short of housing facilities,[23] and the distribution of scarce apartments followed criteria such as age, years of work, and number of children. One sixty-something-year-old man described his situation after he got married in the following way:

> We first rented a house in the countryside where we lived for ten years. Then in 1976 we shared an apartment with another couple. Later we had a small apartment for ourselves. Now we have this bigger apartment. The Institute [danwei] was new when I first started to work there. A lot of new staff and most people had no place to live. The Institute had no houses. Everybody had to wait in line. The Institute would distribute the houses according to age, degree, and years of working, and so forth.

Many people had to initially share residential units. As a teenager, sixty-five-year-old Fang Hongzhu, for example, first lived in the dormitory of his school. When he began to work, Fang moved into the dormitory of the factory, where he shared a room with seven other men. But even married couples sometimes had to live in (separate) danwei dormitories because they could not obtain housing. As told by this woman: "I lived in the dormitory of my factory, and he [her husband] lived in the dormitory of his. We met once a week or every other one. We would meet in parks. We finally moved together in 1973 [after ten years of marriage]." Holding a bureaucratic position could help to access housing, but not necessarily so. Thus, even though Zhu Laoning's husband was a cadre, after she returned to Beijing, the family had to rent a small pingfang house in the countryside beyond Jiuxian-qiao. She explained:

> My husband was a cadre but he didn't feel like asking for a house because the work unit did not have many. So we had a ten-square-meter room until 1979. Then we got a small apartment, and afterwards we got this apartment in 1986. At that time the danwei distributed houses according to working years. We were in school for many years, so the workers had better and bigger houses than we had. Their children were older than mine, which was also an advantage they had. I got married when I was twenty-five, later than they did. I gave birth when I was twenty-eight and twenty-nine. My children were small, that was the reason why I couldn't have a big house.

In the case of people who were lucky and received a danwei room or apartment, women nonetheless derived only limited advantages from the combined work-housing design of the work unit. Single women tended to live with their parents (if they were in the city), and after marriage women were more likely to reside in housing provided through their husband's work unit. Sixty-eight-year-old Mrs. Li described the distribution process of apartments in her danwei in the following way:

> I could get in line and wait for an apartment from my danwei, but there were more than a thousand people in my company, and houses were few. Male comrades were less than female ones, 60 to 70 percent were women. So the leaders liked to give houses to men first. Most of the female workers got married to men from other companies. They could get a house through the husband's danwei. It was difficult when a couple worked in the same company.

This meant that women frequently continued to face long commutes. He Yuehua and her husband received an apartment through his danwei at Jiuxianqiao, but she worked in the south of Beijing: "My workplace was very far. I had to leave the house before 6:30 a.m. to arrive there at 8:00 a.m." Nevertheless, given the insufficient housing that the older generation had often lived in for many years, my informants considered the newly introduced Communist planning style of combined work and housing a favorable solution to people's everyday problems, since usually at least one spouse spent less time commuting to work.

Socialist Subjectivities: Work and Revolutionary Struggles

The centrality that the danwei gained in urban residents' lives can only be fully understood when taking into account the ideological importance of wage labor during the Maoist period. After the Communist revolution in 1949 and the introduction of the centrally planned economy, the socialist subject was defined through wage labor. Indeed, it was productive labor that identified a person as a fully social being and that was the measure for human worth (Rofel 1999). Urban residents were usually assigned to state-sector jobs, their danwei, which they kept throughout their entire work life. Wage labor was not a means for personal aspirations, consumption, and individual gain, but part of the socialist project that promised an egalitarian, redistributionist order that provided job security, basic living standards, and special opportunities for those from disadvantaged backgrounds (Tang and Parish 2000).

With the demands that the regime made on its workers, and in the case of women, with the double burden of wage labor and housework (e.g., Barlow 1994, 1995; Gilmartin 1993; Gilmartin et al. 1994; Robinson 1985; Yang 1999), people's lives were very busy. Mrs. Fang described how she and her husband had to take care of their four children, work, and attend political meetings: "We woke up and prepared breakfast for our children; we went to work at eight o'clock and were off from work at 5 p.m. But at the time, we couldn't go back home as soon as the work was over; we had to stay and attend meetings. Lateness was not allowed. It was a busy time." All of these activities happened in, or were connected to, the danwei. In effect, it was this combination, or merger, of work and private sphere that made the work unit such an all-encompassing and dominant feature in urban residents' lives. Moreover, over the years in which they lived and worked together, danwei members formed a close-knit community, as my older informants repeatedly and positively stressed. This is how one woman expressed this sentiment: "The compound was built by the factory. All of the people who live there are from the same factory. . . . We know each other and can help each other. We are from the same factory after all. . . . If we need help, we just knock at our neighbor's door." Mrs. Fang brought it to the point: "The factory [danwei] became our home."

The danwei as an institution of social and spatial organization thus had an important effect on my informants' lives and their subject formation. While the factories in Jiuxianqiao were slow to provide their employees with accommodation, especially private apartments, eventually one spouse did receive danwei housing; the family could thus fully enjoy one of the most important benefits that urban residency implied. Even for those informants who had to wait for a long time for a house, the danwei provided a new identity and sense of belonging; in the long run not only to a social unit, but importantly to one that was rooted in space. In effect, the work unit became the geographical, social, political, and economic center of my older informants' lives. Colleagues were neighbors and often friends; they were the people one saw every day and to whom one turned for help. This social dimension of the danwei was enforced by the (relatively) equalizing character of the danwei: cadres and regular workers lived side by side and were only minimally distinguished in terms of pay and benefits.

But the danwei was certainly also a closely monitored and supervised realm. Privacy became virtually unknown as the state, in the form of the danwei officials, intruded into the most intimate aspects of life. This intrusion of politics into the private sphere reached new heights during the Cultural Revolution between 1966 and 1976.[24] The "ten bad years of great disaster" or "ten-year calamity" *(shinian hao-jie)*, as the period is officially referred to today, are vital to understanding present-day transformations and Chinese people's reactions to them.

Most of my informants who agreed to talk about this still sensitive period in Chinese history were relatively lucky, and only passively affected by the upheavals of the time. One woman's husband, however, was a university graduate and as such was "sent down to the countryside" in 1967, just two months after the couple got married. He could not come back to the city for eleven years. The wife thus had to live and take care of their children alone. This certainly reinforced her dependency on the close-knit community of the danwei. The case of Mrs. Li, on the other hand, shows the negative side of the controlled danwei environment. Mrs. Li's sister was sent to the countryside to work in a village. Like many others, she ended up staying there because her hukou was never moved back to the city. Mrs. Li always felt responsible for the sister and tried to send supplies and food in her support. But Mrs. Li's own situation in the city was not easy either. She explained:

> My father was an intellectual in the old society [before the revolution], which was bad. All of my leaders knew about it. If they wanted to call us rightists,[25] we would be rightists; if they said we were good people, we were good people. As for us, if we made a single mistake at work and somebody saw it, we would be in trouble. Every change in our life we had to tell our leaders and the secretary of the party committee. . . . I had to behave, not only one year or two. From school all through my work life, we were so serious and dared not make any mistakes.

The Cultural Revolution seriously damaged Chinese people's lives: hundreds were killed, families were torn apart, and the entire middle and upper levels of administration were destroyed. Moreover, social relations were deeply affected. Informants repeatedly pointed out how they would no longer trust others as a result of the movement, but also how they had found a few "true friends." The effect on social solidarity and community has been a lasting one: until today people claim that it is because of the Cultural Revolution that mutual help and cooperation have allegedly lessened, that individualism is on the rise, and that people embrace and cherish the new private spaces that emerged in the reform period.

The destructive social effect of the "ten-year calamity" was underlined by the chaos it created in the city structure: to achieve Mao's target of mixing manual and physical labor, and to engage all people in some productive activity, dangerous factories were haphazardly placed within residential zones. Many new buildings were blindly located on basic infrastructural lines, several hundreds of thousands of square meters of substandard housing were completed, green and open spaces eroded, and harm was done to countless cultural relics (Sit 1995). Nonetheless, according to my informants, Jiuxianqiao—far out of Beijing proper—remained relatively untouched by these structural upheavals.

Conclusion: Socialist Reorganization of Space and Society

The economic policies and modes of social organization introduced by the Communist government after 1949 worked together to bring my older informants to the city and to Jiuxianqiao, adjacent to today's suburban Wangjing. Forced industrialization offered new employment opportunities that pulled migrants to the cities where they were assigned to jobs and, eventually, received new housing through the danwei. With the establishment of the hukou system, urban residents' presence in the city received an identity-forming legitimacy that segregated China's population into those who were provided for by the state—urbanites—and those who had to provide for themselves—the rural population.

Generally speaking, the years after the Communist revolution were important for my older informants because many of them arrived in Beijing during this period of intense industrialization. They saw the beginning of the construction of danwei compounds and the overall transformation efforts, with the concomitant atmosphere of revolutionary zeal and thrust. These experiences, together with their sacrifices in comfort, were formative to the older generation. At the same time, the socialist organization and the state intrusion into urban people's private lives led to a dependency on (or supplicant relationship to) state services. Furthermore, it generated a social structure where differentiation was based on politico-ideological factors rather than on socioeconomic ones.[26] The period was characterized by extreme social supervision through the various institutions of control, by a vertical relationship of obedience between subject-citizens and party or government officials, but also by significantly homogeneous living standards and politicized ties between subordinates and superiors in the workplace.

2 REFORMING THE STATE SECTOR, OPENING THE PRIVATE SECTOR

Changing the Suburban Experience

> Beijing experiences big changes these years. We have more roads, bridges, and buildings. Some of the old places, one does not recognize them anymore if one did not go there for just a short while. . . . Some of the state companies, like the factories, are torn down to build apartment buildings. To tell the truth, the state-owned companies don't make any money these days and there are many people out of work. Some people [have to] retire when they are just forty-five years old, which is the best age for people to work and they have big families; they are well experienced and very productive. They have the older generation and children to take care of, but they are retired.
>
> —Xian Dongwu,
> sixty-three-year-old retired worker

ON THE EVE OF THE REFORMS IN THE LATE 1970S, Jiuxianqiao had become the lifeworld for the workers assigned to the factories in the industrial cluster. Most of my older informants lived in the area, either in one of the few available new danwei units or in houses they rented from local farmers in the vicinity. The upheaval of the Cultural Revolution notwithstanding, the geographical, social, and economic center of peoples' lives was the work unit. Jiuxianqiao residents spent their days between wage labor, political meetings, and taking care of their children and the household. There was little spare time for excursions and diversions; entertainment facilities or consumption opportunities were virtually nonexistent. The reforms that were about to be launched would initiate a dramatic transformation with far-reaching effects on informants' lives and on the suburban area itself.

Looking back on thirty years of reform policies in the year 2009, China's transformation seems like a linear development. In reality, the "reform and opening" *(gaige kaifang)* was far from a concerted and uniformly directed project but rather a gradual process of trial and error, as described in the famous saying "to cross the river by feeling for the stones."[1] Four large measures stand out in their dramatic effect on China's urban landscape and on peoples' lives: the reform of the state sector; the opening of the private sector and authorization of foreign investment; the permission to leave the countryside; and the land and housing reforms. Amidst the numerous more detailed measures, these large strategies are the major driving force behind Guangzhou, Shanghai, and Beijing's (and increasingly other cities') transformation into global metropolises with high-flying economies and growing sociospatial differentiations. These policies are also the catalysts for the growing suburbanization in Chinese cities that is in large part a translation of such stratifications into spatial differentiations.

But the focus on policies and larger reform processes obscures how the reforms have actually impacted on peoples' everyday lives, both in practical and in conceptual ways. In fact, my informants' entire life experience has changed. Before the reforms danwei residents were both supervised and provided for by their work unit. Now they have to take at least partial responsibility for their (future) well-being. State welfare provisions have been severely cut, and many people struggle to make ends meet. These existential life changes impinge on peoples' social relations, but also on their experience and use of space. Moreover, as we will see in the remainder of this book, they also play an important role in the formation of suburban neighborhoods.

Both the makeover of the city structure and the socioeconomic transformations that affect everyday life were of great concern to the people in my investigation, as expressed in the quote by Xian Dongwu above. In this chapter, I examine aspects of the reforms and show how they have transformed my informants' lives. The discussion goes beyond housing and the Wangjing neighborhood since the research locale and the people living therein are affected by policies and issues beyond that realm. As will become apparent, urban residents' living situation and experience has dramatically changed. Concomitantly with new privacy, new choices, and opportunities emerged greater uncertainties and problems. At the same time, certain social groups or sectors have not only benefited more from the reform-period changes than others, but government policies have actually encouraged emerging inequalities.

It is this particular role of the state that makes the study of Chinese suburbanization such a compelling case.

Reform of the State Sector

As we have seen in the previous chapter, after my older informants had become urban hukou holders they were part of the urban job-placement process. Upon graduation from school or university they were assigned to a danwei where they usually worked until they reached retirement age.[2] Lifetime job security was the rule; the "iron rice bowl" *(tie fan wan)* guaranteed that they could not be laid off. An unwanted result of this arrangement, however, was an extremely low productivity rate in state-owned companies. Zhu Laoning put it succinctly: "Before the reform, whatever you did, no matter if you worked hard or you were lazy, as long as you went to work every day, no matter if you made a contribution or not, you had the same salary." Moreover, she explained how there were no incentives to work harder, longer, or better. "I conducted some research [for the company] but the money that came from it was shared by everybody. Five yuan each. Our bonuses were the same. If mine was higher, I would have been in trouble." Thus, since the early 1980s a central element of the economic reform agenda was the attempt to improve the performance of the Chinese economy. Various measures were launched with the intention to cut the costs of social benefits and to make state-owned factories work (more) profitably. To "smash the iron rice bowl" *(dapo tie fan wan)* reformers aimed at recommodifying labor by introducing a labor market where workers could be hired and fired according to enterprise needs and remunerated according to productivity.[3] In addition, to address the lack of labor flexibility, discipline, and incentives, lifetime tenure was replaced by a system of successive five-year labor contracts. As an effect, public-sector employees now face considerably higher competition and resulting pressure in their work life. Many of my informants expressed fears of being pushed out of their positions by younger, better-educated, more dynamic employees. One thirty-three-year-old woman, for example, commented: "[The stress comes from] work and new knowledge. New work requires a good educational background. Some low-educated people are in more danger to be fired. Young people often have higher degrees, so older people have to keep on studying. We have more pressure." If they could find the time, people tried to confront this pressure by acquiring extra qualifications such as a foreign language or computer or special technological skills, or they pursued a higher degree in evening and weekend classes. Not a few of them, however, worked eight hours for six days a week and often spent more than two additional hours a day commuting. This did not leave enough time to pursue such goals.

Older workers were not put on five-year contracts, but were instead encouraged to retire early to create vacancies for younger employees (Tang and Parish 2000).[4] They thus depend on their pensions. Despite various pension reforms,[5] for the state-company retirees in Jiuxianqiao this was generally not a problem; informants said that they were able to support themselves.[6] Their pensions were raised every year in adjustment to inflation and price increases. Indeed, the majority of the retirees I talked to were comparatively well off because their danwei, the electronics-producing companies in Jiuxianqiao, had been relatively important during the Maoist era and also had been able to stay economically competitive in the reform period. Not only were their pensions higher on average than in other state-owned companies, but they were also paid regularly, which is not necessarily the rule. One man, for example, pointed out that his sister's company could only pay half of her pension, since they had economic difficulties.[7] Nevertheless, most of the elderly did not have enough to pay for bigger medical bills, travel, or other great expenses. Limited financial means also curbed older informants' mobility at a time when the danwei provided fewer and fewer daily necessities and the suburb was still lacking a range of basic facilities. Several people thus indicated that they relied on or would count on the practical and material support of their grown-up children, now or in the future.

One worry shared by almost all people I talked to during my research was about becoming seriously ill, having to go to the hospital, and/or buying medicine. "I am still worried that I will be ill, although I have my pension," explained one sixty-year-old retiree. "The state used to pay 90 percent in case of illness; people dared to see the doctor. After the reform of the medical care policy we have more problems with it. Some retired people don't like to go to the doctors because they have only 700 or 800 yuan (US$93 or 107) salary per month."[8] Indeed, the changes in the health care and insurance system have been among the most important reforms that resulted from cutting the overhead costs of state-sector employers. Portrayed as a measure to improve the quality of care, in effect it has meant that state-provided medical services have been cut back and private health providers gradually stepped into the void.[9] The commoditization of services, in turn, restricts the new quality-services to only a few, since the majority of urban Chinese cannot afford to pay the market-driven prices.[10]

The issue loomed large on my informants' minds. In reaction to this preoccupation about their health, especially older informants stressed how they exercised regularly to avoid illness. Important in this context, the health issue was also linked to the experience of space and to socioeconomic stratification: while many of the long-term old residents emphasized the suburban location's better, that is, healthier, environment in comparison to the inner city, some of the increasingly wealthy living in private apartments in Wangjing actually pointed to the *unhealthy* living environment of the locale that they thought was caused by construction and bad planning. The seemingly unrelated issues of health reforms and suburbanization thus came together in an unexpected way: rising medical costs and cuts in state benefits resulted in a new and differentiating experience of the suburban space. But the issue of health reforms and space had another dimension. While they could not move their residents to healthier locations or districts, better-off danwei could at least improve the compound's environment and microclimate by adding green space and trees. They also installed public exercise machines that proved particularly popular among the older residents. Thus, health has become a severely stratified issue, where economic success is directly linked to the available means and facilities of care and well-being. Yet, the apparent perks and benefits provided by wealthier danwei also physically reflect the larger policy shift toward self-responsibility: instead of providing all-encompassing health care, the danwei now provides the means for residents to take care of themselves. The built environment, the suburban space, thus becomes a mirror of this change.

Besides work contracts, pension schemes, and the health care reforms, the most compelling measure connected with the reform of the state sector has been the massive layoff of workers, especially after 1997.[11] Among my suburban informants several older people had stopped working because their companies reduced their personnel in the reform period. Ms. Zhang, for example, explained that she should have retired when she turned fifty-five, but since her company "didn't make any money" she had "left" when she was fifty. This meant also that her pension was paid irregularly. She and her husband relied on his salary and occasional monetary gifts by their children. More problematic, however, was the situation of the Wu family. While the *dingti* policy was still in place, Ms. Wu had given up her position in the factory for the benefit of their oldest son. A couple of years later Mr. Wu agreed to retire early from the same company because it was in financial troubles. Since then, the company has closed down and their son remains unemployed. Because the company went bankrupt, the family only received the minimal living allowance from the government. They relied on the occasional support from their daughter who worked in another state-owned enterprise. In recent years, Mr. Wu had developed health problems. To earn some additional money to cover medical fees, Ms. Wu and her son started a small business together, selling household wares in one of the Wangjing markets. The family, including daughter and son with their spouses, lived in the parents' forty-square-meter apartment that they had bought from the danwei in the early 1990s at a highly subsidized price. The negative effects of the economic reforms have thus renewed the importance of kin relations, a point I will further discuss in chapter 3.

In sum, the reform of the state sector has dramatically transformed Jiuxianqiao residents' living situation and life experience. While the state—theoretically—still provides basic amenities and provisions, informants' overall situation depended to a large extent on the economic performance of their work unit in the reform period. But even in better-off danwei, the new policies and regulations introduced previously unknown uncertainties, and it has become necessary for people to provide for themselves. This, in turn, importantly affected informants' social relations; social networks of support with children, neighbors, colleagues, and friends have to be built and maintained. Moreover, the transformations have significantly impacted on people's experience of and command over space. The suburb offers both advantages/opportunities and disadvantages/obstacles to individuals' efforts in securing their livelihood.

Opening the Private Sector

In the reform period, more and more private businesses, markets, and shops have popped up outside of the enclosed danwei compounds and farmers' houses of Jiuxianqiao. The Wu family, mentioned above, was only able to set up their small business because since 1978 the private sector, largely eliminated under Mao, has been gradually restored in an effort to stimulate economic growth and employment opportunities.[12] In the beginning, private entrepreneurs were often met by contempt or distrust, and only those persons who had no alternative means of making a living would *xia hai* (jump into the sea), that is, enter the urban private sector.[13] What made the private sector increasingly more attractive were exactly the simultaneous reforms of the state sector. Especially for early retirees and the unemployed (or laid-off) the private sector has offered new opportunities. In addition, rising costs of living and shifting social responsibilities from the work unit to the individual have put even employees in stable positions under economic strain.

Indeed, almost all of my older informants had found some form of private-sector job after they retired from the public sector. Few, however, set up their own businesses such as the Wu family; instead, they went through a series of informal employments. When I asked people why they continued to work after retirement from the state-owned company they initially often answered that they could not get used to not working any longer. Yet, after a while, informants admitted that they really needed the extra money, either to save for their future (especially possible medical expenses) or to support their children.

It was, however, not always easy for the elderly to find a new job. Since the beginning of the reform period, people's different skills and qualifications played out much more than before. Zhu Laoning, a radio technology engineer, was rehired by her own company after retiring at age fifty-five. Later she worked for several years in two different joint-venture companies until she finally chose to retire for good. Ms. Wang, in contrast, had difficulties finding an appropriate job because she had not received higher education.

> After my retirement I tried to go and work in other companies, but my skills were far behind. There are so many automatics. The technology is beyond my power to catch up with. I did everything, according to the demands; I can do simple things. I managed the construction material depot of the Australian Embassy when it was under construction. I was the guard of the building. . . . There are all kinds of demands from the society, if you are daring enough. I was a cosmetics company storehouse manager, making a record of the incoming and outgoing goods. I have worked for seven to eight years after my retirement. I also worked for a hotel; room management,

administration, and cleaning. I found it was not interesting at all, since I
was a skilled worker. They told me that different kinds of work have different characters, so I said okay. . . . [Now] I don't work any longer.

Besides the lack of education, another hindrance or difficulty to
overcome for older residents around Wangjing was the commute to
the new job. In the emerging suburb, at the time, there still existed
few if any new employment opportunities. Positions such as those
described by Ms. Wang above were usually located in the inner city.
Not a few of my older informants revealed that they eventually gave
up such jobs (or the search for one) because of the strain the commute
took on their health.

The private domestic sector role is complemented by the rapidly
growing number of joint ventures.[14] Over the years, foreign and joint-
venture businesses have expanded in location and scope, offering
more and more jobs for urban workers as well as for professionals.
These positions, even low-qualified ones, are often better paid than in
the public sector, but usually offer no or fewer benefits than the public sector.[15] Yet, among my older informants only one man had left his
job in the state sector before retirement and ventured into the private
sector early in the reform period. As an engineer with a university
degree he was able to find a job in different joint-venture companies,
first at Siemens and later at Ericsson. The daring had paid off: he and
his wife were among the few older owner-residents in the privately
financed apartments around Wangjing.

Generally, younger informants were much more likely to work in the
private sector. Since 1985, jobs are no longer automatically assigned
through the government; graduates are responsible to find employment themselves. Several of the younger people I talked to, who now
worked in private or joint-venture companies, had initially taken up
a job in a state-owned company. Here they were able to gain some
work experience, but they also learned about the (still predominant)
reality of working in the public sector. Quite a few of them pointed out
that they left the state-owned company because they were bored, fed up
with incompetent colleagues, felt like they were wasting their talents,
or wanted to pursue better career opportunities. Thirty-five-year-old
Ning, for example, had held a job in a ministry after graduating from
university. But she told me, "I found the work in the ministry was not
very interesting. I only read the newspaper and drank tea all day. I

thought it was a long way for me to run and I didn't want to waste time. My husband was a colleague of mine and he had the idea to establish his own company, so I helped to realize it." Others changed into the private sector, either full time or as a second job ("moonlighting"), solely to earn more money. This was the situation of Tang Shan, a thirty-one-year-old woman, who had studied electronics. After graduation, she worked in a state-owned machine factory but had recently changed to work for a foreign company. Asked about the benefits of the change, she answered that she could make more money. Nonetheless, she later specified: "Although the salary is high in the foreign company, the work I do is simple, which is not good for my future career. I studied electronics, but now I am working on an assembly line. My work has nothing to do with my major."

The situation was quite different for several other workers in their thirties who had been laid off from their factories. With middle school or secondary technical school degrees they had more problems finding new employment, and several of them had thus become private entrepreneurs. Similar to the Wu family, Wang Hong rented a sales stand in a suburban market where he sold hats, gloves, scarves, etc. While he could get a small income from the business, he, his wife, and one-year-old son had to live with his parents in their forty-square-meter two-room apartment because they could not afford to pay for their own house.

Wealthier young couples that I talked to in Wangjing frequently engaged in the strategy "one family, two systems" (yijia liangzhi), according to which one spouse works in the public and one in the private sector, to improve their financial situation while not losing out on state benefits. Among my informants, it appeared that women were more likely to enter the private sector than men. This might have been caused by special opportunities that the urban labor market offered to young, educated women in the reform period,[16] but it also reflected gender ideologies that considered men's contribution to the family economy more important than women's. The dual-income strategy is especially important in the context of housing provision because the public-sector spouse is likely to have access to subsidized housing.

All in all, the opening of the private sector has had positive as well as negative effects; it influenced my informants' lives in very different ways. On the one hand, the private sector offers new employment opportunities, often with significantly higher salaries. These, however, also come with less security in terms of tenure and benefits, and with higher pressure due to the competitive environment. On the other hand, for laid-off workers, the unemployed, and those in badly paid positions, the private sector often is a last resort to earn some extra income and to make ends meet. Overall, the private sector has played a decisive role in the stratification of present-day Chinese society and thus in the suburbanization processes underway.

Migration

In the midst of Wangjing's sleek vision of Chinese modernity, migrants—who live in substandard housing and work as construction workers, salespeople, or nannies—were a vital part of this new suburban zone. With their work, their everyday life practices, and their social positioning vis-à-vis other suburbanites, they importantly contribute to the transformation of Chinese cities and the urban living experience.

The reasons why migrants leave the countryside are complex. Migration systems theory suggests that migration is embedded in broader processes of economic, demographic, social, cultural, and political change; it is an integral part of globalization and social transformation. Migration is a way for individuals and groups to sustain or rebuild their livelihoods under conditions of rapid change (Castles 2000). Indeed, the reasons migrants in my investigation gave for their decision to leave the countryside and try their luck in the capital were a complex mix of economic incentives, new desires, and ideologies.[17] The further into the reform period, the more complex and diverse the reasons for peasants to leave the countryside have become. The growing social, economic, and spatial differentiations of Chinese society, however, have a vital impact on the phenomenon.

While the hukou system of residence permits remains officially intact in China, much of the state control has lessened in the reform period.[18] In cities, the emergence of the private-sector economy, and especially retail trade and personal services, offers job opportunities even for migrants without proper documentation.[19] Yet city governments have been reluctant to either build the infrastructure or give migrants legal access to urban amenities that would ease social problems (Jie and Taubmann 2002; Tang and Parish 2000). Without urban registration migrants face numerous obstacles: they are prevented from entering into certain occupations and trades; they are denied subsidized work-related housing, medical care, pensions, and social security; they are often forbidden to buy or build property; they and their offspring are excluded from, or charged exorbitantly to attend, local educational institutions; they are excluded from community- and work-based political, social, and recreational activities. Moreover, lacking proper documentation, stable residence, or secure employment, migrants may be considered criminals and subjected to fines, deportation, or even arrest (Gaetano and Jacka 2004). Thus, many migrants in the city are forced to live an uncertain existence on construction sites, in market stalls, on the streets, in rented rooms, or in makeshift settlements, located especially on the urban periphery.

Indeed, in Wangjing migrants usually lived in simple brick houses that they rented from the local rural population. Some of them were employed in local shops and restaurants, but the majority worked as private entrepreneurs in the various temporary markets in the suburb. These were usually designated outdoor areas or cheaply put together structures set up by the local government that filled the district coffers with the income produced from renting out stalls or selling sales permits. In the course of suburban redevelopment the markets were closed or taken down as easily and quickly as they had been put up. Salespeople were usually given a one-month notice during which they tried to find a new place to work.

One of the popular suburban markets in Wangjing was a combined indoor and outdoor affair. The outside area was the size of a soccer field, on what seemed to have been in the past the yard of an industrial plant. Every day vendors and customers streamed into the square to look, bargain, trade, buy, and sell everything from toilet paper to herbs, paper decorations for the Chinese New Year, clothes, fruit, electrical appliances, aquarium fish, flowers, puppies, fake antiques, cigarettes, and so forth, as well as freshly prepared food, such as dumplings, fried rice, tofu, and meats. The sales stands were all makeshift structures; sometimes an old bedstead or a table, sometimes moveable carts with window panes around a cooking device. The inside part of the market, in contrast, initially did not attract much attention from customers because it was crammed, steamy, and badly ventilated (Figure 3). Shortly after Chinese New Year in February 2002, however, the outside area and all of its permanent structures were razed, having been designated as the site for yet another new edifice. From that time on, some of the previous outdoor vendors rented stalls in the market hall to sell their wares and produce. Several food sellers propped up their stands on the sidewalk at the rear entrance of the hall.

Over lunch I frequently chatted with these vendors, among them a friendly couple in their sixties who were from Harbin, in China's north. Their story was exemplary of many others: shortly after the wife had retired, her husband was laid off from the clothes factory in which both of them had worked. Apparently, their pensions were paid irregularly; she only said, "It was hard to make ends meet." Since their daughter was not able to find a job, in 2001 the entire family decided to come to Beijing. Soon after, the old couple began to sell pancakes in this market. They rented a small brick house in the vicinity for which they paid 200 yuan per month. They also had to pay 15 yuan every month to the administrative bureau of the market. While they felt their life was better than in Harbin, it was still not easy: "It's [still] hard to make ends meet. We are five people in the family, and we have to pay for the house and [also] to be allowed to sell [the pancakes] here." When I asked them what they would do if the market would be closed, they shrugged and said they would look for another market and nearby house to move to. Indeed, just before I left the field in the fall of 2002, the market hall was torn down and the migrants scattered in all directions.

Figure 3. This suburban migrant market offering fresh produce was torn down during my time in Wangjing in 2001.

Besides working in small businesses, cottage industries, and temporary markets, migrants are a major factor in the transformations of Chinese cities and, by extension, in the development of suburbs: they are the ones who construct the new buildings and structures. Migrant construction workers are often organized groups from specific locales. They usually live and work on location and after finishing a project either move on to the next construction site or return to their home places. Nonetheless, they are also an important factor in the suburbs' everyday life, for example, as customers of local markets and restaurants or food vendors. But since migrant construction workers usually do not rent housing or engage in individual economic enterprises, in the present study their situation is not specifically addressed.

Land and Housing Reforms

Among the major changes that have affected city structures, and concomitantly urban citizens' lives, since 1978 have been the reforms in the housing sector. In the 1980s, the national government realized that the continuous housing shortages in Chinese cities were closely linked to the welfare character of housing provision. Neither local governments nor enterprises or individuals had an interest in the construction of housing because funds could not be recovered (Ye S. 1987). Subsequently, a series of experiments were launched to reform the urban housing sector.[20] Initially, efforts concentrated on improving and expanding the existing public-housing stock. To this end, the financial burden of housing construction was transferred from the central government to the danwei.[21] It was during this time that the electronics companies around Jiuxianqiao built residential quarters for their employees. Until then, the majority of them had lived in shared apartments without private bathrooms or kitchens, or in simple one-story brick houses in the vicinity. Evidently, the changes strengthened rather than diminished the role danwei played in housing provision. At the same time, the Chinese urban population did not equally enjoy the improved housing situation since the capacity for work units to provide new houses to employees now depended completely on their own financial situation. Danwei that performed well in the new market-based economy, such as most of the electronics companies in Jiuxianqiao, could provide housing, while those that performed badly had a reduced capacity to invest in new housing. Inequalities in housing provision thus increased substantially (see D. Bray 2005; Tomba 2004; Xing 2002).

In the 1990s, government policy shifted to stimulate commodification of residential real estate.[22] The Second National Housing Reform Conference in 1991 decided on three initiatives: first, rents were to be raised to cover the costs of maintenance; second, sitting tenants were to be encouraged to purchase their apartments on installment plans; and third, an increasing share of new housing was to be offered in the market. Wage rates were gradually increased, and families accumulated substantial savings. Confronted with growing inflation and China's immature financial institutions, the purchase of a home became an attractive investment; even more so as a secondary property market emerged in the second half of the 1990s (D. Davis 2000; Wang and Murie 1996).[23]

With the growing availability of mortgages, in the 1990s most of the older Jiuxianqiao residents bought their houses.[24] Most of these purchases, however, were made at drastically reduced prices.[25] Even with increased wages, the majority of danwei employees would not have been able to afford market prices.[26] The government thus differentiated between commodity housing *(shangpin fang)* for those who can afford to pay market prices and subsidized (or economy) housing primarily provided through the danwei. Moreover, a dual price system was developed for selling old (and new) work-unit housing: the "cost price" *(chengbenjia)* with discounts for years of service, age of housing, etc., and the standard price *(biaozhunjia)* set by the government housing authorities based upon local financial conditions and usually substantially lower than cost price.[27] Alternatively to buying their own residences, employees could also buy newly built houses while the work unit carried the largest part of the construction or purchasing costs. This option played a major role in public-sector employees' access to new residential complexes that were constructed during this time in neighboring Wangjing.[28]

Besides the housing reforms, the second major impact on Beijing's urban landscape was the (re)introduction of land prices in 1987, which has dramatically affected locational decisions throughout the city.[29] At the same time, industrial land use has declined and the amount of land used for commercial and residential purposes steadily increases (Wu and Yeh 1997; Yeh and Wu 1995). Today's spatial structure is more and more based on land value. In effect, the "hard edges" of cities that segregated rural and urban populations during the Mao-era "as clearly as a moated city wall" (D. Davis 1995, 2) have eroded and we can find urban-rural sprawl. Pushed by the real estate industry that has become the most important engine of economic growth in China (Zhang L. 2004), the focus of development of property complexes has increasingly shifted to the urban fringes because of rising land prices in the inner city. In Beijing, areas beyond the Third Ring Road, which were formerly considered "the suburbs" or even countryside, experienced sustained growth after 1990. Now this area is unquestionably part of the city proper, which is roughly defined as the zone within the Fourth Ring Road. The suburban area between the Fourth and Fifth Ring Roads, where Jiuxianqiao and Wangjing are located, has become the center of the latest residential construction projects.

Conclusion: The Transformed Urban Experience

The various reforms since 1978 have dramatically transformed Chinese urban residents' living situation and experience. In contrast to the Maoist era, when differentiations were based on a person's "revolutionary background," the importance of one's danwei, and personal relations to superiors, in the reform period citizens' social and economic conditions and social positions have been "reshuffled." Work units are increasingly differentiated according to economic success rather than political importance. At the same time, however, the growing marketization of various state services is beginning to favor the part of the population who have financially profited from the reforms. Workers and lower-level state-sector employees have to either accept significant cutbacks in benefits and social welfare or look for alternative incomes to purchase these in the market. In addition, after twenty-five years of being fixed in the countryside, peasants are able to migrate to urban centers where they attempt to get a share of the emerging wealth. Feeding the transforming (or developing) urban labor market, migrants' presence in cities questions prereform political, social, and economic dichotomies. Besides these socioeconomic transformations, it was the land and housing reforms that effectively altered the urban landscape. They gave rise to functional and spatial differentiations, and, in fact, to suburbanization.

The suburbanization process in China could thus be attributed to the growing importance of the market. Chinese suburbanization, however, is a much more convoluted process. Indeed, while the land and housing reforms have subjected the previously little differentiated urban landscape and the construction of housing to market mechanisms, both the danwei (employers) and the state remain importantly involved in housing provision and thus in the ongoing transformation processes.[30] But the involvement of the state in the suburbanization process does not end here. In connection with the transformations of the housing sector, government policies have had a great impact on China's urban society, in fact, supporting the ongoing class-formation process. A number of reform policies have put a certain population segment—namely, the emerging middle class—at a definite advantage over others. This happens not by coincidence or as an unfortunate result, but with the full intention of the government.

In the following chapter I will discuss the different forms of housing available around Wangjing, how they differ not only in architectural design but also increasingly in residents' lifestyle. By way of examining the lives of Wangjing residents in more detail, we will further see how the suburb has developed during the reform period, how residents are differently affected by the transformations, and what strategies they employ to counter the more disruptive changes.

3 DAILY LIFE IN WANGJING

From Exclusive High-Rise to
Crumbling Compound

BY 2006, Wangjing was a fairly well-established suburb with different housing options ranging from medium-priced to more upscale complexes, increasing numbers of restaurants, cafes, bookstores, and individual shops, and an exclusive shopping mall. The suburb was still changing and expanding, but in the central area the dust of construction had settled, and planted trees and flower beds sprouted roots. Ample roads, numerous buses, and a new subway line (finished just in time for the Olympic Games) connected the suburb with the inner city. At the time of my research in 2001–2, however, the locale was still in the making. Vast areas of this former green belt around the capital had been leveled in preparation for construction projects. The then recently finished six-lane Capital Airport Highway dissected the urban fringe diagonally, separating the old industrial cluster Jiuxianqiao in the east from the new Wangjing Development Zone in the west. On the edge of the freshly paved loop of ample streets, which projected Wangjing's future expansion, one could still get an idea of how the locale had looked before the blitz of development. Here, a narrow dirt road ran between rows of old buildings. On the left stood apartment blocks from the 1950s that had once belonged to a state-owned company; now run-down and obviously not taken care of, they were still partly occupied. Across the street, a maze of abandoned small factories and neglected enterprise lots was mixed with small brick houses, some of which had been turned into makeshift shops and restaurants. The ominously painted character *chai* (demolition) marked these structures for near-future destruction. Along the road, piles of garbage rotted in the sun, and a small, open canal was the only sewage system. The back alley stank horribly as soon as temperatures rose in spring. This was poorest and most dilapidated part of the entire suburban zone; it appeared to be the symbolic far side of Beijing's modernization enterprise. No foreigner and no newly wealthy Chinese trod down these streets without the shiny facades of fancy shopping malls and without newly planted trees to swallow the dust storms of Beijing. This road not only seemed to reflect what China had left behind on its way to modernization, but also the cost of that endeavor: the people left out from the newly emerging wealth (Figure 4).

The transformation of the former industrial zones on Beijing's fringe comes as a result of the land and housing reforms described in the previous chapter. Both farmers' small brick houses and the typical Soviet-inspired concrete buildings that marked China's urban landscape until the 1980s are by and by replaced by modern, colorful high-rises. The new residences come in an array of price, quality, style, service, and location, catering to consumers in different socioeconomic positions.[1] The difference between expensive and low-priced residential neighborhoods is clearly evident even from the outside. Not only location and architectural style, but also overall decoration, amount and design of green space, as well as cleanliness of the usually enclosed compounds are visible physical markers that distinguish them (Figure 5). Less evident are differences in property value, services, and social composition.

Figure 4. In 2001, the edge of Wangjing still showed what the area had looked like before the recent blitz of development.

Beijing people emphatically differentiate between individual neigh-borhoods' status, but these distinctions are not always clear-cut. The category most determinedly set apart by all informants was that of the "rich neighborhood" *(furen qu)*.[2] Nonetheless, depending on individu-als' own standing and perception, this could refer to either exclusive garden villas in resort-like areas in Beijing's outskirts or to the new upper-medium-level apartment complexes that have been built around Wangjing. More important, beyond such varying subjective percep-tions, and due to the persistent importance of the danwei in housing provision, distinctions of this kind cannot be taken as representations of sales prices. In the mid and lower categories of housing, private and public sector notably intersect. While housing in the medium category is commercially developed, the way residents obtain their units varies and makes these neighborhoods quite socially diverse. Some of the units in this category are sold in the market as commodity housing to individual buyers. Others, however, are bought or constructed with the help of the housing provident fund[3] by large work units with good resources, such as large profitable firms, major banks, and govern-ment agencies and institutions (see Zhang L. 2004). Buying in bulk, the danwei can negotiate better prices than individuals and are thus able to resell the units to employees at substantially discounted prices.

Figure 5. Upscale residential complexes are visibly distinguished by many large windows, overall architectural design, and landscaping efforts at the compound. [2001]

At the same time, lower-level neighborhoods include commercially developed units sold through danwei, government-sponsored complexes in distant locations for people resettled from inner-city locations, specially subsidized housing for people under a certain income level, and finally commercial residences sold in the market and targeted at the lowest financial bracket of urban residents. As a result of this mix of private and public spheres in housing construction and distribution, residents of mid-level complexes could have purchased their units for a significantly smaller price than what is paid in a low-level commodity compound. This circumstance highlights that present-day stratifications in urban China run much less along the state-market dichotomy than along markers of wealth, access to resources, lifestyles, and, ever more important, levels of consumption, all of which find a visible expression in housing.

While fancy up-market villas remain a dream that only a few very rich Chinese can afford, an increasing number of more reasonably priced, middle-income apartments of good quality have been built in immediate suburban areas such as Wangjing. However, even among these mid-range complexes there is a range of prices, types, and styles from which buyers can choose according to their means and tastes. In this chapter I will first describe the different types of housing available in Wangjing, and then discuss in more detail the lives of and differences among residents. What will become apparent is how housing choices, lifestyles, and socioeconomic stratification in China have become intricately linked and mutually reflective processes. Instead of straightforward economic indicators, increasingly it is residential neighborhoods that represent specific social status groups in China's urban social fabric.

Suburban Residential Choices

Mid-Level Commodity Complexes

Throughout the research period, ever-new mid-level residential complexes mushroomed around the Wangjing suburb. What was intriguing about them was the effort that was put into creating distinct communities. Each of the projects aimed at a specific style, reflected in the design and the name, apparently not only to attract buyers but also to forge owners' identification with the place. One of the complexes that caught my attention, for example, was a project with the English name "Heart Ocean." It was going to occupy one of the last lots available in a mixed residential and commercial block. I had visited many times the outside vegetable, fruit, and miscellaneous goods market that occupied the corner property where the complex was going to be built. In two days, the makeshift structures around the market were torn down, migrant workers with horse carts drove away the neatly cleaned bricks, and a fence and sales office were set up.

According to the clerk in the sales office, Heart Ocean was designed as a "European style complex," with apartments selling for 5,500 yuan (US$733)[4] per square meter. There was a 20 percent down-payment requirement, and the most expensive unit cost 800,000 yuan (US$106,667) in total. The compound promised facilities such as an underground parking lot, coffee and retail shops, as well as a gym. When I asked what kind of people the project aimed to attract, the salesclerk assured me that "with the availability of mortgages to Chinese people today, the apartments are affordable to everybody."

Another complex, "Ocean Pearl," had its name announced in English and Chinese. The compound sticks out in this suburban landscape because of its relatively small size, consisting of only six buildings and 212 apartments. The sale of units had started a couple of months before, and there were only fifty units left. Remarkable about this small neighborhood is its distinctive feature—extra-large living rooms in apartments that, as the eager salesclerk pointed out, were marketed to young wealthy couples without children.

One of the most fascinating new complexes at the time, however, was one block down the same road: "Saint Angel Shenxin" stands out because of its mixture of European styles. The fence around the compound is decorated with marble plaques depicting legendary Greek-style scenes with naked women and amphorae of wine. The common ground between the complex's four main apartment towers features a gothic-style building in the shape of a church that houses the compound's administrative offices. On top of each apartment tower a gilded cupid statue aims with bow and arrow into the distant horizon. The main entrance to the complex is closed by a four-meter-high, pointed arch-shaped iron gate with gothic ornamentation.

The complex had caught my attention early on because of the advertising posters around the compound. These depicted various Caucasian people—a middle-aged couple, a young man in a business suit, an elderly couple—who happily gazed down on the patch of green lawn between them. There, two over-large Chinese and Caucasian babies in diapers giddily spread their legs and arms and beamed with big, bright eyes at the observer on the street. The photo collage was surrounded by the words (in Chinese characters) "Environment" *(huanjing),* "Water" *(shui),* and "Air" *(kongqi)* (see Figure 6 for a later version of the advertisement). The real estate agent in the sales office informed me that there would be over one thousand apartments in thirty-one different styles within the compound. Each of the apartment towers had its own distinctive style, which the saleswomen described as overall "European romantic." The apartments ranged from 67 to 277 square meters in size, and their average price in 2002 was 5,360 yuan (US$715) per square meter. Among the amenities offered by the complex would be a supermarket, dry cleaner, swimming pool, gym, library, and a restaurant that was scheduled to open in June 2002. The entire complex was supposed to be finished by the end of 2002, and only one hundred apartments were left for sale. The project aimed to attract white-collar workers and businesspeople. So far, apartments had predominantly sold to couples, and only a few to families.

Sales representatives of the various complexes happily presented their glossy advertising brochures. These typically tried to lure buyers with slogans that referred to a cleaner environment in the suburb,

Figure 6. "Environment," "green space," and "water" are the catchwords on this advertisement to attract potential buyers to this recently finished expensive compound. [2002]

the nearby airport, the convenient commuting distance to the inner city and the CBD, and, more recently, the proximity to the (then planned) Olympic City to the west of Wangjing. The developer of the last project, Saint Angel Shenxin, had published an entire magazine that, centered around the complex, propagated a whole new lifestyle, explaining basics about health, sports, and nutrition, but also about community and family life. I will come back to the naming/framing and advertising for the new commercial complexes in chapter 5.

"Wangjing New City" (Wangjing Xincheng), the residential complex at the heart of the suburb, consists of two gated communities: the first one with "commodity" apartments *(shangpin fang)*, and the second with a mix of commodity and "economy" units *(jingji shiyong fang)* sold at a subsidized price. Altogether Wangjing New City is home to about twenty-five thousand people. It was built by the Beijing Cheng-shi Kaifa Jituan Youxian Zeren Gongsi, one of the largest state-owned construction corporations in the country.[5] Several of the residents in this complex told me that they actually decided to buy an apartment here because the developer was a state-owned company. They felt it was "safe" and that the facilities would be better than in other complexes at the time (Figure 7).

The first neighborhood consists of twenty-six buildings with twenty to twenty-nine floors. It was completed in 1997 and praised as the first fully commercial high-standard complex catering to Beijing's growing

Figure 7. Wangjing New City, the first "middle-class residential compound" in Beijing, rises above the still relatively empty ample roads of the suburb. [2002]

middle class (Tomba 2004). Accordingly, most residents referred to it as a "middle-class compound" *(zhongchan jieceng qu),* but some people I talked to in the city referred to it as a "rich people's place" *(furende difang),* pointing to the relativity of the socioeconomic differentiations in urban China at this point. The majority of the almost six thousand units in the first Wangjing community had been sold on the free market by the end of 1998. With an average price of 5,000 yuan (around US$667) per square meter, the apartments were expensive, but actually not much above the city's average of 4,764 yuan per square meter in 2002. Buyers, however, had to have enough money at hand since bank mortgages did not yet exist at the time.[6] The second neighborhood of only around three thousand units was completed in 1999. Similar in quality, location, and services, the prices of these units ranged from 4,000 yuan per square meter for the subsidized units to 5,500 yuan for the "commodity" units.[7] Buyers in this second development have generally been mortgage payers. Since most of the units are fairly large, the end price for the "economy" apartments was not significantly lower than for the commodity ones (Tomba 2004).

Wangjing New City is one of the biggest complexes in the suburb, covering a plot of more than one square kilometer. Encircled by large roads, the walled compounds each have four gates with security checkpoints and a barrier across the street. Incoming cars and pedestrians are usually announced. Inside the first compound, a winding road inscribes a loop around a central, small mall with various shops, two restaurants, Ping-Pong facilities, and a gym. Next to it there is a paved square with a fountain. Various benches, seats, and pavilions are loosely arranged around it. This central area is strictly pedestrian; security guards watch closely that no car and no bike enters the space.

Most of the apartment towers have small shops and facilities on the ground floor. There are hairdressers, small restaurants, a travel agency, kiosks, beauty salons, another gym, a flower and present shop, and more. The buildings are relatively plain, without any distinctive stylistic markers. As new apartments in China are usually sold completely empty (even without bathroom appliances), they varied strongly in their individual interior design and decoration. In marked difference to old danwei housing, however, they were brighter and more spaciously laid out. Moreover, all the new apartments that I saw during my research had tiled kitchens and bathrooms with Western-style toilets, and wooden or tiled floors. Visitors were always asked to take off their shoes when entering these apartments. As this never happened in old work-unit housing, the slippers assembled at the entrance doors of the new mid-level units became somewhat of a symbol of the residents' improved socioeconomic status.

On weekdays, the Wangjing New City compound was quiet and lonely, apart from midday when the central square was populated for about an hour by small children and their nannies, most of whom, judging by their clothes and dialect, came from the countryside. They were joined by a few old people who sat in the sun before disappearing into the buildings again. On warm evenings the compound became livelier when the mostly young and middle-aged couples went for leisurely walks. Weekends, in contrast, were busy times. The compound became crowded: young families and some elderly strolled about, went window shopping, sat on the benches, or played with children and pets. Nonetheless, there was not much communication between the residents, an impression confirmed by people I talked to, who unanimously said that they hardly knew anybody in the neighborhood and were not interested in meeting other residents.

Wangjing New City's good-quality apartments, high levels of services, and a green environment within a reasonably short distance from the city are intended to attract a relatively well-off and educated group of residents. Upon its completion in 2000, the general manager of the state-owned enterprise that developed the complex described it as "modern and culturally advanced." The neighborhood should become "a model for other residential developments in Beijing and the rest of the country" (Tomba 2004, 3). Owner-residents were mostly nuclear families, typically young couples with or without child, and sometimes retired parents. Commonly, they were employed in skilled positions in the public sector, but also in private or international ventures. As indicated above, the size of the "economy" apartments resulted in sales prices that have effectively prevented lower-income groups from moving into the complex.

Mid-Level Economy Compounds

Besides the mid-level commercial complexes, there are also several new mid-level compounds in Wangjing that have been financed by work units, or in which danwei bought substantial numbers of units (such as the second community of Wangjing New City). These apartments were then sold at preferential prices to the work unit's employees. One such neighborhood is Hua Yuan in a lot just north of Wangjing New City. The complex was built in the mid-1990s by several educational institutions, which resold residential units to their employees at a discount. Hua Yuan's residents, therefore, were teachers, editors, and professors in various schools and universities throughout the entire city. The majority was relatively young (thirty to forty years old).

The compound covers a roughly ten thousand–square-meter property on one of the major roads through Wangjing. Like the new commercial compounds, it is enclosed by a wall and fence with three gates guarded by security personnel who announce visitors. Inside the compound, about twenty twenty-floor high-rises lie scattered on one side of the main road, while on the other side there are five two-story houses that have been split up into individual apartments. The buildings and apartments are similar in style to Wangjing New City. Units range in size between 50 and 120 square meters and were offered to employees according to age and family size. All were sold at highly discounted prices. One family who lived in a roughly sixty-square-meter apartment told me that they had bought it in 2000 for 80,000 yuan (US$10,667), having received discounts for both of their ten years of work. Thus, they had paid about 1,300 yuan (US$173) per square meter, as compared to an average price of 5,000 yuan (US$667) in the Saint Angel Shenxin and Wangjing New City complexes described above.

Between the buildings are lawns, small paths, and a few nooks with benches, bushes, and Chinese-style garden elements. In one corner of the neighborhood is a parking lot, with above- and underground facilities. On another side sits a combined kindergarten, primary, and middle school building. There was only one small provisions store located within the compound, but several of the high-rises had small kiosks on the first floor that sold telephone cards, soft drinks, snacks, and ice cream. Just outside the main gate of the compound, a new supermarket had opened a couple of months before my research. All of this is comparable to the Wangjing New City complex, just slightly smaller in scale (Figure 8).

Similar to the atmosphere in other new complexes, during the week the compound was very quiet. On weekends it became lively and crowded with the predominantly young families with small children. While some of the couples chatted with each other, these were usually short interchanges and greetings. This resident confirmed my impression: "As for the neighbors, everybody has to work during the

Figure 8. A new midlevel compound offers "economy" units and style comparable to many commercial complexes in Wangjing. [2002]

day and we all come back home late at night, go see our parents on the weekends, so we can hardly find the time to meet each other." The residential neighborhood organization offered activities for its residents such as a health club, dancing, and music, but none of the people I talked to in this compound took part in them, claiming that they were at inconvenient times and that they were too busy anyway.

In sum, Hua Yuan offers its residents housing and a living environment that closely resembles the commercial complexes described above at roughly a quarter of the price. Categories such as "mid-level" or "low-level," used to describe residential communities as explained in the introduction to this chapter, thus refer much more to physical markers and status conveyed through them than to the real purchasing price of an apartment. It is in this sense that I will use these labels throughout the book.

Lower-Level Commodity Neighborhoods

Reflecting city planners' ideas of turning Wangjing into a middle-class suburb, only a couple of housing complexes built in the late 1990s catered to lower-income homebuyers. Since Beijing's successful Olympic bid, residential projects have become even more expensive in this suburb, and it is unlikely that more affordable housing will be built.

The lower-level neighborhoods were clearly of a much plainer style than even the simplest mid-level housing in the suburb. Nanlu Yuan, for example, consists of five straight rows of box-shaped, low-quality, five-floor buildings. After only a couple of years, their exterior already looked run down, with the paint coming off in parts of the facade and rust on window frames and roofs. The small paths between the buildings had minor greenery to each side, but there was no significant green space, no garden, and no children's playground in the compound. The environment was not very well taken care of: some of the shrubs had dried up and garbage littered the ground. A fence enclosed the neighborhood, but its main entrance gate always stood open and I never saw any security personnel. Although property management agencies created by development firms should take charge of public security, environment, and community services, lack of funding often interferes with fulfilling such responsibilities. For the same reason, security teams are often understaffed, and the agencies cannot afford any high-tech surveillance and tracking devices (Zhang L. 2004). As a result, residents protect themselves by installing metal bars around their windows and small balconies—a radical visual difference to the mid-level complexes in Wangjing.

Residents in such low-level neighborhoods usually have very diverse backgrounds. Most of them live on modest salaries from the public or private sector. Some people, however, have additional incomes, for example through a second job. Often, they can eventually improve their overall household economy and move to better neighborhoods. Other residents, in contrast, might have been laid off from their state-owned companies and no longer receive salaries, but rely on family and a complex social network for support instead. Thus, even within the lower-level communities, socioeconomic stratification processes continue to differentiate residents; public and private sector have different effects on people's lives (Zhang L. 2004).

Old Danwei Compounds

A description of the Wangjing residential landscape would not be complete without mentioning the remaining old danwei compounds and the scattered pingfang houses that once accommodated the rural population when this was still hinterland. Most of the danwei compounds that remained in the Wangjing suburb at the time of my research had been built in the early 1980s. Although of differing size, these compounds were all designed in the typical work-unit style: rows of identical, evenly spread out, parallel, five-story, walk-up apartment buildings on both sides of the main street of the compound. Inside, residential units were all of a similar design. What visibly distinguished them from newly constructed commercial apartments were the barren cement floors and untiled kitchens and bathrooms. Several units I visited were also dark and damp. Residents, however, put effort into improving their homes according to their financial means (see chapter 5). Yet the complexes' dirty hallways with their worn-off paint and bare, low-intensity light bulbs for illumination stood in stark contrast to the tile-floored and elevator-served new housing complexes.

As in the new neighborhoods, around the buildings in the danwei compound there were usually small recreational areas, a kindergarten, a primary and middle school, and some shops and service stores. All this was enclosed by high walls with one or two gates that used to be guarded by security personnel, but subsequently just stood open.[8] Since the reforms, differences among the old complexes derive from the economic success of the "mother-company"; while some looked run-down and slightly desolate, others had been renovated and improved and were well kept.

One of the nicer such compounds was Hong Yuan, erected in the early 1980s as the residential quarters for the employees of several of the electronic-parts factories in the area. At the time of the research, 4,337 families, or 13,180 people, lived in Hong Yuan. More than 60 percent of the residents in the compound were over sixty years old and depended on their pensions.[9] The average income of the working population was said to be 1,000 yuan (US$133) per month. Management and service offices' financial expenditures were covered by the electronics companies, which had put the money into building the residential complex. Residents had purchased their apartments since the early 1990s at below market prices. The price was determined mainly by buyers' length of employment in the danwei. Ranging from 20 to 60 square meters in size, the cheapest unit had sold for just about 10,000 yuan (US$1,333), while most of them cost 40,000 yuan (US$5,333).

Hong Yuan had seven so-called work stations (branches of the local residents' committee), each staffed with two employees who were responsible for health care, child care, employment for laid-off workers, and care for the elderly in the community.[10] In addition, the work

stations took care of family issues and acted as mediators in communal conflicts. They also offered free social activities to the residents,
which were normally led or taught by volunteer community members.
The majority of the people living in Hong Yuan were (former) work
colleagues. Life in the compound today was strongly marked by the
retired residents, who could be seen all over the *xiaoqu* (small residential neighborhood) involved in one of the various activities that were
offered: chess, dancing, gymnastics, card playing, and so forth. People
I talked to gave me a sense of a "pensioner's paradise":

> After the building of the community, we organized some groups, such as the
> singing group, folk dance group, disco group, kungfu, and sword-practicing
> teams. In order to prepare for the Great Olympics, every community has its
> own English class and calligraphy class. It is fine. We have plenty of activ-
> ities. We can play around after the meals. We also have gym facilities for us
> to do some exercises. This area is very good; they offer the retired men and
> old grannies a place to play.

But Hong Yuan was in many ways a "model community"; other old
danwei compounds in Jiuxianqiao and around Wangjing were rather
drab places with no such facilities and special activities for the retired
population (Figures 9 and 10).[11]

Their specific features and services notwithstanding, all the old
work-unit compounds in the Wangjing area and their retired residents

*Figure 9. One of the few old state-owned residential compounds remaining in
Wangjing in 2001.*

appeared a little like being in a different time. Even though the Hong Yuan compound, for example, had been renovated and changed, once one stepped through its gates, life appeared slower and quieter. Wherever one looked, people were chatting with neighbors on their way to run errands. This stood in stark contrast to the newer residential complexes, where anonymity of living was actually one of the positive qualities that residents mentioned. The communal atmosphere within the old danwei compound was further underlined by the growing changes and increasingly faster pace of life just outside the compound's walls. Residents' mobility (especially of the elderly) reflected the discrepancy between the modern new suburb and the old compound: almost all of them said that mainly out of economic reasons they hardly ever went downtown; neither did they move much around Wangjing. Their lives revolved around the *xiaoqu*.

Pingfang Houses and Villages

Even more out of place in the "brave new suburban world" appeared the few remaining islands of one-floor, brown brick houses (pingfang) that had been typical of the countryside. These were usually comprised of only one room and had outside kitchenettes and no private bathrooms. Huddled together, and accessible only through a labyrinth of small dirt paths, these used to be the houses of the agricultural

Figure 10. A renovated old state-owned compound in Jiuxianqiao. [2001]

population within the Beijing municipality. Now in the shadow of the ever-rising luxurious new apartment complexes, the pingfang areas were generally in unsanitary conditions; as they were bound to be torn down in the near future, the city seemed to have given up on the provision of services such as garbage collection, for example (Figure 11). Yet, the pingfang houses offered the only accommodation to migrants who worked in the suburb. When they were demolished, these temporary residents scattered in search of new places, most often moving further out of the city into the more rural hinterland.

Villages beyond the suburb have actually developed a dual character: while maintaining their rural appearance, increasingly more of the inhabitants are forced to give up their land (and farm work) for new construction projects. Some find employment in the city and commute daily to the capital to work. Others depend on income generated by renting their houses or rooms to the migrants who, without a residence permit, are excluded from the urban housing market. This renting, moving, tearing down, however, is a perpetual process since the city continues to grow outward into this hinterland, and practically every month a new village on the urban fringe is marked for destruction. For migrants, therefore, housing in the suburban area is generally

Figure 11. A former farmer's house now rented to migrants who worked in one of the suburban markets. [2001]

neither safe nor stable but instead a constant search for new temporary solutions.

To conclude, the suburban landscape is a highly dynamic zone, an area in constant flux. It offers diverse types of housing in differing compounds or neighborhoods, ranging from new exclusive gated communities on the upper-medium end of the economic spectrum to affordable neighborhoods catering to lower-income buyers, from new mid-level economy units to old state-subsidized compounds and prereform structures such as the pingfang houses. Not surprisingly, even though publicly known as a "middle-class" area of Beijing, Wangjing is in fact home to people from a multitude of social, economic, and educational backgrounds, who live in the suburb for very different reasons. Consequently, the social, economic, and spatial transformations of the city in general and of this suburban space in particular do not affect all residents alike. Suburbanization is multiply experienced. This is an important difference, or departure, from suburbanization processes elsewhere. In the United States, for example, after World War II, improvement of transportation, growing affluence, the rapid rate of urban growth, and growing dissatisfaction with the city itself, together with lower tax rates in the urban fringes and racial tensions, led especially white Americans to choose outer-city locations over minority-dominated central-city residences. The resulting suburbs were characterized by low density, large lots with single-family homes, extensive automobile infrastructure, and racial and class homogeneity (see Zhou and Logan 2005, 2008).[12] In China, in contrast, the specific historical, political, and economic conditions of urban transformations make for the development of very different, and much more diverse, suburbs, even if there is a certain homogenizing momentum. Especially the way public and private sector continue to intersect has a decisive influence on the suburbanization process by favoring certain population segments over others. As will become apparent in the remainder of this book, however, Chinese urban residents are also agents whose decisions impact on the city's transformation and on the shape and form of the suburban realm.

Wangjing Residents

Almost all urban residents that I talked to around Wangjing had bought their apartments. Yet how they did so and the reason why they had purchased their houses strongly diverged. At the same time, some suburbanites—notably young people with low-income jobs and migrants—lived in the area but, for different reasons, were *not* home-owners. In this section I will describe the inhabitants of the different residential choices that existed in Wangjing at the time of my research. What emerges from the discussion is a picture of increasingly distinct residential communities with characteristic lifestyles, a point that will be further explored and elaborated on in the subsequent chapters.

Residents of Old Danwei Compounds

Elderly informants in the old danwei complexes said that because of their many years of work, they had received considerable discounts on the sale price for their apartments. Sixty-three-year-old Ling Dawen, for example, explained: "We have bought it from my husband's company. It was very cheap. My husband started to work in the 1950s; our working years together are more than sixty-five years, so we got this house for 10,000 yuan (US$1,333)." In other old danwei compounds, the average forty-square-meter apartments had sold for 30,000 to 40,000 yuan (US$4,000 to US$5,333). Despite such substantial discounts, some retirees whose pensions were not very high had received support from their children to purchase their homes. While loans and mortgages have been widely available since the late 1990s, retirees especially might not qualify for them.[13] Thus, among the fifteen residents whom I surveyed in one old danwei compound,[14] only two had bought their apartments with a loan and one of these had actually been taken out by an adult single daughter who still lived with her retired parents. In another case, several children had pooled money to purchase the unit for their parents, a practice I heard of repeatedly.

Residential units in the old danwei compounds were for the most part sold to sitting tenants. Thus, homeowners were predominantly older work-unit employees or retirees. Some people, however, rented or sold their units to either children or strangers. An example of this arrangement was thirty-nine-year-old Wang Jianling. Wang was not able to find a highly qualified (and well-paying) job because the Cultural Revolution severely disrupted her education. After she became unemployed, Wang was given a job with the neighborhood's residents' committee.[15] Her husband worked as a driver for a state-owned company. With their low salaries, the couple could certainly not afford to buy an apartment. Instead, they rented their unit from Wang's parents-in-law, who had purchased it from the danwei at the substantially discounted price of 10,000 yuan and lived with their other son in his bigger house. Another young resident was Pan Suming (age thirty-two), who also worked for the residents' committee. Yet, she was in a better financial position than Wang Jianling since her husband worked for one of the better-paying electronics companies that had built the compound. With the financial support from their parents and the money they had paid into the housing provident fund since 1998, they were able to buy a small apartment in an old danwei compound from a couple who left to live with their son.

Wang Jianling's case demonstrates how an unfavorable economic situation impacted on the younger generation's perspective of home-ownership, even in the significantly more affordable secondary housing market. At the same time, it shows that the old generation's favorable access to subsidized public housing could significantly ease the negative effects of the reform of the housing provision system for their children's generation. Thus, good family relations are extremely important, if not essential, for many younger people's well-being. A difficulty, however, is the lack of available apartments in the old, more affordable danwei neighborhoods. Pan Suming was lucky to have found her apartment;[16] many new employees of state companies and adult children of danwei residents were actually forced to (and at times also chose to) move to different, often commercially built housing complexes if they wanted to have their own place. These were likely to be in distant locations as the number of affordable housing complexes around Wangjing was limited.

Yet frequently children continued to reside with their parents even after they got married, because they did not earn enough money to afford apartments sold at market prices and/or their employer did not offer any housing support. It usually took a few years of saving money through this kind of cohabitation before young couples could finally buy their own house. After they got married, Pan Suming and her husband had also lived for a couple of years with his parents before they could afford to move out. Similarly, among the fifteen residential units surveyed (see above), thirteen (86 percent) were occupied by at least two generations of residents. Two of these were middle-aged parents with a small child; the others were retired parents with adult children. In two units, adult children had only recently moved into their own apartments. In five (38.5 percent, or 33.3 percent of the total units examined) of the thirteen two-generational households, adult children were married and lived with their spouse in the parents' house. Three of these (20 percent of the fifteen households I surveyed), in turn, had a small child, that is, three generations cohabited. In this context, it is important to keep in mind that the majority of apartments in a typical old danwei compound are only forty square meters in size and often have only two rooms. Thus, in the multigenerational homes that I visited, there existed no living room, but only two bedrooms, one of which was used by the young family. Guests like me were usually attended to in the small hallway/entrance space, which was also where the family ate. In other cases, the old generation's bedroom served as a sitting room where the bed stood in one corner and a table and some chairs were squeezed into another.

Research in the early 1980s (Unger 1993) and early 1990s (Whyte 2005) showed that some two-thirds of all households in China's major cities consisted of nuclear families, and between 35 and 47 percent of the children were married. In contrast to popular perceptions that Chinese families usually are composed of three generations (grandparents, parents, children, or stem families), the data revealed that actually only one-quarter of urban Chinese families followed this model. Scholars (e.g., Davis and Harrell 1993; Treas and Chen 2000; Unger 1993; Whyte 2005) have attributed these residence patterns less to culture or "tradition" than to the temporary lack of alternative accommodation. Similarly, most of my interviewees—both parents and married children—expressed the desire to live in separate households. Because of the lack of housing and financial means, however, they accepted coresidence, at least temporarily. Ms. Ma (age sixty), for example, was actually quite upset when I asked her about her living situation:

> My daughter doesn't live with us, but my son does. He has no house. To tell the truth, apartments are really expensive in Beijing; the most expensive in China. How can salary-class people afford to pay for it? We don't like to live together but we have to. The old people should have their own place; so should the young people. We have to save money and also ask for loans from the bank. . . . To tell the truth, the houses are so expensive, I have to let them save money for their own house. I won't stop them if they want to move out. My son-in-law has his apartment. My house is only fifty square meters; too crowded.

In the past, multigenerational residence was mainly due to the overall lack of available housing. With the reform-period increase in housing construction, however, today coresidence is much more likely to be economically motivated. Yet more and more families are able to fulfill the ideal of separate households, at least after some years of saving funds through cohabitation.

Importantly, even after setting up their own households, married children and parents maintain close mutual contact; they deliberately keep interdependent households, more so than would be the norm in most Western societies (Unger 1993, 40). This applies to the interchange of monetary gifts, but also to help in everyday affairs and social support. Such connections are motivated by notions of filial piety,[17] but are also enforced by the reforms of the social security system that has transferred responsibilities from the state to the individual and the family. Not surprisingly, these connections were especially strong or important among the less economically well-off, and thus particularly relevant and observable among residents of the old danwei compounds. One should not assume, however, that such support only flowed from children to parents; quite on the contrary: since state-sector wages are based on a steep seniority system and daily expenses are rising, many adult children remain financially dependent on their parents. Thus, several of my younger, married informants relied on their retired parents for special expenditures, especially for their child. Wang Jiangling, for example, pointed out that she did not support her retired parents. "On the contrary, they give me money. The computer and my daughter's stuff are all bought by our parents."

The interconnections between parents, adult children, housing, and financial support were well illustrated by two of my informants, thirty-one-year-old high-school classmates Tang Shan and Caroline.[18] Tang Shan, who studied electronics, had recently left her state-owned company and found a job in a joint venture. Tang's husband worked on a construction field in the northwest of China, where he could earn more money than in the city, and came back home only occasionally. Despite their double income, the couple could not afford to buy their own house. Instead, they lived with Tang's parents, who had bought their danwei apartment, and thus tried to save as much money as possible. Because of their financial situation, Tang and her husband had also postponed having a child. All they strived for was to have their own house. "It's my aim [to have my own house]. All my works and studies are for realizing this dream." When asked why the house was so important to her, Tang explained, "It will change the quality of my life and I may be able to have a child." But to realize this aspiration, Tang and her husband needed the support and interconnection with their parents. For Tang's parents, in turn, it was "only natural" to support their daughter and her husband. The mother, who was retired, cooked for the entire family so that Tang Shan "could concentrate on her work." Tang contributed a small sum to the household's monthly expenses, but the parents insisted that she save most of her income for an apartment.

Caroline, on the other hand, had studied international trade. She was first employed in a state bank. Later she worked as an accountant in different foreign companies, and she was with a Canadian telecommunications company at the time we met. Her husband was a telecommunications engineer at Siemens. Because both of them worked in foreign companies with higher salaries, the couple had been able to buy a small, one-bedroom commodity apartment, and they were planning to buy a bigger one soon. Caroline even considered purchasing a car. Despite living in a separate household, the couple spent every weekend at their parents' houses, something that, Caroline assured, "just comes naturally." The couple usually brought snacks and small presents and occasionally treated their parents to a restaurant visit. At the same time, Caroline made it clear that she would have to rely on her parents or in-laws to help her once she and her husband decided to have a child. From a pragmatic point of view, one could therefore say that Caroline nurtured a social network on which she knew she would have to rely in the near future.

Some old danwei residents actually received daily visits from their adult children; many of them just dropped by after work, but several also regularly took their meals at the parents' houses because they claimed to have little time to go shopping for groceries and/or to cook. Again, this supports studies from the 1980s and 1990s (Unger 1993; Whyte 2005) that showed that even when family generations lived apart, they tended to interact almost like stem or extended families. Chinese researchers have called this arrangement "networked families" (wangluo jiating), which is said to have become more common during the 1980s and 1990s when, as explained above, state-provided social services were cut back. Although young couples and their elders prefer to live apart, they want to live near each other in order to be able to carry on such "networked" arrangements. Davis and Harrell (1993) and Unger (1993) report that families actually maneuvered to acquire housing that would enable one or more of the married children's homes to be clustered near the original home. With growing socioeconomic stratification and indeed segregation in Chinese cities, this ideal, however, will become more difficult to realize. Sale prices for apartments rise according to their proximity to the city center and, in addition, certain "fashionable" suburban areas, such as Wangjing, have also experienced sharp price rises.[19] None of the adult children of elderly danwei residents in my research who had moved out and been able to purchase housing (either commodity or economy units) actually lived physically close to their parents. Although the kind of "networking" described above remained intact, it was at the growing cost of spending more time to overcome large distances.

The long distances to workplaces or to children's schools that result from moving to residential neighborhoods far from the city center have also become a very concrete difficulty in the organization of everyday life of the younger generation. Despite ownership of an apartment, some adult children actually stayed with their parents in what was now (in contrast to the prereform era) a more conveniently located danwei compound throughout the week. Again there was a socioeconomic bias in this circumstance: less economic means and access to preferential housing (through working in a successful company) resulted in less conveniently located and less well-developed residential options and a much lesser likelihood to own a car.

Apart from the direct monetary (i.e., cash) or indirect (coresidence) support that parents extended to their married children, another important aspect of their close relation was daily child care. Since most young husbands and wives work full-time, and most often at least one of their parents (usually the mother) is retired by the time of the birth of a grandchild, grandparents were needed and available to take care of the child. In some cases, grandchildren lived with the grandparents and were registered in their household to get access to better schools in the vicinity. Thus, one grandmother explained: "They [her son and daughter-in-law] have bought their own house, but it is far from my little baby's [granddaughter] school. It is a newly developing residential area."[20] But some parents also just did not have enough time to take care of their offspring because of their busy work schedules.

Networking support between parents and married children in my sample appeared to be guided by practical considerations of convenience and necessity. These networks existed equally with sons and daughters, or the other way around, with parents of both husband and wife; they were not determined by the traditional connection between parents and married sons. Interestingly, but maybe not surprisingly, though, the younger generation with less financial means mentioned retired parents more frequently as a source of support than the young, affluent couples living in Wangjing who were more likely to rely on paid services.

Even though the nuclear family is the preferred, and increasingly realized, residential pattern, this should not conceal another reality: once parents reach old age and became frail, or after one spouse dies, they usually move in with their married children. An important factor influencing this living arrangement is that elderly pensions are usually very low, and some (those who worked in collectives or whose danwei went bankrupt, for example) do not receive pensions at all. While there is also a "traditional" expectation that parents will move in with one of their children (usually the oldest son) to be taken care of in old age, this notion appears to be waning. One reason is that the one-child policy makes this arrangement overly burdensome to a couple who would have to care for four older people. But even among the current generation of seventy- to eighty-year-olds, who almost always had more than one child, some people expressed doubts about or hesitations to move in with their adult children. They thought their lifestyle and their ideas were too different from their children to allow living together harmoniously.[21] Only relatively few adult children, however, could pay for a place in a retirement home or for live-in service personnel to take care of old parents. Thus, at least partly due to economic necessity, frail elderly parents have little choice but to move in with their children. When they had several children, choice of coresidence appeared not to be influenced by gender, but parents usually lived with the child who had the biggest house and the best financial means.[22] In some cases, parents took turns in staying with each child for a certain period of time. After moving in with adult children, the old danwei apartment that the parents likely owned was either rented out or sold. Income thus derived often contributed to the newly formed multigenerational household's economy. These arrangements, of course, also applied to the young, wealthy couples living in commercial housing.

Older danwei residents thus play a vital and dynamic role in transitional Chinese society by providing housing and/or various other forms of support to their grown-up children. In terms of spatial mobility, however, their situation was quite different. Living in the old suburban danwei compound in the reform period has presented elderly residents with new logistical problems. During the Maoist period, the integrated lifestyle of the work unit rarely called for leaving the compound or the immediate neighborhood. There was nothing one had to buy that was not available around the compound, and in addition, there was not much time or opportunity for leisure activities that would involve traveling throughout the city. Since the reform period, this has significantly changed. Nowadays, there are farmers and small-goods markets throughout Wangjing of which danwei residents happily take advantage. Nonetheless, in 2001 more specialized goods, such as clothes and electronic articles were not available in this developing neighborhood. Obtaining them required trips to the city center. In contrast to the Maoist era, public transportation has significantly improved, offering frequent bus services to the inner city. Ms. Li explained:

> [Transportation] is improving year after year. We didn't have so many buses but [now] there are more and more of them. No. 420 takes us to Wangfujing [downtown] directly. It is convenient. We buy vegetables at Jiuxianqiao. It is near; we can go there by bike. We can also go shopping at Erqi, Huajiadi, and other places in this area. But if I want to buy something really nice I have to go to Wangfujing, Longfudasha, Blue Island, or Xidong'an Market.

The cheapest buses, however, took over an hour to reach a central-city destination, and faster ones were more expensive. In addition, riding cheap buses remains quite an experience: old, dirty, and polluted, without any comfort, and rarely a place to sit. Even for me, a younger person, these trips were physically exhausting.

Asked about how they moved around the city, several danwei residents named the bicycle, but also the bus. Very few said they would use taxis, because the price was too expensive for them, such as this woman who explained, "I seldom take the taxi. I take buses in order to save money."[23] In consequence, the majority of the elderly danwei residents actually said that they did not go to the city very often. If they did, maybe once a month or every two, many of them relied on children who had cars to pick them up. Besides, they depended on the danwei to organize outings for them, as this woman described: "Several days ago, our factory organized for us to go to Fengyang Zhuozhou, to visit the Film City. We had a bus for free. . . . Our factory always organizes some activities for us although we are retired." Younger danwei residents, in contrast, usually used bicycles or the cheapest public buses as transportation methods.

In conclusion, old danwei complexes were dominated by elderly, retired residents. These owned their apartments and received a pension, which, together with the remaining social benefits granted by their danwei, allowed for a relatively secure livelihood. The few young residents of these danwei compounds were in one way or another intricately linked to the older generation: they lived with old parents in their apartment, or rented or bought units from old residents. The connection between the two generations in the old danwei complexes was further strengthened by other reciprocal exchanges and services that continued even if the young people eventually moved away: retired parents provided child care and sometimes material support to their adult children and in return received material, logistical, and eventually old-age support from them. In fact, the two generations were mutually dependent on each other. This dependency, or "networking" as it has been called, is further enforced and even exacerbated by the spatial transformations of the city in the post-Mao era, including suburbanization. Daily life in the reform period involves overcoming larger distances and, with the diversification of urban functions, a growing necessity to reach different places within the city. In this regard, residents of the suburban old danwei compounds, who generally earn less money, have faced new challenges. While the older people more or less retreated behind the walls of the compound, the younger generation became even more reliant on their parents for support to confront these changes.

Residents of Mid-Level Compounds

As I have described elsewhere (Fleischer 2007a), inhabitants of the new commodity complexes belong to the new class of "chuppies"— Chinese urban professionals employed in skilled positions, especially in the public sector, but also in private or international ventures. The most obvious difference between them and the residents of danwei compounds was that while the majority of the latter (especially older

people) had been assigned to the area, the former had consciously chosen the location and the complex in which they lived. The predominantly young, affluent couples with one or no child were actually quite
specific about their reasons to move to Wangjing, that is, their choice
was well founded and reflected upon. Among the attractive features
of the area they named a better environment in the suburb, more
ample space, less noise and pollution, better "quality" of people, and
the convenient location in relation to points of attraction in the city,
such as the CBD, for example. Several residents also cited variations
of the old saying about Beijing's cosmologically inspired city structure
in imperial times that I mentioned in the introduction. "The east is
better than the south, comparatively; as you know the north is better
developed than the south. The government focuses its attention on the
north, the infrastructure is better than in the other places." Allegedly
the north also had better feng shui[24] and my informants were willing
to pay a price for it: "If you can choose, north is the best place, but the
price is more expensive. For the price you buy an apartment near the
North Fourth Ring Road you can buy one near the South *Second* Ring
Road." While the north of the city has a geographical advantage in
terms of its climatic conditions,[25] with these quotes we can also see
how history connected to present-day developments: the historical layout of the city still influenced peoples' choices of residence and, in the
end, city planning and development. Chinese cosmology met imperial
city planning in the market sphere. I will come back to the importance
of location in the changed urban landscape and the status attached to
specific places in chapter 5.

Importantly, since the real estate market took off in 1992/93, Beijing,
like other Chinese cities, experiences residential segregation (see Gu and
Liu 2002); Hu and Kaplan (2001) speak of "zones of affluence." But, as
I have pointed out in the description of residential choices available in
Wangjing, so-called mid-level zones of the city remain at least for now
interspersed with lower-level housing and less affluent residents. Due
to the system of unequal distribution and differential prices of housing, however, *within* new residential compounds Chinese people find
themselves more and more living with others in similar life situations
and of comparable income strata and, often, age. Among the affluent
young couples in Wangjing, living with similar people was actually a
criterion for selecting where to settle. Twenty-nine-year-old Huijing, a
resident of Atlantic Place, for example, explained: "There are about

two hundred apartments in the compound. A lot of young people live here. It is important for me to choose a kind of house where nice people live." Wen Hou (age thirty), who lived in the same compound, made it even clearer: "Most of the people here work in foreign companies or joint ventures. They have a good educational background, which is important for me. . . . It's a good place for young people."

At the same time, residents of the mid-level complexes also embraced the newly found anonymity of these living areas that stood in stark contrast to the old courtyard house or danwei compound–produced control and supervision of the Maoist period. Twenty-nine-year-old Ma Li, a resident of the Wangjing New City complex, for example, said: "I have no idea of others [neighbors]. I don't think people like to associate with each other. It's not like living in a traditional courtyard house (siheyuan). People don't know each other very well here." Even though he had been so clear about the type of residents he sought to live with, Wen Hou confirmed this attitude: "We seldom interact with other people in the community. I know some of my son's classmates' mothers live in the community. . . . When I lived with my parents and in the school dormitory, a lot of people peeked into my private life. I have my own space now."

A 2002 survey by Market-Expert, a Shanghai-based market research firm, found that 44 percent of mainland urban families did not know their neighbors' names, while 63 percent did not have any contact with the people next door (Fang 2003). This presents quite a change from the living situation in hutong neighborhoods (small alleyways), where residents knew each other very well, as described by an elderly couple, still living in an old courtyard house, whom I met at a housing fair: "Our neighbors are our friends. We like the old lifestyle where we meet the neighbors in the street and everybody knows everybody else. In the evenings we sit in front of the house and chat with each other." But the contrast was also apparent in comparison with the old danwei complex where people stressed the communal atmosphere and camaraderie among residents. Nonetheless, with increasing numbers of people moving in and out of such compounds, these also lose their close-knit matrix of social relations, as reflected in the surveys mentioned above.

In contrast to the young generation of old danwei compound residents, among the young, affluent couples living in mid-level housing around Wangjing, being close to parents or parents-in-law was not a criterion for their choice of residence, nor were they dependent on their parents for child care. The reasons are twofold. First, since they were financially sound, all of the young couples I spoke to had household help, including nannies for their children. Quite a number of them actually sent their child to boarding schools, liberating themselves from the daily task of taking care of them. Second, because they had few financial worries, this group of young couples relied on private cars or taxis to overcome distances within the city. For them, physical location was not a limiting concept. On the contrary, most of the young professionals traversed the city frequently and widely to take advantage of the various facilities and amenities it offered, ranging from educational institutions to sports facilities to entertainment venues. Ma Li expressed this sense of independence based on owning a car: "We only have one park around here; it is Wangjing Park. Chaoyang Park is another one but it is quite far from here. As for me, it doesn't bother me too much because I have my own car." Ownership of a car, or the frequent use of taxis, of course, also made it easier to regularly visit parents in other parts of the city.

While the young professionals did not rely on their parents for financial or social support, they had similarly close relations to parents as less financially well-off residents of old danwei compounds described above. In their case, however, it was clearly the children who took care of the retired parents by taking them out to restaurants, driving them to places in the city, inviting them to their houses, and financially supporting the purchase of a house or their travel and vacations. Few of the young professionals had their parents permanently living with them. This, however, might have been caused by the fact that most of the commodity homeowners I talked to were in their early thirties, and their parents were therefore likely to be still able to live independently and take care of themselves. For those who had invited their parents to live with them, the suburban location could pose a problem, as became apparent in Xiu Lan's story. Xiu Lan, a middle-aged woman, worked in Haidian, in the northwest of the city, and had recently bought an apartment in Wangjing from her danwei. Yet, Xiu's elderly and frail parents, who lived in a small, old work-unit apartment further inside the city, required her daily attendance. Moving with Xiu Lan into her new, more spacious suburban apartment in Wangjing would remove the parents from their accustomed surroundings. They would live in a place where they neither knew anybody nor had many elderly coresidents, something Xiu did not want for her parents. Therefore, instead of moving into her new apartment, Xiu and her husband actually rented it out and lived with her parents in their old house.

Very few of the homeowners in the commercial complexes I visited around Wangjing were older than fifty years. The most important reason for this was, of course, that the elderly had fewer chances to financially profit from the economic opportunities of the reform era. They were, therefore, usually not able to afford commercial housing. In the Wangjing complex, however, I met one exception: fifty-five-year-old Liu Dongtian and her husband, Zhang Renqing (age sixty), who worked for a foreign telecommunications company. The company had financially contributed to the purchase of the new house, even though the couple already owned their previous danwei-connected apartment, which was located further away in the city proper. Present-day (foreign company) employment and previous work-unit membership clearly put this couple into the very privileged position of owning two houses. Renting the old apartment to relatives, they could even make some extra money on the side. Liu Dongtian explained their living situation:

> We have another apartment near Yabaolu [within the Third Ring Road]. Our apartment [here] was bought with the help of my husband's company. The company paid part of the money, and we paid a part; for the rest, we asked for a loan from the bank. My husband's company was buying housing for its staff. A lot of people like this area. His company is located at Jiuxianqiao close to here, so we chose this place. The reason why we didn't choose Atlantic Place was because the management fees there are very high. Some of his colleagues chose Shunyi county [beyond the Fifth Ring Road]. Whichever place you chose, the company paid for you. Several of our good friends live in this same building, so we can take good care of each other if we need help. We also bought the old apartment. It cost only 30,000 yuan. Working years helped reduce the price. . . . I like this [apartment]. The old apartment at Yabaolu is our house in the city. I have relatives who live there now. Compared to people my age, I have good living conditions. Our house was not enough when my children were small. Later on, the company helped us solve that problem. I got what I needed. . . . I had a lot of choices before we bought this apartment. We chose this place at last.

While Liu Dongtian and her husband certainly appeared overprivileged, this kind of intersection of the public and the private sector, or economic and commodity housing, is quite common, especially among the affluent. Indeed, as becomes apparent by examining more closely the living situation of several residents in new mid-level economic housing complexes, access to subsidized housing is an important factor behind this social cluster's economic rise. Rui Lan, for example, was a thirty-three-year-old editor in a university publishing house. Her husband had his own company and was working in Canada at the time. The couple had a five-year-old son. Rui Lan had bought the apartment from her danwei at a heavily reduced price. She planned to live there for the three years her husband would spend abroad, after which time they would have saved enough money to buy a bigger commercial apartment. Renting out the current place, it would generate an additional income. Similarly, Zhang Jie, age thirty-four, worked in an international cosmetics company. Her husband was a teacher in a local middle school. They had bought the apartment from his work unit at a time when they otherwise could not have afforded to buy a house. When we met they had lived there for five years. With a significantly improved financial situation due to her promotion and his pay increase, and planning on having a child soon, they had begun to look for a new, commercial apartment they wanted to buy around Wangjing.

In fact, the majority of residents I talked to in mid-level economy complexes had one spouse working in the public sector and the other in the private one. Living in apartments they had bought at preferential prices, they were saving money in advance of buying new, commercial houses that would suit their wishes. While they praised the high quality of residents in the neighborhood, they appeared all too aware that the compound offered neither the luxuries nor the prestige of a commercial one. Once they had bought their new house, the rent received from the work-unit apartment would pay for the mortgage or otherwise contribute to their monthly income. Thus, the public sector supported these urban residents not merely by providing them with subsidized housing, but in fact by substantially contributing to their climb up the socioeconomic ladder.

Living in Lower-Level Compounds and Pingfang Houses

Since there were only a couple of low-level commodity neighborhoods in the Wangjing suburb, my contacts here were the fewest. The account of the Fangs, a family I met in one of these neighborhoods, might serve as an exemplary description of residents' lives in these compounds.

Fang Aimei, in her early fifties, retired early from a state-owned company to avoid layoff; this way, she had the right to an immediate payment of her small pension that otherwise she would have had to wait for without any income until reaching the official retirement age. At the time we met, she worked as a household employee for a couple in Wangjing New City. Her husband meanwhile held on to his danwei job. Due to the economic difficulties of his employers, however, he received his salary irregularly, and the work unit was not able to provide housing. Nonetheless, with the help of a married daughter living in Germany, the family had been able to buy an apartment in the Nanlu Yuan neighborhood where the price per square meter amounted to 2,000 yuan (US$267). The apartment was small but, Aimei assured me, much better than the pingfang house where they had lived before because neither she nor her husband had been offered housing by the danwei. It was in fact the first time in her life that Aimei and her husband could enjoy the comforts of an apartment building. Similar to the mid-level compound residents, though, she complained about the people in her neighborhood, who were of "low quality" *(suzhi di)*, she said. Not surprisingly, she did not have many social contacts within the *xiaoqu* where residents were highly diverse as regards their economic, social, and educational background.

As becomes apparent from the Fangs' story, residents in low-level commodity housing generally are low-income earners who do not have privileged access to housing through their employers. Instead, they importantly depend on some form of outside support, either through sideline occupations, private entrepreneurship, or children. While some of them might eventually advance financially and subsequently move into newer, better neighborhoods, without the backing of the public sector they are generally in a far less secure living situation and usually more exposed to the whims of the market.

Still more left to their own devices are the migrants one can encounter in Wangjing. Even if they hold a temporary residence permit, migrants have only limited options to find accommodation in the city since they remain excluded from the more affordable public-housing sector and few can earn enough money to buy commodity housing. The still widespread public perception of migrants as not trustworthy, or even as criminal, because of their unregistered residence status further excludes them even from the secondary housing market. Migrants therefore rely on renting rooms or houses from the rural population living in the suburban realm, who often depend on this source of income. Due to the continuous expansion of the city into the urban fringe, many farmers have lost their land and are no longer able to live from agriculture. Since they often reject low-paid and strenuous jobs, they have difficulties finding nonfarm work. Renting rooms or entire houses to migrants has, therefore, become an essential source of income, especially since these former peasants are still required to pay grain tax in cash.

One of the younger migrant women I met during the course of my fieldwork was eighteen-year-old Xiao Mei from Hunan province, who sold household wares in a local market. Xiao Mei had come to the capital together with a classmate after they finished middle school, "to try my luck *(kao yunqi)* because at home there is no work, not even in the fields," as she explained. Initially she and her friend found a job working in a shop for household goods. But after she had learned the trade and saved a little money, she decided that she could earn more money working on her own. She then rented a sales stall in a market and was her "own boss." When I met her in 2001, she shared a pingfang house on the far edge of the suburb with three other young women she had met in Beijing. Each of them paid 50 yuan per month. Within the fourteen months of my research, however, Xiao Mei changed her accommodation three times: once because she thought she had found a better location, once because her landlord raised the rent, and once because the house was scheduled to be torn down.

As explained above, when the pingfang houses are torn down, migrants have to look for new accommodation; this is likely to be located further out of the city, not infrequently in the villages beyond the suburb. Several of the migrants I met during my research in fact lived in such locations. For example, two migrants I met lived in a village an hour away by bus from the market in the center of the suburb where they worked. The almost identical one-story brick houses they rented consisted of a four-by-five-meter room. One couple who had brought their teenage son to the city had divided the room into two halves with furniture and curtains. The parents slept on one side and the son on the other. Besides two bedsteads, a closet, shelf, and small desk for the son to study, there were some stools and a folding table. The kitchen was in a small brick construction just outside of the house. It was just high enough for a small person to stand upright and contained only a stove and a small table. Another square structure contained the toilet. In summer, the families washed themselves outside in the small space between the house and the kitchen. In winter, they had to take turns inside the house.

Simple and quite far out of the city as these houses were, these migrants considered themselves lucky to have found the places. Nonetheless, there was no stability in their housing situation either. When I visited them in the spring of 2002, after they had lived there for about a year, it was rumored that the village was going to be torn down within the next months to make way for an expansion of the Capital Airport Highway, and the migrants had begun to look for new accommodation. Frequent change of residence, therefore, was very common among the migrants. Even so, the migrants were confident they would find a new place to stay, not only because of the local farmers' need for cash income, but also because local—district, township, and village—governments earn considerable administrative fees from their presence there.

Conclusion: Living in Suburban Wangjing

As a result of the land and housing reforms, in the reform period Chinese cities' fringes experience sustained growth and urban sprawl. What emerges is a dynamic suburban zone. Around the old danwei complexes that are dominated by elderly, long-term residents of the area, new neighborhoods are incessantly rising. For geographical, historical, and economic reasons marketed as one of the prime locations in the capital, Wangjing thus experiences an explosion of mid-level gated apartment compounds that draw ever-larger numbers of affluent homeowners. Nonetheless, the suburb is also the location where some of the millions of migrants who leave the countryside in search of a share of the new urban wealth find employment and housing as they remain excluded from more privileged and more tightly controlled spaces such as the inner city.

Due to ongoing social and economic stratification processes, life in the various residential neighborhoods differs quite dramatically: young "chuppy" couples or nuclear families with busy work schedules and active agendas cherish the "quality" of fellow residents while seeking the anonymity of the private-property complex. In contrast, increasingly elderly and retired former state employees live in variously networked family arrangements of mutual support and retreat into a communal setting where people know and help each other. Migrants' lives, in turn, are characterized by frequent change of housing and workplace and by flexibility and uncertainty, and they appear to have nothing in common with the other Wangjing residents. Nonetheless, through their rent and labor they contribute in essential ways to the growth, shape, and life of the suburb. Maybe it is this importance that gives at least some of them the confidence to claim permanency in the city, an issue I will come back to in chapter 4.

The altered urban structure affects the daily lives of all residents, state employees, the affluent, and migrants alike. The details of these effects and, importantly, people's ways of dealing with them, however, differ significantly. Even more divergent is the influence that different social groups have on the transformations themselves. While old danwei residents appear to retreat behind their compounds' walls,[26] and migrants are pushed ever further out of the city, mid-level homeowners actively "play with" or embrace the transformations by frequently cruising the city to enjoy the many new commercial, entertainment, and leisure possibilities it offers. As we will see in the next chapter, they also continuously search for new property locations and types that suit their changing—by implication, improving—lifestyles.

Viewed from the outside, these residential groups thus appear to be increasingly different from each other while sharing distinct characteristics among them. The question remains, however, whether people in the individual neighborhoods share more than coincidental coresidence. Do the different groups of suburban residents form distinct identities? Do they show recognizable dispositions? Do they have an emerging consciousness as groups opposed to and divergent from others? More generally, how is the new experience of voluntarily shared space connected to ongoing socioeconomic stratification processes in contemporary urban Chinese society? These are the questions I will address in the next chapter.

4 SOCIOECONOMIC DIFFERENCES

Emerging Market Forces, Diverging Values

AS WE HAVE SEEN IN PREVIOUS CHAPTERS, growing socio-economic stratifications in present-day urban China are increasingly translated into spatial differentiations: inner cities have turned into high-tech versions of a globally imagined modernity, but suburbs remain zones where old and new, "winners" and "losers" of the reforms, live relatively close by. Shared suburban space does not necessarily mean shared lives, as walled, gated, and safeguarded neighborhoods tend to segregate residents into ever more distinct communities where they live with "people like us." How should we conceptualize these residential communities? How and why have new neighborhoods and associated lifestyles taken on such importance in post-Mao society that real estate developers spent significant means on creating not merely residential communities but "cultural milieus" (Fraser 2000; Zhang L. 2004)? Are residential communities merely coincidental groupings of strangers, or are they formative elements of a more profound social transformation and differentiation process akin to class distinctions?

Marxist class analysis has tended to emphasize social differentiation based on people's relationship to the means of production. In the context of China's current transformation process, "traditional" relations of production have become notably confounded as people work several jobs and in different sectors. Categories such as "worker," "employee," or "entrepreneur" are not clear indicators of a person's socioeconomic standing and status; neither is the association with the "public" or "private" sector. In this chapter I argue that it is precisely the domains *outside* production that are formative in the cultural production of social differentiation in China today.[1] One such domain is residential communities.[2]

Examining structuration processes outside of the workplace and relations of production, of course, brings Bourdieu's (1977) concept of *habitus* to mind. Habitus is defined as individuals' internalization of social norms, understandings, and patterns of behavior. It is integral to the formation of class-specific subjects. While habitus does not determine action, it ensures that people are more likely to act in some ways than in others. Even more, and this is especially illuminating in the process of class formation, habitus is both the product and the generator of the division of society into groups and classes. Habitus is shared by people of similar social status, but varies across different social groups. Habitus thus gives individuals a sense of how to act in specific situations, without continually having to make fully conscious decisions (Painter 2000).

The problem with applying the concept of habitus in the Chinese context, however, is that it is based on dispositions that are acquired or developed in a *long-term* process. Yet in urban China formative structures and institutions, systems of reference, and social relations have radically changed throughout the last decades. The changes of the reform period differentiate groups along lines of generation, gender, and socioeconomic position without guiding sociocultural patterns for corresponding values and behavior. From where do the emerging socioeconomic groups get their "dispositions" when the social, cultural, and economic "fabric" of Chinese society has shifted so significantly?

During my fieldwork a sociology professor from Beijing University commented in a conversation with a fellow researcher that people obviously lacked necessary knowledge and needed guidance in questions of lifestyle. He therefore suggested that academia should develop a manual of appropriate lifestyles for different income groups in present-day Chinese society. Similarly, in 2001 the new magazine *Vision* was published by a Shanghai-based artist. At the (for most Chinese) steep price of 45 yuan (US$6), the magazine featured page after page of photos from around the world that were accompanied by short articles about fashion, lifestyle, and travel, all interspersed with advertisements for mainly western consumer goods. In a launch interview the editor revealed that his main aim was to "educate people's taste."

What these examples point at is the processual character of present-day stratification in China. Socioeconomic differentiations are growing but are not (yet) clearly identifiable by corresponding lifestyle, tastes, and values. At the same time, there exists an apparent desire, or perceived need, for clear markers of such distinctions in contemporary Chinese society. Given the nascent nature of socioeconomic differentiations in China, here I suggest that community and consumption are even more important spheres of shared experience through which distinct social groups are formed.[3] While we cannot speak of fully developed classes with specific habitus in present-day Chinese society, nonetheless a close analysis reveals ideologies, behavior, and values that are increasingly linked to socioeconomic positions.

We have already seen the emergence of new forms of community life. Below, I will analyze the three different groups of Wangjing residents' changing patterns of identification, behaviors, and values that can further illuminate how the growing marketization of society affects personal attachments and social relationships. As will become apparent, differences in lifestyles, identities, and consumption behavior are indeed beginning to separate the three groups. These are, however, differentiations in the making. If we understand class as a process, a "social and cultural formation" (Thompson 1966, 11) then the emerging group-specific values and behaviors can be understood as markers of difference within this process. Thus, residential communities are not merely coincidental groupings of strangers but formative elements of a more profound social transformation and differentiation process akin to class structuration. The question remains, however, if this process might also lead to the development of group consciousness or basis for concerted action.[4]

Danwei Residents

Localized in a Different Sense of Time

In comparison to the young, affluent residents of mid-level commodity housing, residents of old danwei compounds led a much simpler life. As we saw in the previous chapter, while the residents owned their apartments, these were small, if not crammed, and often of low quality. At the time of my fieldwork in 2001/2, the elderly's pensions, and continued connection to the danwei, allowed them to provide for their living. Exceptional expenses, however, were a challenge. Low education and socialist work practice gave few of the older men and women the opportunity for employment after retirement, which would have been a means to improve their living standard.

The retirees also led a very "localized" life. In contrast to the residents of commodity housing, old danwei residents lived in this part of the city because this was where the work unit they had been assigned to was located. Their lives unfolded predominantly within the realm of the danwei compound and its direct vicinity. While they certainly also moved within the larger city, this happened only occasionally. For older, retired state employees, time and space merged in a specific way that set them apart from other Wangjing residents. Their "other-timing" was, on the one hand, related to retirement, that is, a daily life not organized around work hours, but instead around meals and social activities in the compound. On the other hand, this "other-timing" was also caused by their connection to the danwei/state-owned company, which functioned according to a different time than privately owned enterprises.[5] Not in the position to actively participate in the current modernization project, elderly, retired danwei residents stood somehow "outside" the new negotiations of space in the urban landscape. This does not mean, however, that they were passive subjects. To a certain degree, the elderly could *choose* to withdraw from the newly developing realities of competitiveness because of the continued support they received from the state. From this position of secured, albeit frugal, retirement, the elderly danwei residents of my study were able to support or assist their children. Either by offering them (cheap or free) accommodation or by taking care of the grandchildren, these former state-employees actually did take an active part in current socioeconomic restructurings as they enabled their children's performance in the free job market and adoption of the new disciplinary regime. At the same time, through their "withdrawal" the old danwei residents also created meaningful identities that stood in contrast to demands of present-day consumer society, but were coherent with their own Maoist habitus, their socialization to frugality and sacrifice. Generally, despite their relatively moderate standard of living, the elderly danwei residents I spoke to expressed contentment with their living situation.

Since I think this is central to understanding older residents' self-identification and position in present-day urban Chinese society, I will here present the life-story of Zhu Laoning as an example to illustrate the elderly's values and frames of thinking. To recall, when we met, Zhu Laoning, a retired radio technology engineer, was sixty-three years old and lived in Xin Yuan. Her life, the experiences of hardship in her childhood, living and believing in the ideals of the Communist revolution, and her attitude toward the transformations of the last years reflect the sentiments of many elderly women and men I talked to around Wangjing.

Zhu Laoning, a Retired Danwei Resident

Zhu Laoning was the oldest of six children. Her father passed away in the early 1950s when Zhu was thirteen, and her mother had to raise the children by herself. This proved difficult since she had no education, but she eventually found a job in a clothes factory. Studying diligently, and enduring much hardship, Zhu Laoning and several of her siblings were nonetheless able to attend university, helped by the socialist system of free education and a small monthly government stipend. "All our fees were paid for, including our food. The government gave us 12.5 yuan each month." Zhu Laoning chose to become an electronics and radio technology engineer.

After she got married, Zhu Laoning and her husband were assigned to work in two different cities and lived separated for ten years. Zhu delayed childbearing for the first three years of marriage because she felt that she had to pay back the government its investment into her education, and she also supported her younger sister's university education. Zhu showed a strong sentiment of obligation in this question: "I began to work in 1964. . . . We had our first child in 1967 because I thought that we should concentrate our minds on our work. It was not easy for the government to educate us for so many years and we shouldn't bind ourselves to our families."

Because of the demands of both her and her husband's jobs, Zhu Laoning arranged for her elder daughter to live with another family to whom she paid a monthly fee. "Our younger daughter went to primary school and our elder child lived in another family. We paid 30 yuan a month for her, which did not include the meals and health care. Altogether she needed 60 yuan a month, half of our family's income." The financial burden was oppressive, especially since Zhu Laoning also supported her mother in Tianjin. Because Zhu and her husband were highly paid workers, they did not get financial support for their children's education from the government. "I never got any [money]. We belonged to the high salary class at the time. [University] graduates could earn 56 yuan. We had been soldiers, so we got extra money from the army. Our salary was higher than others', so the government wouldn't give us any special allowance for the children." The couple was fortunate, though, in that Zhu Laoning's father-in-law was able to give them some money, which enabled the family to send the younger daughter to a dormitory school.[6]

After her retirement in 1994, Zhu Laoning continued to work because she liked to, but also for financial reasons. "I retired in 1994 and was reemployed by my danwei for one more year. Then I found myself a job in another company for two more years. I like my work; I was busy and [even] had to do extra work." Zhu Laoning was content with her life after retirement. While she was not wealthy, she had enough for a comfortable living, especially since she owned her apartment, and her danwei still flourished and was able to provide basic services. In addition, Zhu Laoning's older daughter was financially well-off and was able to support her when she needed money.

> My life is pleasant. I have no burden financially, and my daughters and I will help each other when we lack money. My elder daughter has 100,000 yuan (US$13,330) per year. She has a house and car. . . . She will send her child to me when the child is on vacation, because my husband likes to go swimming, so does the child. They go to swim at the Lido Hotel every day. I have been going to dance in the morning since 1999.

At the same time, Zhu stressed her frugality and the fact that she and her husband did not need much in life to be happy.

> We eat steamed buns in the morning and have two dishes for lunch. We also have simple food for dinner. My younger daughter has dinner with us. . . . We travel twice a year. . . . I will meet with my brothers and sisters twice a year. We will go to Anshan [where her sister lives] this year. My house is too small to meet them here. . . . I have 1,600 yuan (US$213) per month. My husband and I need 1,000 yuan (US$133) for our monthly expenses. We save 1,000 yuan each month and the other 1,000 is our travel fund. My elder daughter always gives us money for our travels.

Asked how she overall evaluated the reforms, Zhu gave a positive but critical reflection. She began by pointing out the tremendous changes that she had experienced in her lifetime and how living conditions had improved from her generation to her daughters': "Our living condition is improving. My daughter's salary is very high. . . . We didn't have much food to eat. We had to use rationing coupons to buy some meat. One kilogram was not enough for the entire family. So we had to ride our bikes to go to another market. Now we have so many shops and markets." But Zhu saw the negative side of the transformations as well. Especially important to her seemed to be what she perceived as a growing lack of ethics and morality in contrast to her generation's selflessness.

> Today only a few people get rich. There is unfair competition. Some people are not honest and get rich. I wonder if they sleep well at night because the money they have is illegal. We are honest people; our money is clean. My daughter earns her salary according to her work. . . . [After retirement from the state company] I worked for a private company that was making laser machinery. I told the boss, "You cannot cheat. Every part of the machine should be made according to the standards." . . . I also teach my children to respect the truth and to never cheat. . . . But people are becoming more and more pragmatic. The relationships between people are now characterized by indifference. Not like our generation. We preferred to be unselfish and to give [to others]. Now people are working for money. It is said that the amount of money you make is a measure of a person's ability. We never questioned our salaries. Now people are calculating. . . . People earn their money according to their work. There is no charity; you don't get money for nothing.

Nevertheless, despite these critical tones, generally Zhu subscribed to the idea of being paid according to one's performance. Maybe this was because she herself had experienced colleagues' unpunished laziness.

> The new system is not the same as the old one. You can earn more money if you do more work. I think it is good. If the lazy people are treated the same as the hard workers, how can society develop? We earned the same, no matter what kind of title you had. The others would talk or argue if you had more money than they had. Now our salary increases according to our title. I am a senior engineer. I could get a 50 to 60 yuan (US$6.7 to US$8) increase. As for common workers, they could get 20 to 30 yuan (US$2.7 to US$4). Now they no longer argue. We had low salaries before the reform, while the state took care of our houses, pensions, and medical insurance. No matter if we worked hard or not, the result was the same. Now we have to work hard for our future, otherwise we won't have as good an apartment as other people have, we won't have enough money when we get ill, and our old age won't be guaranteed. Our hard work can buy us a good future. There won't be any lazy people.

Several themes emerge from Zhu Laoning's narrative, which were common among the elderly who still lived in work-unit compounds: First, Zhu Laoning was old enough to have had at least some childhood memory of the time before the Communist revolution in China, and she definitely experienced the difficult early years of the People's Republic. She grew up with a strong sense of obligation to work, and to support her younger siblings, as well as to pay back the country that enabled her to study. From this point of view she accepted the ten-year-long separation from her husband, the burden of working and raising children at the same time, and even giving her daughters away for some time. Now in her retirement, she felt relatively secure because her danwei was still flourishing and she could rely on the payment of her pension. In addition, she had at least one daughter who was able to help her out when she was short of money or in need of help. This was the background for her perception of the current transformations, which she evaluated as overall positive. Nonetheless, we can also read out of her statements a strong sense of difference between her life and those of her daughters.

While Zhu Laoning's experiences were characteristic of the group of elderly residents of old danwei compounds, there were also important differences among them. For example, supported by a family that valued education, Zhu Laoning had been able to finish high school and to receive a university degree. Many other informants of the same age had not been able to do so because of their bleak economic situation or, in the case of women, often because of a gender bias. Zhu Laoning's high level of education, however, did not matter much in the era before the economic and social reforms, as salaries and the distribution of houses were based on years of work experience. That is to say, several people in this group who had received a lesser education still had a very similar lifestyle to hers, based on the provisions made by the danwei. Some elderly with fewer qualifications, Zhu Laoning pointed out, actually had a better house and pension than she did.

What seems striking in Zhu's narrative is how she manages to draw a connecting line from her generation to the present: by highlighting socialist values such as dedication, selflessness, and frugality, she elevates her generation's moral standing vis-à-vis a perceived self-interest and cunning in the present. At the same time, she acknowledges that the system of equal pay during the socialist period invited freeloaders. But by portraying herself as an honest, hard-working person, she implies that people like her would also be successful in today's pay-for-performance type of remuneration. She thus effortlessly combines the better of two systems to validate her own transformed (and in public discourse often devalued) subject positioning. I will return to this issue below.

Given the commonalities and differences, what distinguished the (elderly) danwei residents from other people in Wangjing? Why were they so different that one could identify them on the street? Did they share more in common than residence, and if so what was that? Did they identify as a group as opposed to others? These are the questions I will examine in the following section.

Speaking Bitterness, Evoking Progress and Modernity

The lived experience of daily life in reform-period China is marked—at least for the older generation—by what Bourdieu (1977) terms the *hysteresis* of habitus, that is, the lack of fit between the social conditions for which an individual was socialized and the social conditions of the moment (see Fleischer 2006). As Shevchenko (2002, 847) observes in the Russian context,

> Individuals who grew up under state socialism with its relative income equality and social guarantees, and who mastered skills tailored to this particular social context, could not help but experience a sense of disorientation when this social environment was replaced with one which required assertively entrepreneurial behavior, a certain adventurousness and a number of other qualities which were not a part of their cultural tool-kit.

Similarly, Pine (2006) points out that in the normal life course, the senior generation trains and guides the younger, who in turn eventually takes over these roles in relation to their juniors. With the postsocialist changes in the economic system in Poland, where she did her research, especially the resulting deindustrialization has turned this relation between the generations upside down: It is often the elderly who rely on the younger generation for help and advice about how to confront postsocialist challenges. Worsening the older generations' sense of loss, of mismatch, is the restructuring of state-provided services, from education to leisure, to employment, and other systems involved in providing what Giddens (1990) calls "ontological security" (see also Shevchenko 2002).

In China, the reform period has undoubtedly provided ample occasions for discontent. Besides larger social problems, such as inflation, rising prices, increasing layoffs, growing socioeconomic differentiations, and concurrent downsizing of state-provided services, people have to confront more subjective and personal dilemmas such as the breakup of grown/known collectives and communities, changes in the prestige of one's occupation, and reconfigurations of opportunity structures for current and future generations. Grievances, however, are still difficult to utter publicly in China. No doubt, today we see more open discussions about problems and issues arising from the reforms. In recent years, the government has even publicly acknowledged difficulties that affect people in the countryside and, at least partially, those of migrants to the cities.

With the acknowledgement of peasants' and migrants' grievances in the reform period, their fates have been given a voice in the official language, albeit a limited one. But how does someone deal with the transformations who is neither a peasant nor migrant, who is in no significant or dramatic way affected by the reforms, but who feels nonetheless "dislocated" in the new environment of state-prescribed consumption and competitiveness? What kind of discourse do the elderly engage in to understand their subject positioning in a period when their habitus as "supplicants to the state" (D. Davis 1993), as socialist workers, has become problematic, is questioned, disrupted, or even dissolved. How do the elderly reflect on their subject position in the reform period?

The elderly among my informants commonly began their life stories with a traumatic memory. Women often recalled how gender biases had kept them from going to school. Both men and women described the poverty that forced them to work instead of pursuing higher education. Another theme was recollections of the atrocities committed under warlords or the Japanese occupiers before the Communist revolution. Mrs. Fang, for example, one day invited me to her apartment to tell me her life story. After she led me into her combined living and bedroom with cement floor and barren walls, where she offered me a seat and tea, she started without hesitation:

> I am a retired worker; I am sixty-eight years old. My life is very well, while it was not good when I was a child. My hometown is called Xibaipo. It is in Hebei province and was one of the base areas of the revolution. The Japanese Army treated us according to the policy of "burn all, kill all, loot all." So my father and my grandfather were killed by them.

Here, Mrs. Fang started to cry. It took her about two minutes to compose herself again before she continued:

My life was very hard, our house was burned down to the ground; we had nothing to eat but grass and wild herbs and we had to pick up the firewood by ourselves. I was seven years old in 1941. In 1945, it was better, because the Japanese invaders surrendered. We began to plant in our field and I went to school, which was free; the government even gave me money for it. After I graduated from middle school I went to work.

This links to another recurrent theme in the elderly's accounts: wage labor. As we saw in chapter 1, after the Communist revolution and the introduction of the centrally planned economy, the socialist subject was defined through wage labor. Dedication to work indeed proved to be central to the elderly. Sixty-eighty-year-old Wang Lianzi, for example, explained this attitude by quoting Mao: "As Chairman Mao said, 'Love Your Work, Whatever You Do, and Be an Expert in It.'"[7] Between wage labor, household tasks, raising their children, and attending political meetings, leisure time was practically unknown. But despite the demands the regime made on its workers, in their life histories the elderly all tried to convey that their lives improved considerably in comparison to a more or less explicitly drawn past—usually a mix of memories of and ideologies about life "before the revolution" and "in the countryside." In this way, the old people demonstrated how much they had internalized the ideology of Communist "liberation" after 1949. At the same time, their stories also reflected the reality of lived socialism, namely, the drab and poor rural living conditions that stood in sharp contrast to the restricted and privileged urban realm: they had become urbanites; they had gained access to the benefits of city life. Not surprisingly then, some elderly expressed deep gratitude toward the regime that had indeed "liberated" them.

To illustrate this point, I return to Mrs. Fang's narrative: After explaining how busy she had been in the past with wage labor, household duties, and attending political meetings, Mrs. Fang immediately counterposed this description with a comparison that made her situation appear relatively better:

No matter how hard it was, I was glad to live in the city. I came from the countryside and I thought my life was much better here. I was struggling for the best and took the factory as my home; my work was first, my family was second. We were taught to do this; on my graduate diploma was written "Serve the People!" So I never thought about myself. I was very busy and sometimes I had no time for breakfast.

Until 1986, when she moved into the current apartment, Mrs. Fang and her family lived in simple houses in the urban hinterland where they shared the bathroom with other families. I wondered if she had any regrets or bitter feelings about her life. Working in an assigned job that she would not have chosen herself, the burden of taking care of children while at the same time having to put work first, in addition to the endless political meetings people had to attend, and living with six others in very cramped conditions—how did she feel about her life, and the role the Communist regime had played in it? In contrast to my expectations, Mrs. Fang had nothing to complain about. "I am always satisfied with what I have," she assured me. "I think [about the fact] that some people don't have a house [apartment in a building] like this. I am just in the middle class."

For Mrs. Fang there were three "classes" of people in postreform China: peasants who lived in simple houses, the middle class who lived in danwei-provided apartments, and the wealthy who could afford to buy commercial housing. Compared to where she had come from—the countryside—her evaluation of her life was positive: "I am very satisfied with my life; we have enough food to eat and we play every day. I feel very happy. Nobody dares to bully us now; my country is strong. The burning of my house left a deep impression on me; it was all the fault of the Japanese. [Now] the country is rich and we are getting rich too."

Writing about reference points in East German women's life stories, John Borneman observed that they either dwelled on the hardships and obstacles encountered in the decade after the war or emphasized their own distinct contributions to society. He relates this to the East German state's influence on the identity construction of its citizens. According to Borneman (1997, 109), the state "set the ideational and aesthetic framework in which individual citizen's experiences could be related to the larger group narrative of Germanness."

The elderly people's accounts in my research can be related to a similar framework as the one Borneman suggests for the East German case: Under the Communist regime, up to the reform period, much of the regime's political legitimation was constructed in opposition to the horrendous atrocities committed under the Japanese occupation of the mainland, as well as the hardships suffered by Chinese people before the Communist revolution. The claim to end the social and political injustices of the imperial and nationalist regimes, as well as to turn

China into a modern nation that would be able to fend off intruders such as the Japanese, was the basis for legitimizing the Communist Party's rule, the explanation for its political campaigns and for the required sacrifices in the name of the revolution.

While I expected the elderly danwei residents to feel bitter about their life experiences, their "missed chances" and the hardships they had suffered, the sacrifices they had made, in their own accounts the elderly had done comparatively well. They escaped a life in the countryside, had an apartment, were able to provide for their children, and could now enjoy a relatively good retirement. As one of them said, "My life is better than before. Our life was hard. In fact, it is really better than before. We can only compare with our past, can't we?" This attitude not only reflected the frame of identification that the Communist regime had provided, but also showed the elderly's subjective positioning in relation to history that Lisa Rofel (1999) writes about. In Rofel's research, elderly women's accounts of the past, of their sacrifices and of the hardship they experienced, were regularly recounted by means of "speaking bitterness."

In China, after the Communist revolution a new socialist language recast citizens into workers, peasants, revolutionaries, counterrevolutionaries, and "bad elements."[8] One of the most important "tools" in the reeducation of people under socialism was known as "speaking bitterness" *(su ku)*.[9] "To speak bitterness" implied challenging one's social status. The Chinese revolutionaries instrumentalized the metaphor not only as a means to root out the "five bad classes" that socialism would eradicate but also to transform people's consciousness (Erwin 2000). Speaking bitterness, Rofel explains, was used by party cadres as a fundamental method to teach peasants and later workers how to speak as socialist subjects of the new nation. "Speaking bitterness, in other words, . . . led people to conceive of themselves as new kinds of subjects, as subaltern subjects" (1999, 138; see also Anagnost 1997).[10] Rofel eventually understood that the older women workers in her research population cast their lives in this mode of speaking bitterness in order to assert certain political claims, to express certain nostalgia.

> By speaking this bitterness now, . . . they implicitly expressed a longing for continued recognition that would lend a heroic quality to their identities as women workers. They spoke *as if* they still deserved to be seen as heroic, even though the whole interpretative frame of their actions has been brushed

aside as part of the wrongheadedness of Maoism. . . . The nostalgia, then, is
for the political frame that lent a larger-than-life importance to their labor-
ing activities. (Rofel 1999, 144–45; emphasis in original)

The elderly danwei residents whom I interviewed were similar to
the elderly women in Rofel's research, but in Beijing and more than
ten years later. Speaking bitterness in my investigation had given way
to a discourse of "progress and modernity." The elderly recounted the
hardships and sacrifices they had experienced, and felt importantly
defined through these experiences, as is shown in the centrality of
these accounts, similar to the ones in Borneman's research. Nonetheless, in Beijing by the year 2002 these tales had been turned into something else: proof of how far China had already come, of the difficulties
it had surmounted, and of the conviction that the nation was on its way
to a bright, new future called "modernity." Thus, Mrs. Li explained,

> My mother lived in the old society. A lot of children, her life was hard. My
> life is different from my son's and my daughter's. My life was hard, but it
> is improving. . . . Now it is good. My daughter is thirty-three and my son is
> twenty-eight. Their living conditions are good. We only had 20 to 30 yuan
> per month to support the entire family. Now they can make several thou-
> sands yuan. . . . My life is better than my mother's; my children's life will be
> better than mine.

The elderly had fully embraced the notion that "modernity feeds
on the idea of overcoming the past" (Rofel 1999, 153). Indeed, their
accounts embodied the heart of the modernist projects as identified by
Rofel: "In creating a self-portrait as a triumphal march through time,
[modernity] gathers up the memories of the past into tidy linear narratives that act as mythical guides to that overcoming" (ibid.). While
the elderly portrayed themselves as disinterested in politics, dwelling
on their social activities after retirement and the success of their children, they also repeatedly stressed the amazing changes Beijing had
gone through since the beginning of the reform era.

At the same time, though, they presented themselves as content,
if not grateful, citizens, who—standing a bit back from current processes—mainly wanted to maintain a quiet life, to guard their health,
and who wished the best for their children. Their "standing back" was
caused by perceiving themselves left out of the dramatic changes in
society, of feeling themselves behind present-day developments. One
important topic that brought this sentiment to the fore was the work

ethic. Sixty-three-year-old Ling Dawen expressed the differences in the following way: "The people of my generation were very naïve in their thoughts. Nobody asked for extra payment if the leaders asked us to do extra work. Now people like to know how much you can pay if you want them to do something. We are different. I think it [the changes] is to increase the productive forces. Our thoughts are old." Mrs. Li also reflected on the changes that the reforms had brought upon the generations. Her statement, however, contained a certain sense of feeling lost in the new economic system:

> After the reforms and opening *(gaige kaifang),* there are a lot of good changes. It has little influence on our generation. We are studying it little by little and try to understand it. We are used to the state-controlled economy. At first, we couldn't get on well with these changes. But the new system has already taken its shape, so we have to adapt ourselves to it.

While several of the elderly stressed that among themselves relations had not changed, they did perceive growing differences in attitudes and values between their and their children's generation. Zhu Laoning assured, for example, that within their residential community there were no perceivable changes in solidarity. "Nobody has a note on their door to mark if they are rich or poor. In this area *(xiaoqu),* we [actually] don't have many rich people. We can help each other." This, however, stood in strong contrast to remarks such as the following by Mrs. Wang, who claimed: "Children [today] don't care for their parents as much as they should do." And Mrs. Li observed:

> My mind is more open than my mother's. But I cannot catch up with the young people today. We are between these two generations; we are more conservative than the youth, while more open than the old. We have more traditional opinions in terms of daily affairs and how to get along with others. Sometimes I chat with young people. For example, if someone is drowning, I would jump into the water and save him or her. But they [young people] think a lot about themselves, whether they can swim well enough to save others, or will they drown while saving someone? I think the young people think mostly about themselves.

I detected a sense of separateness, of detachment, if not rupture, between the two generations in these older people's reflections. While most of them evaluated the reform process as a positive development, they also critically observed the results of the new competitive climate on society. They obviously felt a sharp contrast to the—real or perceived—solidarity of the socialist period during which they grew up and matured.

In addition, these latter statements also seemed to express the elderly's growing uneasiness about their generational position in relation to the younger ones. As Ikels (2004) explains, filial piety *(xiao)* has a long history in Chinese culture. Obedience or subordination to the senior generation, production of male descendents, and support of parents in old age were all traditionally part of this concept. Political movements and campaigns, already starting with the May Fourth Period in the 1920s, but especially during the Maoist period, questioned or upset this relation between parents and children. Martin King Whyte notes, "A comprehensive set of institutions was set up to indoctrinate the younger generations into a new set of values" (2003, 10). Notably during the Cultural Revolution, young Chinese were encouraged to attack "traditional" hierarchies, including parental authority. At the same time, however, filial obligations were never a direct target of the Chinese Communist Party's politico-ideological campaigns. In fact, the 1950s Marriage Law made it a legal requirement for children to support their aging parents. Whyte thus concludes that institutions and practices developed in the People's Republic after 1950 actually supported the continuation of strong filial obligations and intergenerational exchanges. He notes, however, that patterns of exchanges were altered into more modern forms (Whyte 2004, 125).

With the economic reforms in China, intergenerational relations and exchanges have become more complicated. Similar to what Pine (2006) describes for Poland (see above), in China's new economic system based on competition and consumption it is not so clear what kind of knowledge or skills the elderly can convey. Younger people might actually consider their parents' experiences outdated or old-fashioned, not a source of respect. Further, since employment, housing, and other resources are now controlled by markets, generally young people have more opportunities to become independent from their parents. Together with new values of consumption, these developments might undermine the concept of filial reciprocity. At the same time, cutbacks in state-provided services and support increase the older generation's reliance on their children for help. With the one-child policy this kind of support more and more often rests on the shoulders of one offspring, a burden of which the elderly are very aware. I would suggest that it is this uncertainty about intergenerational relations that brought the above statements of my elderly informants to the fore.

The Young and Educated

"One Only Has to Pay Some Money"

One evening, Zhang Jie, a group of her friends, and I drove to a newly opened Sichuan restaurant designed and run by an internationally known Chinese artist, which was one of the latest hot spots of the Beijing entertainment scene. Liz and her husband in their station wagon had a hard time keeping up with Liang Yang, who raced across the city in her Jeep Cherokee while listening to Chinese pop music on her high-tech, fashionably colored stereo and wrapped in the smell of the "Armani" perfume dispenser on the front console. After dinner, we went for a beer in a bar next door, which served as a clubhouse for the Beijing Jeep Exploration Team—a group of young people driving around China in their Jeeps in search of ever more extreme roads and trails. The bar was decorated with car parts and memorabilia from previous tours, mostly to the southwest of China and Tibet. All the while, three monitors showed videos of the tours and extreme car races in the Australian outback.

Maybe it was the surrounding decoration, but somehow we started to talk about Chinese people who emigrated to other countries. Liz and her husband thought about emigrating to Canada, which was supposed to be easy. "One only has to pay some money" *(zhi dei fu qian)* they assured me. Liang Yang, however, got very upset about the issue: "I always want to keep my Chinese passport; I am proud of it *(jiu mian zihao)*. I won't leave the country!" Liz weighed in that they wanted to have at least three children, which would be impossible in China. But Liang Yang rebuked her "Of course it is possible! You just have to pay the fine! That can't be an argument to emigrate!"

I describe this scene because it strikes me as a good illustration of the lifestyle of the young, educated couples I met throughout my research, especially in contrast to my experiences in China less than ten years before. In 1993, a lot of Beijing people still wore the blue and green army clothes that had been the standard uniform during the Maoist era, stared at foreigners, at times pointing with fingers and calling out *"lao wai"* (foreigner),[11] while the more daring ones asked to take a picture together. As a foreigner, one was continuously approached by young Chinese who wanted to practice their English. For something like chocolate or ice cream, one had to go to the *youyi shangdian* (Friendship Store), which specialized in imported goods and catered to foreigners and Chinese government employees. The recently opened McDonald's flagship in Beijing drew crowds of people who had to wait in long lines for hours on the street to be able to get inside, where many of them took a bite of the unknown food and left it uneaten.[12]

With these memories in mind, the style, the sense of fashion, and the unmistakable international air of the group of young people described was astonishing, almost overwhelming. But the short vignette of our evening also evokes several of the common characteristics that I found in the young, educated couples' lives: weekend social activities that included meeting with friends, visiting restaurants, driving around the city, and buying consumer articles; the interest in travel, or "exploration," as my Chinese friends called it; a concern about property and investments; and an ambivalent feeling about China, which manifested itself in a quite strong nationalist pride mixed with doubts about being able to realize one's individual dreams, for example, to have more than one child. These were issues repeatedly brought up by the young, educated couples I talked to.

To further illustrate young, educated couples' identifications, values, and frames of thinking, in the following I introduce the life story of Wei Hong, a young, educated woman who lived in a new danwei complex.

Wei Hong, a Young, Educated Woman

Wei Hong was thirty-one years old, married, and had a six-year-old son. In 1990, she had come to Beijing from Kaifang city in Hebei province to study philosophy. After she graduated in 1994, she joined the army and later worked at several public technical and financial research institutes. When I met her, Wei Hong was a secretary in the President's Office of a technical university in Beijing. At the same time, she was preparing to take the exam to become a certified lawyer.

Wei Hong and her husband lived in an apartment they had been able to purchase at a favorable (i.e., nonmarket) price from her danwei, the State Educational Bureau. According to her own account, she was one of the last persons who benefited from this policy that ended in December of 1999. In the beginning of the year 2001, the family moved into the newly built complex while renting out their old apartment, which they had bought from her previous danwei. They chose to purchase the new apartment because they preferred the Wangjing living area, especially its location and the transportation facilities.

Wei Hong's husband was a manager at the Stock Exchange Market. His company was located in Chaoyang district. The couple recently bought a car, and her husband drove to work. He had to leave the house at eight in the morning to be at the company at nine. Some days, Wei Hong's husband gave her a ride to work, which was on the way to his company. Other days, Wei Hong took the university's shuttle bus or the public bus, which brought her directly to her office in about twenty minutes. When the weather permitted, Wei Hong rode her bike to work.

Throughout the week, the couple's son stayed in a kindergarten that was located near Wei Hong's workplace. Wei Hong's husband brought him there on Monday mornings and picked him up for the weekends by car. I asked about the kindergarten of their son, and Wei Hong elaborated:

> The kindergarten of our son is private. It's the most expensive one in Beijing. It's owned by a Doctor of Philosophy who graduated from Beijing Normal University. He lays stress on developing children's potential. My child changed a lot since he started going to that kindergarten, and his changes surprised us. When he was three, small as he is, he could skate. Maybe it's normal in foreign countries. Yes, he can skate very well, he knows a lot of words, and he can count from 1 to 100 and from 100 to. . . . He can count odd numbers and even ones. We could hardly believe it. [But] it's so expensive, about 3,000 yuan a month. . . . My husband's salary is among the highest in China, so he can support the whole family. My salary is my own pocket money, not for the family expense, and sometimes I take money from his pocket. So it's easy for us. Another reason is that we did not pay too much for this apartment. It was not sold according to market price. Financially we have no pressure to support a child and we want him to have the best education. But the price of the kindergarten is really too high for the average income in China and its quality is not worth the price. But it's the best kindergarten. None of the others are as good as this one in Beijing. So we chose it.

When their son was small, the couple employed a nanny since Wei Hong's parents and parents-in-law lived in the south of China and were therefore not able to help with the child. Housework was entirely Wei Hong's domain; her husband was only concerned with their son's education. Wei Hong had therefore hired a domestic servant on an hourly basis to organize their household.

> I am managing the home, including hiring the maid. He [the husband] does not do any housework, except joining in the education of our child. If I ask him to do something, . . . he will take care of it. [But] he doesn't worry about the management of the home. . . . We have an *ayi* [household help] working for us by the hour. My husband is busy with his work and I want to study. We are very satisfied with our ayi's work. She comes to our home two or three times a week and helps to clean the rooms.

Despite the household help, the couple had dinner outside the house most days of the week. Wei Hong's daily life looked like this:

> I usually wake up at about 7 a.m. during the week and go to bed at 10 or 11 p.m. I get off from work at five o'clock. I arrive home at about 5:20 p.m. My child is not home and my husband comes back home late, so sometimes I come home late too. I often go to the swimming pool near the university where I work, or I stay in one of the classrooms to prepare for my exam. My husband will call me if he has time; we'll go to a restaurant or somewhere to play. Then we go home. Sometimes we go to the movies; we don't like to go home directly. [When I go out] I take the buses. I like the new buses that can take you anywhere you want to go directly.

Sports were an important item in Wei Hong's weekly schedule: "I am doing sports for my health. I go to a health club in another neighborhood once a week to dance. I keep up a certain amount of exercise. I also go swimming once a week." During their holidays and most weekends the couple traveled, or tried at least to go out of the city.

> Exploration is very fashionable. . . . My husband and I want to go to a different place each year [during the holidays]. Our child is growing up. Soon we will be able to go to some tourist cities together. We went to see some historical places in the north of China and some beautiful scenic spots in the south. We go to the mountains around Beijing if we do not have too much time or have a rest at home for a few days.

When I asked Wei Hong how she felt about the changes in Beijing, she brought up various issues: the new availability of household service, her living environment, and her house.

> We are new here but we already feel the great changes. When I was young there were no housework services in society. [Now] housework can be divided into tasks [to delegate]. A woman does not need to bind herself to the home. I like this change. The household workers are reliable. Whenever

you call them, they will be there and do the job well. As regards cleaning and doing the laundry, they will finish it on time. When you come back after one or two hours the room is clean and perfect. As for eating, I don't like to spend most of my time cooking. I would rather play with my child and take him to fast-food restaurants, both Chinese and Western food, not very expensive; these problems are solved. And the bookstores, we have several good bookstores in Wangjing New City. You can take your child there and read. But we really lack sport facilities, both for adults and for children. . . . We wanted to move to the east of the city even before my work unit offered these apartments. The reason we want to move to Shanghai is because the headquarters of my husband's company is moving to Shanghai. We want to sell our old apartment and buy a big new house. This apartment is too small, we want a better one. We will sell one apartment in five years. We need one more room. But it is hard for us to realize now. We have to wait.

Asked how she liked Beijing today, Wei Hong expressed mixed feelings about it. She seemed to think more of Shanghai, which might have had to do with the family's plan to move to that city. Nonetheless, reviewing the advantages and disadvantages of Beijing, Wei Hong's sentiment conveyed a special appreciation of the new, modern, bustling city atmosphere.

In Beijing I like the universities, the atmosphere of studying. Culture, media are well developed; newspapers and theater are outstanding. But regarding work conditions, they are bad. Another thing is that there are plenty of opportunities for hard-working people, but the working conditions and services are not as good. I feel these are shortcomings in this city. [But] this city is grand and magnificent. . . . The Olympic Games are going to be hosted here; the city is better every day. If we don't have the chance to go to Shanghai, staying in Beijing is also a good choice, compared to other cities. For work, for life, for friends, it's a good place. The original Beijingers are rare, though. We often meet people who come from other cities. Both the people from the south and the north are energetic people. They are not satisfied with the old life. They like changes. It's interesting to get to know them. I think that is something special about Beijing. I believe most of these people are excellent.

In the ten years since Wei Hong had first come to Beijing, she experienced incredible changes that she described to me.

The Third Ring Road had not opened when I first came to Beijing. It was in 1993. My husband was my boyfriend at that time, and we circled around the third ring by bike. Beijing was surrounded by villages. Da Zhongsi and the People's University were out in the fields. The city double-extended in these years. Another outstanding change is the public transportation and the infrastructure facilities that are much better than before. . . . Another thing is the girl's clothes changed a lot {laughs}. Beijing was covered in deep blue, black, and gray, but now there are all kinds of colors in the streets; very beautiful. The way of living has changed too. There were few people who went to restaurants during the Spring Festival, but now the [restaurants] and tourist spots are filled with people during the holidays. People pay more and more attention to the quality of life.

She continued to reflect on the changes in Beijing's urban landscape:

I agree with the design for Beijing. . . . Beijing is the capital of China and has a long history. I believe Beijing should maintain its traditional construction and morality. I believe Beijing will go back to its own style. . . . No matter if as a tourism city or historic city, Beijing should make improvements in its culture. I know a couple who live in a traditional courtyard house *(siheyuan)*. But the *siheyuan* are being replaced by skyscrapers. . . . I hope we will have a place to show our Chinese culture and let others see the true essence of China. China is losing her character.

This made her talk about her current neighborhood:

This area is developed by several investors. They don't have a long-term plan and design, and it is not a high-level living place. It is just an economical apartment complex for teachers. The interior design of the apartments is lacking, and the distance between the buildings is too close. I think it's a bit disorderly. The developers lack cooperation; they work for their own best interest and have no plan for the whole area. I don't hope for great changes but partial changes are possible.

Even though Wei Hong still worked in a state-owned company and her good financial situation was based on her husband's income, I chose to present her account here because her sentiment, her thoughts, and her discourse reflected the ideas of other young, educated couples with whom I talked in and around Wangjing.

Wei Hong's thoughts and concerns showed that she was a woman with education who did not have to worry about immediate survival and had options and possibilities to form distinct opinions and ideals that I would associate with the new affluent class. There was, for example, the awareness and concern about the child's education beyond the ideal of good grades; the concern about body, fitness, and health, but also self-fulfillment; the ideal of traveling, or "exploration" as Wei

Hong called it. Other themes included an environmental consciousness; thoughts about the way China will develop and retain its traditions; an interest in politics; a strong sense of a need for self-improvement, in this case by studying law after work to receive another degree and further her career; meeting friends in restaurants and public places; planning activities and trips together; considerations about where to live in the city, that is, considerations beyond the price of an apartment, such as environment, design of the place and of the neighborhood, accessibility, and facilities. All these were topics upon which the young and wealthy dwelled.

In contrast to other young, educated, wealthy residents I met around Wangjing, what was special about Wei Hong was that, despite coming from a peasant background, through hard studies she had managed to enter university and, as a result, received an urban hukou that guaranteed a number of privileges and rights. But most importantly, it turned her into a fully legitimized urban citizen in contrast to a poor market woman such as Liang Jiehua (see below). In her early thirties, Wei Hong was part of the last generation of Chinese who received a free education, the only way a person with her family background could afford to get a university degree.

Another difference with other women was that she already had a six-year-old child, which was rather unusual among the young, wealthy couples. The demands of a career in the free market had put so much pressure on women to work hard and perform well that most of them had postponed, although never questioned, childbirth. As regards Wei Hong, employment in the public sector presumably enabled her to have her child while working at the same time. Only now that the child was old enough to stay in a boarding school was she planning her career, seeking employment in the free market as a lawyer.

Citizens of Modernity

Young, educated, and wealthy couples' presentation of self focused mainly around work. They portrayed themselves as diligent and dedicated workers who would bear the burden or stress that came with the responsibilities and demands of jobs in the private labor market, or with the need to and urge for self-improvement through additional education. This dedication to their careers, however, was less a means for the realization of a greater nationalist project, as during the Maoist period, than for the realization of individual aspirations and future well-being. Young, educated couples had thus transformed into, and presented themselves as, "modern" subjects who organized their lives around busy work schedules. Ling Na, age thirty-two, for example, commented on her acquaintances' busy schedules in the following way: "After the opening and reform, it's not easy to get together with friends. I guess it is because people are too busy with their own work to communicate with others. We only have time to talk with colleagues at work. It's dark when we go back home and it's dark when we go to work, so we have little time for friends."

In addition, the young and educated had fully internalized the changed time-space of the reform era. Interviews with them were very much to this point. They expected concrete questions that they answered concisely. Further, they subjected the exchange to a rigid time schedule. After about one and a half hours, the young and educated made clear signs that they considered the interview over by looking repeatedly at their watches or answering only with "yes" or "no." Overall, the young and educated couples presented themselves as people well positioned in modern, capitalist time.

Furthermore, real estate and lifestyle had become a very important topic to the young and educated. They spent a good deal of time on this issue, individualizing and decorating their houses, but also continuously investigating the real estate market and visiting housing fairs. To understand why new commercial housing has become so important in urban residents' lives, we have to look at their previous living situation. Cao Xiangjun and her husband Zhou Tianxin, for example, were among the first to buy an apartment in the Wangjing New City complex. When we talked about what her house meant to her, Cao explained how she had spent her youth in school and university dormitories and was therefore longing to have her own house. This desire was only reinforced by living for more than four years in a damp basement apartment provided by Zhou's danwei. But besides the low quality of the apartment itself, it was the life in the danwei that she considered unfavorably in contrast to their current place:

> My old neighbors worked in the same company as my husband. We cooked and ate together. Your home was mine, mine was yours. We felt happy, although the house was not good. But now we are far [away] from our [old] neighbors, we are no longer just one big family. . . . We were happy to be with friends [in the old apartment], but whenever friends came to ask you to eat with them you couldn't refuse, even if you actually wanted to read

something, for example. You couldn't refuse even if you felt tired or wanted to study. Now I can do everything I want; I have plenty of time of my own. We knew each other when we lived in the old place; there were no strangers. We knew each of our neighbors. You were afraid to be seen if you were doing something wrong. But now, nobody knows us here, people can do whatever they want.

Thus, after Maoist-era surveillance of public and private life, embodied in the work-unit compound, housing today offers private—personal, nonpublic—space. And for this space, the young, affluent couples were willing to spend significant amounts of money and effort in decorating it.

In terms of their financial means, young, educated couples were the best positioned among the three groups discussed here. In a more general evaluation of urban Chinese, or more precisely Beijing, salaries, their income levels positioned them in the middle to upper stratum of emerging income classes.[13] The financial well-being of the young and educated was illustrated by their newly acquired lifestyle: not only did they live in new, relatively spacious apartments that were usually equipped with modern, Western-style furniture, they also used their financial means to frequently visit restaurants, travel, or buy selected consumer goods, such as computers and cars. In addition, Wei Hong and other couples I talked to all had domestic employees to help in the household, they frequently sent their children to boarding schools during the week, and they commuted to their workplaces by private car, company shuttle buses, or taxi.

Based on their financial means, the young and educated couples led a life organized by and based on choice. They lived in the Wangjing suburban area because they had chosen to. That is, the couples had investigated the property market and decided on this residential neighborhood because they considered its position in the north favorable to meet their newly developed values of a more spacious layout, privacy, and a clean environment. In addition, they frequently cited the neighborhood's convenient location in relation to the inner city, especially the new CBD, where many of them worked. Even the couples who had purchased the apartment from their danwei, that is, who did not have as much choice as the others who looked for an apartment in the free real estate market, said that they had wanted to live in the area even before they were offered the house through their work unit.

The young, affluent couples were able to choose their work, where and how they lived, and according to which lifestyle. They also chose when and how to move throughout the city. Despite the stress that young Chinese felt from their competitive work lives, they frequently exhibited a "being on top of the world" attitude. Financial independence and career success put them in charge and in control of their lives, and they were quite confident about their future.[14]

I do not want to suggest, however, that the couples did not also feel constraints and limits. Their thoughts about China's place in the world, about emigrating, and their wish to have more than one child all expressed a difficult positioning in society, a positioning that required negotiation between a modern urban Chinese identity and the framework set by the regime and individual desires. In this negotiated identity, specifically, they felt the limitations set by the regime. However, as I have demonstrated, housing had become a new space of individuality and freedom outside the official confines, one into which the young couples poured a great deliberation and attention.

Housing had indeed become so important that the young and educated were even willing to challenge authority. In the course of the transformations within the city and the development of new residential areas such as Wangjing, there have been several conflicts between developers and homeowners. In consequence, previously unknown public protests are being held, which sometimes even turn violent. While I conducted my research, in Atlantic Place various windows were covered with huge protest posters. I asked Wang Xing, who lived in the complex, about it when I visited her, and she told me that there was a conflict between the developer and the homeowners over particular unfulfilled promises.[15]

Chaoyang district, to which the Wangjing area belongs, has become a battleground for homeowners and developers. Many property disputes take place in mid-range residential complexes where most residents are middle class. The protesters are well educated, with sophisticated organizing power, and many operate their own Web sites and chat rooms. Whether such collective actions by middle-class homeowners will grow into more lasting class-based action remains to be seen.[16]

In sum, the young, educated, affluent residents of Wangjing are hard working, ambitious, and studious. They are very aware of the need to make money in order to secure their own and their (prospective) child's future. At the same time, they enjoy their financial independence and the possibilities money has opened up in the transformed urban environment.

Migrants

During one of my frequent visits to the markets around Wangjing, I met Liang Jiehua, a middle-aged woman from Shandong province. Liang had come to the capital fifteen years before to "learn something" and "gain experience." In Beijing, she met and married an urban resident who worked in the city's horticultural department. She had a thirteen-year-old son. When I met her, Liang had two sales stalls: one in an inside market where she sold young, sporty-style clothes, and one in an open market, where she set up shop three times per week. Offering slightly different (cheaper) clothes, she tried to attract a different clientele than in the first venue, which was taken care of in the meantime by one of her nieces. The outdoor market was also the place where the elderly couple from Harbin (a city in the northeast of China), mentioned in chapter 2, sold their freshly prepared pancakes. To recall, they had moved to Beijing after her retirement and his layoff. Finally, through Liang Jiehua, I met Ling, a woman in her late twenties, who had followed her husband in 1999 to Beijing, since neither she nor her husband had been able to find work in their home province Hubei. Now Ling sold babies' and children's clothes, and her husband worked as a helper in a nearby bread factory.

As diverse as their backgrounds and stories were, these migrants had carefully evaluated the advantages and disadvantages of coming to Beijing and decided that an uncertain life in the capital was preferable to the desolate living situation in their home places. What they had in common was their occupation, private entrepreneur, and their location in the capital—the suburban realm. In contrast to other migrants who have been described in the literature thus far, to my surprise several of these "urban guerillas" (Beynon 2004, 131) claimed permanent residency in the city. Nonetheless, they certainly also shared characteristics with other migrants—evidently since *all* migrants are subject to the same legal (political) regulations and ideological environment.

In the following I will portray key aspects of my migrant informants' lives, such as their identifications, behavior, social relations, and values (see Fleischer 2007b). I am framing the discussion around the life story of Liang Jiehua, who became my closest informant. While her situation is somewhat special—being married to a Beijing resident—it is far from singular, and in many ways her experiences reflected those of the other migrants I met in the markets.[17]

From the Countryside to the City

Liang Jiehua described her decision to migrate to Beijing in the following matter-of-fact way: "I came to Beijing during the Spring Festival of 1986 in order to get away from farm work. . . . My teacher . . . introduced me to [my classmate's] uncle in Beijing and encouraged me to find a job here. So I came to Beijing to work in the clothes factory." In reality, of course, it was not such a straightforward story. It took months of getting to know each other better before Liang revealed more about her background and her motivations to come to Beijing. What came to the fore was an account of failed aspirations and lack of opportunities combined with a certain determination to not simply accept her lot.

Contrary to a widespread notion that all Chinese migrants are uneducated, Liang Jiehua had actually finished high school and even taken the university entrance exam. After she had failed the test for the third time, however, she gave up on her dream to study. "I thought I was going further and further away from being admitted to university and I would never have a chance to study."

While the perception that migrants are uneducated and unskilled has been shown not to be true globally (e.g., Castles 2000), in the Chinese case this is somewhat different—at least until now. Early in the reform period, migrants were indeed mainly young, little-educated, unmarried peasants who could not find employment in their native places and considered the chance to earn money through wage labor in the booming coastal areas more attractive than to toil away on their parents' farms. The generally destitute situation in the countryside, where the dismantled commune system left large numbers of people without jobs, contributed to the exodus of youth who were expected to support their parents and families. The migrants were primarily drawn (and after a while channeled through networks of kinship and shared origin) to the special economic zones where foreign and joint-venture companies offered new employment opportunities. With the continuation of the reforms and the concomitant transformations in China's social and economic structure, however, migration is changing its character.

Growing numbers of studies question previous assumptions and findings about migration in China.[18] The level of migrants' education
might be another aspect of such transformations. While some of the
migrants in the suburban markets could indeed barely read and write,
the majority of people I talked to had actually finished middle school,
some, like Liang Jiehua, had graduated from high school, and a couple
of them had attended technical training colleges. Similarly, in a survey
among one hundred migrant women in Beijing, Jacka (2005) found that
46 percent of them finished junior high school, and 30 percent had
senior high school education. Seven percent had been educated to the
tertiary technical level. While this is not a very high educational level,
it shows that not all migrants are necessarily middle school dropouts.[19]

One of the main problems for young people in the countryside is to
find (satisfactory) jobs once they graduate from school. Liang Jiehua,
for example, began to help her family work their land. This, besides
being tedious, does not hold much allure—today less than ever. She
said, "I didn't like that kind of life at all," but that simple statement
had a large real and ideological baggage. In contrast to the booming coastal cities and special economic zones, life in the countryside is
generally marked by a dearth of opportunities. Villagers have built
local industries, but these can employ only a limited number of people.
Furthermore, many of the earlier projects have failed. At the same
time, nurtured by TV and other media, cities have become the epitome of modernity, evoking desires and nourishing dreams, especially
in rural youth. Peasants and agricultural work, in contrast, are widely
perceived as representing the past, that which is to be left behind, to
be overcome, and to be rejected. The decision to migrate to the glitzy
centers of the new, globally framed modernity is thus also shaped by
discourses about the countryside's backwardness (see Jacka 2005;
Yan H. 2003).

Prevailing gender ideologies are another important factor in the
decision to leave the countryside. Women, for example, are generally
less likely to receive good or higher education in their places of origin,
since in the countryside boys still experience preferential treatment.[20]
Thus, Liang Jiehua was actually lucky to attend high school. Other
migrant women I talked to revealed that they had not continued their
education because their parents instead spent the necessary funds on
a brother. Some also wanted to work to help support a younger (predominantly male) sibling's education.

But issues of gender are even more complex and they also affected Liang Jiehua. At the time of her migration in her early twenties, she was already considered old in her village. Other women were not only married, but some even had a child. This gender ideology apparently contributed to Liang's giving up her dream of studying, but it did not change her perspective on life: while she accepted working in the fields for the time being, her statement that she "did not like that kind of life at all" referred not only to the work, but also to getting married to a villager and having a child; in the end, it simply expressed her dislike of the idea of staying in the countryside. At some point during the research Liang almost sheepishly admitted that going to the city she had also hoped to find "a better husband."[21]

Yet the decision to go away is only the first step for migrants to leave the countryside. Given their general lack of "cultural capital," or "street smartness," their inexperience, often young age, and usually limited (or second-hand) information about life in the new centers of economic development, it is not surprising that migrants commonly rely on networks of kin and fellow villagers to reach their destinations, find jobs, and get established. Liang Jiehua, as we have seen above, found her way to Beijing through her teacher and the uncle of a class-mate who already worked in the capital. As with other migrants from the countryside, she relied on these personal connections to find her first job in the city. Without this introduction she would probably have been less likely to migrate.

> So [when] I came to Beijing, I had a place to live and the uncle had found me a job before I went. The day after I came to Beijing I went to work. There were altogether fifteen workers both from the countryside and the city who were employed. My cousin also worked with me. We lived together in the factory's dormitory and also ate at the factory. The situation was totally different from knowing nobody in Beijing and coming to look for a job blindly. The uncle was the head of the personnel office in the factory.

Similarly, other migrants I talked to had known at least one person who had either been to Beijing or was still there. This was clearly an important factor in their decision to migrate to the capital. Nonetheless, it did not mean that after they had established themselves in the city they remained entangled in close ties with these relatives or fellow villagers. Liang Jiehua, for example, did not stay in her first job for long but soon began an extended journey through a number of different jobs and positions that she usually found with the help of new Beijing acquaintances:

> [After quitting in the factory] I worked in the greenhouse for a year, and one of my coworkers introduced me to her brother who became my husband later. We got married in December 1986. Then I worked in a clothing factory. My salary was very low, it was only 2.5 yuan per day and 0.5 yuan bonus, that is, I had 90 yuan per month. In the clothing factory, I could make 3 yuan for making one suit, I could make three a day, that is, I earned 9 yuan per day. It was very hard work so I decided to change my job again after one year. It was in 1987. I had my son in 1988. In order to take care of my son, I took the material back home and made clothes there. I also made some embroidery at home. I went to a shop to sell cigarettes, sugar, tea, and wine when my boy was one and a half years old, which was too young for him to go to kindergarten, so my mother-in-law came to help me to take care of him. My salary was 4 yuan a day. After half a year I thought it was not a good job so I changed to go to work in a restaurant. They paid me 5 yuan per day, 150 yuan per month. I worked there for another half year.

Finally she set up her own business:

> It was at the end of 1989. My son was nearly two years old. I sent him to kindergarten. I had to bring my son to kindergarten and pick him up again every day. One day I met a girl who came from Henan province in a market that was on the way to my son's kindergarten. She had her own stall and she told me, "Don't go to work. You can have your own business. How much do you make a day?" I said it was 5 yuan a day, so she told me where to get the wholesale. I asked her how much she can make a day and she said 50 to 100 yuan. It was a lot of money. So I resigned from my job and had my own clothes stall at the end of 1991.

Liang Jiehua's account draws attention to the constantly changing and highly unpredictable life the migrants led in the city. This applied both to their work and to their homes: They never knew what was going to happen to either the market in which they were currently working or to the pingfang houses they rented and that sooner or later were all doomed to be torn down. As one woman, who rented a room in a village beyond the suburb, expressed it: "Everything is very much up in the air. I never know how much money I can earn or what is happening with our house. I mean, maybe they will really tear it down and we will have to look for another place."

But the above account of Liang Jiehua also outlines a typical career of the migrants I met during my research: after a couple of years in which they usually worked as employees in the service sector, the migrants decided to set up their own businesses and become private entrepreneurs selling various products in suburban markets.

Finding a Niche in the Suburban "Market Economy"

Besides housing, the urban fringe—suburbs and the villages in the rural hinterland—also offers migrants various employment opportunities. Since the reform period, ecologically harmful state and urban enterprises, for example, have been relocated to the city's outer areas. Here migrant workers can find dirty and strenuous jobs that urban residents usually do not accept. In addition, numerous township and village enterprises employ mostly nonlocal people to do the unpleasant jobs while the local residents work in administration and management (see Jie and Taubmann 2002). Finally, the rapid increase in new suburban residential and commercial buildings has created various demands. Construction workers need food and clothing, and the rising projects require materials for construction and interior decoration. Serving these needs are the many informal markets that have sprung up in the urban fringe and that have become a prime arena for migrants' entrepreneurial aspirations. These markets actually also attract residents of the remaining old residential complexes who generally have limited financial means (both as customers and as salespeople themselves), and even customers from the new, exclusive edifices. Notably elderly parents who had moved in with their adult, middle-class children appear to favor these migrant markets where they can touch produce, bargain, and build personal relationships with salespeople, all important practices at least among the older generation (see Veeck 2000). Thus the migrant markets are in high demand.

In fact, analogous to the housing situation, registered local residents, local governments, and even public-sector work-units all have an interest in renting business premises to migrants to ease their financial problems. Some old residential compounds in the suburbs have literally knocked down the walls around their properties and built small business premises to rent to migrant entrepreneurs to gain cash income. Similarly, even some of the state-owned companies and research institutes that had been planted into the undeveloped hinterland during the 1950s and 1960s, and had remained spatially separated from the city at least until the 1980s, were so interested in the suburban conversion and the establishment of a variety of services that they too offered business premises to migrants.

Migrants in the suburban realm therefore have a positive impact upon the locality: legal residents, the urban labor market, the building industry, and the service sector all profit from the migrants' presence. Despite this symbiosis between migrants and local residents, and the important economic function that migrants have assumed in this environment, however, without legal protection they have no security as regards their housing or work situation. The suburban markets, for example, are generally short-lived affairs. As an official of the local "Office of Redevelopment" *(chongjian fazhan bu)* explained, plans for Wangjing's (re)development had already been laid down in 1993; there was nothing to change about it or any surprises. Now this government office oversaw the different stages in which prereform structures were scheduled to be torn down and land to be cleared for new commercial housing and industrial development projects. The migrant markets certainly had no place in the new suburban vision.

The migrant entrepreneurs, however, were also always themselves scouting the different options and possibilities throughout the city. They discussed and exchanged ideas about different markets and places where they got their supplies. Visiting relatives, acquaintances, and friends in other places, they compared each others' profits and evaluated if they could possibly be better off in a different marketplace. New opportunities arose just as quickly as the old ones disappeared: possibly for every market closed or torn down a new one was opened in another location. These were likely to be a bit further out of the city proper, in an area where (re)development had just begun, but they never seemed to completely disappear. Thus, knowing of the fleeting nature of their business premises, migrants took a flexible approach and tried to continuously improve their conditions through changing locations and maybe being ahead of the next closedown.

In many ways it is private entrepreneurship that offers the, apparently necessary, flexibility to survive in this ever-changing geographical realm and economic niche.[22] As outlined above, the migrants I met in the markets all had initially worked as employees in various businesses and companies. After several years, they had gained experience and saved enough money to start their own business. They chose to become private entrepreneurs because they felt that they would be more in charge of their lives and their future. As private entrepreneurs they were exposed to the whims of the market, but also able to determine their physical and material input. The success of their businesses, the profits they could make, depended solely on their own input, talent, diligence, and effort. Thus, despite certain risks, "being one's own boss" was considered an achievement.

Importantly, as self-employed entrepreneurs the migrants also did not have to deal with or suffer under an employer, and they did not have to worry about work schedules or times. They could accommodate their private lives with their work lives without the need to justify absences, for example. This was all the more important since migrants cannot rely on any state-provided services from which they are excluded. Not infrequently they had to take care of sick relatives or acquaintances or young children or run errands. As self-employed salespeople, they had no problem taking off during the day to do so. As employees, they would either not be allowed to leave or were likely to lose the job if they could not avoid an absence.

Interestingly, among the married migrants there appeared to be a special occupational pattern: while the husbands sought (temporary) employment in local factories, their wives engaged in this kind of private business. With this dual strategy they had one regular, if limited and temporary, monthly income, and one that was more unpredictable. At the same time, more flexible hours allowed the women to attend to everyday tasks that arose from the migrants' insecure living conditions.

In sum, various local conditions in the city's suburban fringe enable the migrants to carve out a niche that gives them a long-term perspective. This new economic space in many ways actually needs and relies on the migrants' labor and money. Importantly, however, it offers no guarantees, but instead is characterized by high uncertainty and unpredictability. Migrants thus have to be extremely flexible and adaptable. While private entrepreneurship does not offer any guarantees or certainties either, the flexibility of the trade, with little necessary start-up money and know-how, with self-determined input and working hours, makes it possible to counter, confront, or circumvent many of the difficulties that arise from migrants' semilegal status in the city. Choosing private entrepreneurship could therefore be interpreted as a strategy that migrants employ to adapt to the adversities they are confronted within the city.[23]

Settling Down

With the frequent changes of work and housing locations, the migrants I talked to could hardly form long-lasting and complex social networks. To counter the difficulties and adversities that the migrant salespeople faced in their everyday lives in the city, they built local relations of support. These, however, were based on being on the same stage of the life cycle rather than on coming from the same native place: young, unmarried women hung out with one another and often shared rented rooms, couples exchanged information about the business and where to best school their children, and mothers helped each other out when they had to tend to their babies.

Liang Jiehua, for example, received help and advice from fellow migrants, but these were not from her village or even from her home province. Instead, she had built relations and friendly ties with fellow market people who were in a similar life situation, were of the same age, and especially with other mothers. Similarly, thirty-five-year-old Yang Fengmei occasionally had to leave her sales stall either to attend school conferences for her son or to take care of her ailing mother-in-law, who (in an exceptional case) had come to join the family in the city.[24] While Yang was absent, her neighbor commonly took care of her business, as Yang did in return when the neighbor had to run errands. Coming from different provinces, the two had formed a friendly relationship based on the fact that they had rented opposite sales stalls and were both mothers of young sons. But even Yang and her neighbor's relationship halted when they went home at night. As they frequently change their homes, forming long-term residential communities was impossible for these migrants.[25] Nonetheless, both had established lasting relations with women and men they had met in previous places of work. Time to see them, however, was rare because of everybody's busy schedule. "We don't have much time to meet. But we call each other every other week or so."

It would be wrong, however, to suggest that the migrants were not connected to their families and other people from their home places. Migrants' support for the family expressed itself in money transfers and material goods sent home. Some had also either left behind or brought back small children to their home places to be taken care of by their parents, which certainly was a vital connection to the native place. Another form of "networking" among migrant families was the support for the migration of other family members. In many cases, after a migrant became somewhat established in the city and found a way of making a living, other family members followed. They initially depended on the help and resources of the already established relative to support them. In the case of Ling, for example, some time into my research her little sister, who was seventeen years old, came to Beijing to stay with her. The sister had finished high school and, with the same bleak job perspectives at home, hoped to find a job in the capital. To start, she helped her sister at the market while she learned *putonghua* (standard Mandarin Chinese). After about three months she was able to find work in the factory where Ling's husband worked.

Nonetheless, migrants' connections with their family and their home place were not necessarily their first and foremost contacts and social relations. This became apparent when I asked some of the migrants whom they would turn to if they needed help. While they answered that they would most likely turn to kin, I repeatedly could observe how stall neighbors loaned each other money, a transaction that requires a certain amount of familiarity and confidence. They apparently trusted their colleagues enough to engage in such transactions. Thus, living and working outside of close kinship or native place networks, the migrants in my investigation had formed relations of mutual support and help that were often grounded in necessity. Importantly, through the formation of locally based networks of friendship and support, the migrants also became more rooted in their new living environment.

A factor that strengthened their grounding in the urban environment, and supported the claim to permanently settle in the capital, was the fact that several of the migrants already had brought or were in the process of bringing their children to Beijing, which apparently is a new development. Without urban hukou the choices for schools are limited, but with the payment of higher fees at least some are accessible to migrants' children. Most small children had been left with parents or parents-in-law in the migrants' home provinces because they did not have the time to take care of them. Once they reached school age, however, several migrants tried to bring their children with them to the city. This was the situation of Ling, who had a three-year-old son whom she had left with her parents in Hubei province. During a 2002 summer vacation Ling brought her son back with her to Beijing and decided to let him stay.

The fact that the migrants in my investigation claimed to permanently settle in the city is not only surprising or remarkable in the face of the real adversities they face in their everyday lives, but also because of migrants' perception by urban residents and portrayal in public discourse. In official and urban discourse migrants are presented as a homogeneous, inferior group that needs to be civilized and transformed by higher moral codes set by permanent urban residents (Zhang L. 2001). As indicated above, peasantry and the countryside in official discourse are usually regarded as lagging behind the nation's march to modernity (Cohen 1993; Zhang L. 2001). Anagnost (1997) thus points out that the readying of the Chinese population for participation in global capitalism has taken place through a state-initiated civilizing process aimed at remaking subjectivities into those appropriate for a disciplined, efficient workforce. "Modernity," in fact, has become the new government legitimation for public surveillance and control. Migrants and the countryside, however, are conceived of as decidedly unmodern. Their lack of legal status only supports negative stereotypes and antirural bias held by urban residents. But it also reinforces people's general perceptions. Migrants speak of themselves as *nongcunren* (peasants, literally "countryside people"), whereas city residents refer to them as *waidiren* (people from outside). In addition, many of the current problems in the city, such as dirt, rudeness, and increasing crime rates, are blamed on the "uncultured" *(mei you wenhua)* migrants from the countryside with their "low quality" (suzhi di), such as in this statement made by a middle-aged woman during my research: "More and more people are moving here, people from all kinds of places. It's a social problem. Beijingers want to go abroad and the other Chinese want to go to Beijing. Nobody can stop them. But it's a big problem of the quality (suzhi) of the people."[26]

Interestingly, the migrants I met during my fieldwork engaged in a discourse portraying themselves as "uncultured," "uneducated" peasants, through which they effectively justified the socioeconomic position they were in, only to juxtapose this narrative with one that centered around hard work and honesty. They had built a very strong sense of moral virtue, of being good people who worked hard for their living. Migrant market women, for example, frequently pointed to female customers who were allegedly prostitutes, remarking, "They are bad women. I would never do *that,* no matter how poor I was. I would rather die than do *that!*" Several of the migrants I talked to also prided themselves in being honest salespeople. They did not try to convince someone to buy clothes that did not fit or did not look good, they were willing to exchange products that customers returned, and the customary bargaining was conducted according to very specific rules.

As outlined above, migrants are generally not treated very well or seen in a very positive light by the permanent residents of Chinese cities. It has become quite common to blame crimes and problems in the metropolis on the migrant population. Many urban residents I interviewed blamed the dirt and pollution in the city on the "uncultured" migrant population who did not know how to behave properly. Reports of crimes in the city committed by people from the countryside were standard fare in local newspapers. But when I asked the market people if they had experienced any form of maltreatment, or if they felt looked down upon, one of them said: "Some [people] look down on me, but I can look down on them the same and I can give back in words. I think it is all about who you are, not where you are from. If you are a good person or not."

"It's all about who you are," "if you are a good person or not," these statements reflected a general attitude that I observed in the migrants I talked to: this discourse of diligence and honesty contrasted them from the official and public discourse on the *liudong renkou* (floating population).[27] In fact, together with their laments about their difficult life, this discourse was a new form of "speaking bitterness." The suburban migrants' form of speaking bitterness was one that stressed the hardship and effort they put into improving their living conditions without complaining. They had thus internalized the state's recent emphasis on "self-development" *(ziwo fazhan)* and on the improvement of "human quality" *(suzhi)* as vital ingredients in national development. They had adopted the claim that migration to the city is the key to "self-development" and high quality for young rural people, statements that are common in the mainstream media (see Jacka 2005). Portraying themselves as morally valuable, self-developing persons, the migrants had thus forged a positive self-identification in the face of societal scorn and discrimination.

Closely related to the perception and self-identification of migrants to the urban realm is the question of modernity, which looms large over China's present-day transformations. Once I asked Liang Jiehua to compare her life in the countryside with how she lived in the city. She answered: "I am busier [than my siblings in the countryside]. My income is higher and my life is more comfortable than theirs, but my life is [also] very tense. They work in the field and can take a rest whenever they want to. Their life is more relaxed." Despite the fact that she worked almost every day from early morning until late night, constantly felt tired, had experienced urbanites' scorn, and portrayed rural life with a certain "nostalgia," devoid of hardship, Liang was very clear in that she preferred urban life. One of her most adamant "proofs" of what she had gained was that she had not even seen a train nor had she known TV before she came to Beijing. Her current house, even though small, with an outside bathroom, and located far from the city in a hinterland village, she considered an improvement to where she came from, because it was made from bricks. And there was always the hope, through hard work and thrift, to improve one's situation. Liang and the other migrants I met had apparently discovered and embraced the trappings of modern life in the capital. Maybe it was not so surprising that they did not even contemplate returning to the countryside.

Conclusion

The young, educated couples living in commercial housing, the elderly danwei residents, and the migrant market people, as discussed here, were part of the emerging socioeconomic stratification process of Chinese urban society. Wangjing residents were set apart from one another by age, education, status, residence, access to resources, and the amount and kind of choices they had to design their lives. In addition, the three groups of residents showed attitudes, convictions, sentiments, and ideologies, born from their individual trajectories and influenced by shared experiences that in turn reinforced the socioeconomic divisions that existed between them.

Besides forming distinctive, socioeconomic groups, the differences among them also translated into diverging circles or scales of movement. Specifically, young, wealthy couples who lived in Wangjing traversed between their residences, their place of work in the inner city, and places of leisure and entertainment throughout the urban area. Migrant market people circled between the markets within the research area, the places where they bought supplies that were spread throughout the city, and their residences, which most often lay further out from the built-up zone. Elderly danwei residents, in contrast, predominantly moved within the suburb, gravitating around their residential danwei compound and its vicinity. The Wangjing area as a whole was thus marked by the crosscutting of these circles, the movements in and out of the area, into the inner city, and the hinterland. Socioeconomic differentiation, or class structuration, had a real and symbolic spatial dimension to it. The way in which space and consumption are intertwined with the process of stratification is the focus of the next chapter.

5 CONSUMPTION AND THE GEOGRAPHY OF SPACE AND SOCIAL STATUS

RESIDENTIAL COMMUNITIES have a formative impact on emerging lifestyles in contemporary urban China. At the same time, housing is the point where the emerging class structuration of society is closely intertwined with consumption: When they buy a house, urbanites also choose the real or perceived lifestyle associated with different residential complexes and locations. Yet the purchase of commercial housing in specific locations also points to another important aspect of consumption: its link to place. Not simply for the obvious reason that we must consume things in place, but in the more important sense that consumption is a place-creating and place-altering act (Sack 1992). Consumption is, in fact, among the most important means by which we become powerful geographical agents in our day-to-day lives. In the Chinese case, the way urban residents consume goods, housing, and indeed lifestyles today has an important effect on the reconfiguration of space and society. The preference for certain places and styles, for example, is influenced by a variety of factors, not all of which are necessarily rational. In addition, these choices transmit specific messages.

In this chapter I show that the consumption of space has turned into a marker of difference, an indicator of the new class structuration in reform-period China. Consumption behavior, in fact, plays a crucial role in the reconfigurations of social space in present-day urban China. Below, I discuss the way in which consumption importantly differentiates Wangjing residents. Not only their consumption power but also their attitude toward consumption notably set the three groups apart and further underlined their growing separation. But it is especially the consumption of housing, that is, the intersection of consumption behavior with spatial practices, that reinforces the stratification of urban society: prestigious suburban residential complexes serve the middle and upper-middle income groups to underline their real, and claimed, elevated social positioning in society. The result is what I call the geography of space and social status.

Stratification through Consumption

The introduction of capitalist goods, ideas, and practices in reform-period China has triggered a consumerism that "reconfigures relationships and self-identities from the ground up" (Chen et al. 2001, 12). Especially the 1990s were characterized by a state-sanctioned and transnationally produced valorization of consumption. Consumption has, in fact, become a central aspect of Chinese (urban) life, and one that is actively supported by the government. After the initial stage of economic reform that concentrated on the "liberation of productive forces," the more recent drive away from "heavy production and light consumption" *(zhong shengchan qing xiaofei)* was hailed as the necessary "liberation of consumption forces" to sustain economic growth (Yi 2002, 14). To stimulate China's low consumption rate of 60.3 percent in 2001 (in contrast to a world average of 75.3 percent),[1] the Tenth Five-Year Plan declared that to improve people's living standard was a "crucial factor in expanding domestic demand" (People's Daily Online 2001). In 2002, the National Bureau of Statistics suggested lifting any remaining consumption-restricting regulations, raising salaries, containing public expenditure by privatizing social services, and encouraging the wealthy to spend on tourism, higher education, cars and other means of transportation, as well as on financial and insurance services, all with the intention of increasing the overall private consumption rate from 60 percent of GDP to 68 by 2005 (Liu G. 2002; Tomba 2004). Yet, when President Jiang Zemin stressed the importance of the policy to "build a well-off society in an all-round way"[2] during the 16th Party Congress in November 2002, this also reflected the widely held position that a large middle class is essential for China's political and social stability. To this end, Jiang called for expanding the purchasing power and status of significantly larger groups of urban employees and professionals. Shortly after, Premier Wen Jiabao also suggested expanding consumer credit and boosting consumer confidence (Collier 2004).

The results of these policies have been far-reaching. In Beijing, annual per capita income in 2000 was 15,000 yuan (US$1,875), while the annual disposable income of urban households reached 10,349.7 yuan (US$1,284). At the end of 2000, savings deposits in Beijing totaled 292.32 billion yuan (US$36.54 billion), of which 266.33 billion yuan (US$33.29 billion) belonged to urban households (Beijing tongjiju 2001). At the time, a new development plan for the city set as its target the increase of per capita income to reach nearly 20,000 yuan (US$2,400) by 2008 (a rise of 6 percent annually) (*China Daily* 2002b).

As Tomba (2004) explains, it was especially employees in the public sector who have benefited from these government policies to boost consumption. In Beijing, the city with the largest number of officials, the effects of these measures is thus most notable. Pay raises, for example, more than doubled average salaries between 1995 and 2000.[3] In addition, scientists and teachers have experienced a rise in prestige and remuneration because academic institutions with hardening budget constraints and the need to recruit full-tuition-paying students compete to enroll them (Tomba 2004). Yet, new government policies resulted not only in financial gains. As we saw in chapter 2, public employees also have privileged access to education, welfare, and housing, since all of these are connected to the type of danwei they work in and to their administrative rank. The public sector thus generates new wealth: high-income households in Beijing have an above-average number of members employed in the state sector and a higher level of education and professional training (Lin and Bian 1991). The common "one family, two systems" strategy of my wealthier informants therefore apparently paid off.

It is important, however, to note that while overall per capita income is rising in Beijing, income disparities are growing too. A survey of salaries in eighty-six occupations conducted by the Beijing Statistical Bureau in 2001 showed that employees in some of Beijing's more lucrative occupations earned almost seven times as much as employees in low-end professions. The gap is, in fact, widening by 160 percent year by year. About four million people, that is, 39.4 percent of all workers in Beijing, earned more than the average, while 30 percent earned less than 15,000 yuan (US$1,875) per annum (*Business Beijing* 2002). Wage differentials, consumption power, and the disparate access to education, welfare, and housing thus increasingly differentiate and distinguish the urban population. It is the translation of such distinctions into physical and spatial markers that underlines and enforces present stratification processes.

Decorating Modernity

In Borneman's (1997) research on East and West Germans' identifications, he found that West German people, in contrast to East Germans, related their life stories to events such as the monetary reform after World War II, the purchase of a private car, and vacation time—signs of a growing prosperity of the Federal Republic as a country, as well as of the West German people individually. In my conversations with elderly danwei residents in China, I could observe the emerging identification with similar topics of prosperity. Mrs. Fang, for example, referred to postreform China as a country that was becoming rich, and other people mentioned their own improving life situation or the growing wealth of their children. In the exceptional case in which they owned a car, that was one of the first things the elderly mentioned after introducing themselves. In this way, the elderly danwei residents' accounts not only reflected the growing trend of consumption, but also the fact that in contemporary urban China socioeconomic differentiation and social status are increasingly linked to consumer goods and identified with consumption power.

Unlike the German case, these identifications are intimately connected to a specific cultural context: the modernization project on which China has embarked since the late nineteenth century. China's semicolonial experience of the nineteenth century spurred modernization attempts such as the May Fourth Movement, but in the early twentieth century also gave birth to the Communist Party. Developing a nation-state and society that was on a par with, or "as modern as," the former Western colonizers was one of the main driving forces behind the Chinese socialist project and its appeal to the people. Socialism held the promise that China would reach that "modernity" faster than these nations had themselves, if not overtake them. Since the reform period, the unacknowledged disappointment in the alternative project of socialism has popularly been converted into a desire for wealth, symbolized by consumer goods and consumer spending. The availability of such goods is taken to be an indicator of China's arrival in "modernity."[4]

Since few of the elderly had the economic means to engage in conspicuous consumption, the elderly's sense of personal life improvement, of arrival in "modernity," majorly centered on the type and size of housing in which they lived. After the years of residing in small, cramped, and damp simple houses, often without running water and with outside toilets, to now live in and *own* an apartment—no matter how simple in standard—was a considerable and tangible improvement of their living condition. Sixty-two-year-old Shao Xiaolei lucidly described this process of improvement:

> I feel great. I was worried about my food, clothes, and house. The houses before were small, wet, and dim. Now we have big bright houses. People did not dare to think about good houses at that time. Now the government is trying to meet the demands of the citizens who want to have better apartments. People are happier.

Especially since the 1990s, an additional indicator of success or improvement is the way a house is "decorated" *(zhuangxiu),* which can mean anything from a picture on the wall to the installation of a Western-style toilet. Mrs. Fang, for example, appeared to consider the quality of "decoration" as a proof of the life improvement of her children: "Their houses are decorated very well."

While the "decorating fever" (Tang X. 1998) is certainly the result of the lures of a growing consumer culture, for danwei residents with limited financial means "decoration" is a simple means to improve one's house and living environment. In addition, decorating one's house has become a way to express personal tastes and preferences, individualizing private spaces in an almost symbolic act of rejecting the Maoist standardized aesthetic of austerity. In this process, how *much* the elderly could invest in the "decoration" of their house did not matter as much as the act itself. Mrs Xia (age sixty-two), for example, related:

> I have always been living in the dormitory, but the first place I lived was in the countryside after I got married. My window was facing the field and I had to go outside for the toilet and to wash myself. A lot of flies in the summer. Now we live in a building and have our own toilet. Our standard of living is rising. We have decorated our house, although in the most simple manner.

Yet, despite the desire for better housing and decoration, generally the elderly claimed that consumption was not an important aspect of their lives. This was for two reasons: first, the elderly did not have a lot of spending money, and second, under the socialist system they had also been trained to save and be frugal. Sixty-one-year-old Hen Xiewei's statement brought the economic restrictions on consumption to the fore: "Our life is simple. I seldom take the taxi. I take buses in order to save money. I don't go to restaurants, because it's expensive. I can eat fast food." Limited financial means thus significantly reduced danwei residents' choices in life—in regard to participating in today's consumer society, as well as in regard to their living situation. When I asked Wen Haitian (age sixty-five), a retired factory worker, what he thought about his danwei compound his answer strongly brought out the lack of choice he had in this question. "The environment is okay. I'm very good at adapting to all kinds of environments. It's not a question of liking it or not. I cannot change it, so I have to adjust myself to it."

At the same time, however, my older informants' emphasis on frugality, and their willingness to sacrifice their own pleasures, reflected their socialist upbringing. This attitude toward consumption was expressed by Liu Wenhou (age fifty-six), a retired worker who was now a consultant to his former company. "The ways of spending money are also different. They [his children's generation] spend money easily. We seldom buy anything." Similar to Zhu Laoning's narrative, as told in chapter 4, the old generation of danwei residents made sense of their transformed subject positioning in the reform-period society with its climate of consumption and instant gratification by emphasizing their thriftiness.

In sum, while the elderly were also susceptible to the "lures" of consumer society, their limited financial means as well as their different socialization restrained their full-scale participation in it. Rather, the elderly danwei residents invested in modest "decoration" of their houses, indicating the desire to improve their living environment. At the same time, these small changes gave people the sense that something had changed in their lives. Generally, though, instead of paying too much attention to personal acquisitions, the elderly claimed that more important to them was the overall rise of living standards in China, a symbol of its arrival in "modernity."

The Consumption of Housing

Miller (1998) has criticized anthropological studies of consumption (e.g., Baudrillard 1981; Bourdieu 1984; Douglas and Isherwood 1979) as too mechanical in their focus on the relationship between an individual and society (or social space) within which individual expressions derive meaning and potential. He points out that these studies concentrate heavily on possessions and the communicative functions of possessions. Miller notes, in contrast, that shopping (which we can here read as consumption) is neither about possessions per se nor about identity per se. Miller insists that consumption is concerned with obtaining goods or imagining the possession and use of goods. Since many goods are consumed in a short time, however, consumption is of a "transitory nature" (Miller 1998, 141). Miller therefore suggests that consumption should be understood as a social process that is born from and relates to specific social relations and historical moments. Shopping, for him, becomes a quintessentially social act: an act of sacrifice, a means of saving through thrift, and a way of expressing and constructing bonds of love and devotion. Rather than creative, cognitive, "cultural" resistance, shopping is a socially meaningful, powerfully affective practice that builds and expresses strong bonds of love and devotion.

The emotional aspect of consumption that Miller highlights became strikingly apparent when I asked Cao Xiangjun what owning a house meant to her. She said, "I feel I have my own house. I decorate it in my own way and I feel comfortable to live in it. I think it is my home *(jia)*. I don't take it only as a dwelling *(fangzi)*." *Fangzi* (apartment, dwelling) here obviously stood for something exchangeable, nonpersonal, to which one did not have an (emotional) connection. *Jia* (house, home), in contrast, signified something one had an emotional attachment to, but also a sphere where one felt free, independent, at ease. The emotional dimension is further underlined by the fact that *jia* in the Chinese language also means family. Fraser (2000, 29) states that housing is "the material symbol of having a family and has always been viewed as the source of safety and happiness in Chinese life." In the politically uncertain climate of China in the reform period, the importance attributed to residence is therefore not surprising. Housing has become a newfound valuable private space, an inside that is importantly outside of official surveillance. But even more, through choosing their own apartments, the young and affluent made this private sphere a space where they felt they could live and express individuality and freedom.[5] Cao Xiangjun's description of the changes in housing conveyed this very clearly:

In my grandparents' generation, all of the buildings were the same; no character, no decoration. Bare cement floors, a wooden bed, wooden chairs, and tables; every family was the same. But in my generation we have decorated walls, wooden floors, sofas, and all kinds of other decorations. It's more similar to the pictures in the foreign magazines and movies.

Yet, despite the importance attached to and emotion invested in this newfound private space, my young and affluent informants around Wangjing all indicated that they considered their present residence a compromise, a solution for the time being. This was independent of their present financial situation or of the type of housing in which they actually lived. But couples who had significantly improved their financial situation seemed to be especially self-conscious about the neighborhood, pointing out its shortcomings, such as this thirty-something-year-old woman: "It is kind of difficult for shopping because we have few supermarkets here, let alone a shopping mall. I have to go downtown if I want to buy anything, like a country girl. I think it's not very convenient for me."

When they bought their houses, most of the young professionals had only limited financial means. In addition, at least until the end of the 1990s, there were also only a few choices in the developing real estate market. Wangjing belonged to the first cluster of medium- to high-priced residential areas in Beijing, and the young and wealthy considered it the best option at the time. Nonetheless, with growing wealth and, importantly, the purchase of a car, home owners started to look for other, newer, and more costly projects that would offer an even more exclusive space in terms of environment and living area. Wen Kaiqing (age thirty-four), who lived in Atlantic Place, for example, thought about eventually moving to another, meaning "better," place:

> If I can afford it, I would like to live somewhere where it is easy for shopping and convenient for transportation. We plan to buy a better apartment and rent this one to others. We have to save money to pay for the first sum of money before we move into a new apartment and pay the rest of the money every month with the money our old flat makes. Transportation and shopping places are important for us. I don't understand the developers who built such a densely populated living area without building any shopping centers; they will surely make money from it, because the newly opened supermarket is flourishing. They have so many people here and no shops. It's easier to make money than in downtown. People would rather shop here than going to town, because it takes hours on the way.

Criteria for choosing specific locations throughout the city and individual residential communities within Wangjing were thus relative concepts connected to the individual's life situation. An indicator of the emerging class structuration of Chinese society, the changing perspective equally applied to the affluent urban residents' evaluation of neighbors' "quality" (suzhi). This process of shifting sensitivities became evident through the experiences and narratives of Lili, Cao Xiangjun, and her husband Zhou Tianxin, who lived in the mid-level Wangjing New City residential complex.

Lili, a thirty-something single graphic designer who had worked for several years for a foreign advertising company and was now studying art, had lived in various places throughout Beijing. Two years ago, however, she bought an apartment in the Wangjing residential complex, and she was delighted about her new living place:

> Wangjing gives me the best impression of all the places I have lived in. First, it's clean. Second, it's well greened. Third, the people have a high quality *(suzhi gao)* in Wangjing. I seldom go out anymore since I have moved to Wangjing. I cannot bear the sight of narrow dirty *hutongs* and smelly public toilets. I want to run back home.

Cao Xiangjun and Zhou Tianxin had bought their apartment in the Wangjing residential complex one year before Lili. Zhou explained how at that time they did not have many choices in the incipient real estate market. Wangjing struck them as a good compromise: "The house was comparatively good, although we did not have as much choice as there is today. The people who could afford to buy a house here [in the complex] were white-collar workers and had good incomes, and we felt that the community and people were good."

At the time when Cao Xiangjun and Zhou Tianxin bought their apartment, their respective careers were just beginning to take off. Cao was promoted at the Japanese investment bank where she had started to work two years before. Zhou had sold his expanding IT company to a state-owned group while continuing to work as its director. The move provided him with guaranteed salary, pension, and social benefits. When I met the couple in 2002, their financial situation had significantly improved, and they were thinking about buying a new apartment. Interestingly, now they pointed to the "*low* quality" (suzhi di) of the other residents in their living complex as one of the reasons why they wanted to make a change. As their friend Tian Ping put it: "They [Cao and Zhou] are not new money like the other people [here] who got rich overnight. They depend on their stable salary and they are well educated." Apparently, Cao and Zhou had "outgrown" this middle-class residential complex. To these young urban residents with well-paying jobs, consumption of housing had thus turned into an everlasting hunt for a better, more suitable place. What they were looking for, they said, was a *more* convenient location, *more* amenities, *better* environment, *bigger* space.

Zhang L. (2004) points to the fact that in present-day China it is a social taboo among the newly rich to ask exactly how and how *much* money one makes because many business transactions are done outside of the official realm. It was indeed remarkable to note the difference between older public-sector employees, who immediately revealed how much they earned or how high their pensions were without being asked, and the young, affluent couples predominantly working in the private sector and living in commercial housing, who remained vague even when asked directly about their incomes. In this circumstance, Zhang notes that if "it is the case that the production of wealth is kept secret and intentionally made opaque, then the viable way to assert and maintain one's status is through conspicuous material consumption" (ibid., 11).

Consumption, indeed, had become a major aspect of wealthy urban residents' lives in China. Nonetheless, based on my interviews, I would claim that for the majority of the newly affluent, consumption actually extended less to consumer goods than to a lifestyle. In fact, many of my informants stressed that they did not have the time to go shopping for clothes and other goods. They were too busy working and studying in the after hours. Although they engaged in various new and costly leisure activities (such as traveling, joining gyms, taking in movies and expensive restaurants), saving money to buy better housing was higher on the agenda than excessive consumption. Therefore, I suggest that in Chinese stratifying urban society where socioeconomic differentiations are only becoming apparent, the consumption of space has turned into a special realm and housing is one of the prime markers of socioeconomic status. More important than ownership of a car, travel and leisure activities in general, children's schools, or clothing styles, where and how one lives is an indicator of one's financial wellbeing. It was this function of housing as a status marker that drove my informants to constantly look for new residences—places that would better match and represent their improving socioeconomic position. And it is in this sense, as I will show below, that the consumption of housing, and the preference for suburbs like Wangjing, is a social practice, embedded in and reflecting on the reform-period urban environment. Indeed, apart from a status marker, housing has become a major constitutive element in new identity formations, especially among the young, educated, and affluent Wangjing residents.

Saving for a Child's Future

Migrants from the countryside who worked in the markets around Wangjing had the least financial means to participate in today's consumer culture. Liang Jiehua, for example, drank hot water instead of tea because, she said, she could not afford it. In other conversations, however, she revealed that she had bought a computer for her son, even though she stressed that it was a very cheap and simple one. In addition, she also sent her son to a more expensive middle school in the Wangjing vicinity instead of the cheaper one close to the village where they lived. She thought that this school was better and would give her son a greater chance to pass the university entrance examination.

This kind of indirect spending, not on themselves but on their child, was a very common pattern among the migrants I talked to around Wangjing. None of them owned any of the common signs of the new urban Chinese consumer culture: no cell phones, no beepers. Even in the worst summer heat, when the temperatures in the nonventilated market hall rose to forty degrees Celsius or more, the salespeople did not invest in an electric fan. They did not frequent restaurants, always took the cheapest buses, and when buying their vegetables on the attached open farmer's market, bargained "for their lives." On most of the women I saw two, or maybe three, different outfits despite the fact that they were in the clothing business. The only consumer article some of them had bought was a television set for their house.

I wondered whether the migrant market women were actually able to put some money aside to save, but also if they had any insurance in case they got sick, or any form of provision for their old age. Liang Jiehua told me:

> Once my husband retires, he will get a pension from his danwei, as his father does now. But I don't get anything. I don't count on my son to support us one day. That is the problem of the one-child family. He will have his own family to support, his wife has her parents, and then us too? That

would be a big financial burden for him to support both parents. We try to put some money in the bank to save for later.

When I asked if they were really able to save money, she said that they tried to but actually did not have enough to put something aside. In this aspect, Liang Jiehua for once was in a less favorable position than other migrants since her husband's danwei salary was very low. Other migrant couples, where both husband and wife worked as private entrepreneurs, usually earned more and were therefore able to save money. Nonetheless, the downside for them was their lack of any kind of social security; their *need* to save was higher than in Liang's case.

A large part of migrants' money, in fact, appeared to go into the education of their children. Without urban hukou, the choices for schools were limited, but with the payment of higher fees at least some were accessible to migrants' children. Most small children were left with parents or parents-in-law in the migrants' home provinces because they did not have the time to take care of them. Once they reached school age, though, some migrants tried to bring their children with them to the city.

As described in the previous chapter, after a summer visit in 2002 Ling brought her three-year-old son back with her to Beijing. After he had lived with her for two months, she decided to let him stay and was planning to send him to kindergarten in Beijing. She explained:

> I am not going to send him back home. The educational system there [home province] is very bad. I want to send him to a kindergarten here in Beijing. But I have to bring him there and pick him up every day, so I have to find a place close by. I found one, but it's not so good. It's okay. It costs 200 yuan (US$25) per month. There is a better kindergarten for 400 yuan (US$50). I am not sure yet what to do.

As a result of the strong divide between countryside and city, which the explosive growth in the (coastal) cities has only exacerbated, migrants who work in cities realize that the only chance for their children to have better prospects in life is to receive a good education. This, however, is less likely in their home provinces than in the city.

In September 2002, the Beijing Municipal Education Commission released a new rule that allowed migrant workers' children to attend public schools for a "moderate transregional schooling fee." Fees for non–hukou holders used to be very high and came with so many troublesome procedures that many migrants who could not rely on family members to take care of their children had to send them to urban private schools of questionable standards, or at times even took them out of school completely.[6] The new policy presented migrant families with a better option. Difficulties, however, continued to arise through the hukou system. Local governments are responsible only for residents in their own regions and do not have the budget to provide education and health benefits for children from other regions. Even though some schools are willing to accept migrants' children, they are charged extra fees that their parents cannot afford. Nonetheless, the migrants in my investigation made every effort to have their children attend schools in Beijing. Not surprisingly, school performance and costs of education were a repeated topic of conversation among the migrants. One woman revealed: "I am worried about my son. He does not study. He still has four more years in school. I don't think he studies hard enough to get into university. If he does, though, we will have to pay for his university. The better the school, the more expensive the tuition fee."

Migrants' "investment" in or dedication to their child's future surely also had a certain degree of self-interest; who else could they possibly rely on in their old age? The migrants also knew, however, that they could not necessarily count on their child's support. With the one-child policy, couples now have to attend to four parents—a significant burden that not all of them will be able to take on. Why, then, did migrants put their limited resources into the education of their children with no guaranteed returns?

As we have seen above, migrants around Wangjing engaged in a discourse portraying themselves as "uncultured," "uneducated" peasants, through which they effectively justified the socioeconomic position they were in, only to juxtapose this narrative with one that centered around hard work and honesty. Feeling alienated from urban society, migrants turned the education of their children into an object of consumption because it embodied their desire to become integrated into urban society. Since they themselves did not have many chances and opportunities to significantly improve their own living conditions, education would provide the "cultural capital" (Bourdieu 1984) that might enable their children to do so. The projection of a significantly different and better future for their children was the mechanism that the migrants used to create a powerful ritual "antidote" to their alienation from urban residents and their own uncertain living situation, even if they themselves might not directly benefit from it. This sentiment was expressed by Shu Honghua, a forty-year-old saleswoman from the northwest of China, who felt that her own living situation, her work options, her education, her life was influenced by being from the countryside. But as regards her son, she was convinced that they had overcome the rural background and that she was able to provide him with the necessary education that would enable him to advance in life. Besides being a very real instrument to improve their socioeconomic situation, the ideal and pursuit of education for children had thus also become a symbolic strategy that, in tandem with migrants' self-portrayal as hard-working and honest people, became a means to counter the public and official discourse of the "floating population" as the inherent "other," in opposition to the educated and cultured—"modern"—urban residents.

Deferring their own comfort and aspirations or desires to their children, migrants inhabited a very different world than both danwei residents and the young and educated who lived in the suburb. In their exclusion from conspicuous consumption and hopes for the next generation, migrants somewhat resembled the old people in work-unit compounds. In contrast to them, however, they could not retreat behind the "protecting walls" of the danwei unit with its (limited) welfare and security net. Their flexibility, necessary to meet the uncertainties of their living and work situation, on the other hand, made migrants emblems of the regime of "flexible accumulation" brought about by the Chinese government's project of rapid economic growth and integration into the global economy.[7] While the suburb offered the migrants (preliminary) housing and a business niche in which they could eke out a living, at the same time the suburb also represented all the insecurities of their urban existence. Despite their important input and significant impact on the space and everyday life in the suburb, migrants' agency in the urban transformation process was of a fleeting nature and, thus, rather emblematic of their exposure to the whims of the market.

Modernity and the Global Scale

In the specific cultural context of reform-era China, it is not only the way space is reconfigured that influences social relationships, but also the value that is assigned to specific spaces.[8] In the process of moving from plan to market in China, space has become commodified. Through the introduction of scales of market values, space, which was formerly largely undifferentiated in terms of function and value (apart from the distinction between city and countryside), has become graded or scaled along parameters such as west and east (or interior and coastal areas), rural and urban, urban fringe and urban center. During the Maoist era, Chinese citizens were immobilized through the household registration system and fixed in specific places in a national development hierarchy with Beijing at the top. Today, however, space and people are redefined and repositioned through qualities such as young/old, educated/uneducated, inside/outside, and backward/progressive, and are ranked in a hierarchy of modernity and exchange value (Chen et al. 2001, 16).

It is this kind of spatial ranking, of attributing value to physical location and imbuing it with prestige and status, that becomes an important factor in the Chinese residential differentiation process.[9] Within Beijing's social fabric, "Wangjing," for example, has apparently become a marker of wealth: during my research, when I told people where I conducted my investigation, they frequently commented "Ah, the rich people's place." Apart from affordability and the factual advantages and disadvantages of certain locations, I claim that it is this implied status that was a major incentive for the young and affluent couples to buy an apartment in this particular area of the city.[10]

The primacy this ideological aspect had over more concrete considerations becomes surprisingly apparent when one takes a closer look at my informants' reasons for moving to Wangjing. While residents said that the convenient traffic connection was one of the attractive points of Wangjing, in reality they spent a lot of time between their homes and their companies. Many of them said it took them about an hour to get to the CBD. People I spoke to who lived in the south of the city, for example, needed only around twenty minutes to reach the same place. As mentioned in the Introduction, with the increasing construction and development in Wangjing, various residents commented on the rising frequency of traffic jams in the northeastern part of the city. Less popular residential neighborhoods in the south of Beijing, therefore, might actually offer more concrete advantages in these terms. Nonetheless, my informants insisted that it was better to live in the northern part of the city. Referring back to the imperial city layout, the south was still (or again) considered a "poor people's" living place despite growing numbers of new and costly residential complexes. Thus, living in Beijing's north automatically lends—real or desired—prestige to the residents. Present-day urban transformations do not start on a blank sheet of paper. They are deeply entangled with historical processes and ideologies that transcend "pure economic forces" such as the land and housing market.

Socioeconomic and spatial differentiations of the reform period, however, have another dimension that adds further importance and complexity to the consumption of housing: the quest for modernity. Wealth, consumer power, and monetary value in China today are increasingly translated into indicators of status, and by implication, of modernity. As Jeffrey (2001, 25) suggests: "Whereas Maoism equated capitalism with immorality, today we find a discourse (both official and popular) of the market as a civilizing practice that implies and confers proximity to the modern." Various scholars (e.g., Ballew 2001; Rofel 1997; Schein 2001) have further pointed out that the new modernity of consumerism in China has a decidedly global twist:

> In the era of enthusiastic and officially mandated "reform and openness to the outside world" *(gaige kaifang)*, the reproduction of space is a consummately global process, one proceeding for its own re-representation to the "evaluative gaze of foreign capital," in Anagnost's phrase (1994, 279). This evaluative gaze of global capital represents a primary principle which gives shape to the space in Chinese metropolises. (Balew 2001, 255)

Cities, in fact, are increasingly the sites where the new consumer culture, modernity, and global capital intersect. Especially metropolises such as Beijing, Shanghai, and Guangzhou are, in Schein's (2001, 225) imagery, "widely viewed as glittering markets of a world of goods imported from the catalogs and store shelves of global modernity." Schein calls the present Chinese urban sentiment "imagined cosmopolitanism," which to her appears to be an almost egalitarian notion since even window shoppers can dream that they take part in the new global consumer culture. In contrast, I would maintain that the growing integration of China into global economic flows is an ever more important aspect of how Chinese society is stratified today, or of how citizens are differently positioned in the new socioeconomic reality. Not everybody has the same access to the globally envisioned modernity.

To add complexity to the ways in which time, space, and mobility are experienced in the current phase of global capitalism, Doreen Massey introduces the dimensions of class, ethnicity, and gender into her "power geometry" model. She writes that "different groups have distinct relationships to this anyway-differentiated mobility; some are more in charge of it than others; some initiate flows and movement, others don't; some are more on the receiving end of it than others; some are effectively imprisoned by it" (1993, 61). Similarly, in China, access to and consumption power over the new modernity with its global twist increasingly differentiates Chinese citizens and defines social status beyond mere economic potency.

Rising (and new sources of) incomes have made a visit to McDonald's or Pizza Hut an affordable experience for more and more urban residents, and fake foreign-branded consumer articles have taken the distinguishing edge off a "Gucci" purse or a "Burberry" coat. The real estate market, which is deeply enmeshed in the complicated web of international and national speculative transactions, however, has become an ever more exclusive and privileged—if not privileging—realm. As Fraser (2000) observes, housing is a key element in the social, political, economic, and cultural configuration and in the discourses that reflect and shape relations between people and places, goods and power.

While certain companies (and government branches) continue to provide (or subsidize) housing for their employees, more and more Chinese are seeking to buy commercial apartments in the real estate market, either as investments or to improve their living situation and social status. In this process, however, there is nothing "egalitarian": the better the house, the more amenities and facilities the complex, the more convenient and prestigious the location, the more expensive the unit. Chinese citizens' reform-period redefinitions are thus increasingly turned into repositionings—socioeconomic differentiations that are translated into spatial differentiation.

In addition, as I will show below, Chinese citizens at the dawn of the twenty-first century not only are differently positioned in spatial terms, but also have differential access to and control over space and its meaning. The study of this process of reconfiguration produces what I call the social geography of space and status, which makes evident the relative position of Chinese citizens in terms of space, power, and socioeconomy.

"I Wish My Children Could Live like Americans"

As I have discussed, my elderly danwei informants most commonly compared today's living situation with the lives they had when they were young, or even with their parents' generation—a contrast that was most likely favorable to the present. Here is what Zhou Heping had to say:

> My mother was a worker in a cigarette factory. . . . My father also was a worker, looked down upon by others. . . . We didn't have money to see the doctor; it was the old society. Now we have hospitals. The vicious old society. [During that time] the people were at the bottom of the world; now we are the owners of society. It is a difference like between sky and earth. How can you compare it?

But a few elderly also evoked "the world" as a measure: "It will be better and better. The Chinese people will have a better social position. Friends from all over the world will trust China and become our friends. China will be stronger and have more and more friends," commented Mrs. Li. What we can read out of this statement is the wish for China to be accepted in the international arena, to be an equal partner to other countries. Again, this reflects China's quest to liberate itself from the subordinate status it was subjected to during its semicolonial period in the nineteenth century, and out of which also grew the Communist project of modernization. Evoking this theme today, for many of the elderly the comparison with "the world" predominantly signified reaching "Western" living standards, as Mrs. Fang expressed so clearly: "I wish that China will be as well developed as the United States, and our life as good as Americans'. We still have a long way to catch up with them. I wish my children's lives will be as good as theirs. I can hardly wait for that day." "American life" here stood abstractly for a certain—imagined—living standard fed by the news and media.

This, however, was the only kind of "scale" to which the elderly subjected themselves. They hardly distinguished in terms of importance between different cities in China or different places within Beijing itself. Socialized during the Maoist era, the elderly held on to a view of urban space as a continuous and relatively undifferentiated entity. They apparently did not want to ascribe value or status to physical locations within the city, and they presented themselves as (relatively) indifferent to the glamour that the world beyond China

had in the eyes of the younger generation. While many of them studied English in their community classes, citing the upcoming 2008
Olympic Games as their motivation, this was not due to an "imagined
cosmopolitanism" but, they said, because the government encouraged
the population to do so. At least partially protected by continuing state
benefits, elderly danwei residents could present themselves as not
evaluated by or subjected to "the gaze of foreign capital" (Anagnost
1994, 279).

From the outside, the elderly in their state-provided safety net were
certainly influenced by China's growing integration into the global
economic system. Even state-owned companies have to compete in
the market today, and unprofitability will lead to inevitable layoffs and
closings, which in turn will clearly affect the elderly's lives. Nonetheless, I would suggest, in order to make sense of their marginal position
in the reform period, the elderly constructed themselves as "outside"
of the new system; the "evaluative gaze of global capital" allegedly
only worried them in relation to their children.

Not to Be Somewhere Else

According to Rofel (1997), the Chinese state aspires and claims to
enact a faithful reproduction of Western modernity. Yet, she alerts
us, the state carries out its program in sites and through bodies that
hold memories of past spatial relations. The wealthy, young, and
educated residents of Wangjing, however, were too young to have
clear memories of the time before the economic reform period. They
repeatedly stressed that they grew up during the reforms. In their
early thirties, they had actually spent their first years of life during the
Mao era. As discussed above, they remembered when their family was
able to buy a refrigerator or other consumer goods, but that would
certainly not have left them with a specific idea of the life and politics
of the period. If they did not have concrete memories of time past,
how then were young, educated residents interpreting modernity in
the Chinese context?

When I asked Cao Xiangjun what "modern" meant to her, she
answered: "It means a richer life. Yes, our life has greatly improved. . . . Chinese are getting closer to the international society.
More opportunities and more freedom." Indeed, young, educated, and
wealthy Wangjing residents' "modernity" had a very decisive international aspect to it: They either spoke or studied English (or other

foreign languages, for that matter), and several of them had traveled abroad. They read magazines about Western lifestyles, decorated their apartment accordingly, and followed international politics and China's role therein. Based on their "cultural capital" (knowledge and skills) and their "economic capital" (financial resources) (Bourdieu 1984), their physical space of maneuvering had practically no limit. They not only traveled widely through city, nation, and beyond, but also claimed to have chosen to stay in China, even though they had the means to go abroad. Emigrating might have been more difficult to realize than they portrayed it, but the fact that the young, wealthy Wangjing residents considered going abroad to be an unwanted possibility indicated that they were quite aware of their power of choice in the global negotiation of place. To me, the Western student, they presented a version of deliberate preference for China over the rest of the world, and through this discourse they performed a political act: they valorized their Chinese reality as equal, or even as better than, my "Western" possibilities.[11] This sentiment was also evident when Wei Hong explained her rootedness in Beijing and China:

> I remember that going abroad was hot when I was in university. Chinese believed that the ground was covered with gold in foreign countries. But nobody thinks so anymore. People are going abroad to study the latest management knowledge, feel the great atmosphere, and then go back to make China better. A lot of companies send their staff abroad to study. As for me, I would rather earn more money in China and travel abroad, or study there. I could never put all my hope and future, all my career ambitions in a foreign land. People my age experienced the "going-abroad fever." Many overseas students now want to come back home. It shows that Beijing is very attractive. Some people say that there are more opportunities in China; building up one's career in America is very hard. With China's entering into the WTO, the position of this city is rising in the world; the partition between countries is disappearing. Beijing is more and more international. The changes of Beijing show the great changes of China. [China] surprised the world by its fast speed of development.

Pierre Bourdieu (1991, 236) pointed out that the "labor of categorization, of making things explicit and classifying them" is a central mechanism for defining the meaning and order of the social world. Various other scholars (e.g., Borneman 1991, 1997; Foucault 1972) have shown that naming and framing in fact not only describe, reflect, or represent social order, but in turn shape and reshape power relations among different groups. Indeed, the character of the new commercial housing developments that my young, affluent informants lived in or aspired to underlined residents' distinctiveness. Names such as Saint Angel Holy Fragrance (Saint Angel Shengxin) or Atlantic Place brought to mind a world beyond China. "Star-Sea Jewel" (Xinghai Mingzhu) obviously represented a special treasure, an exclusive fantasy of great riches and glory. Clearly these were metaphors laden with meaning beyond mere residence, intended to imbue the housing complexes with exclusivity and individuality, and to express residents' separation from "the masses" of Chinese society (Figure 12).

New commercial developments also commonly used the word *cheng* (city) in their advertising descriptions.[12] *Cheng* in Chinese also means "wall." While the traditional Chinese city was a walled one, one of its specific characteristics was that, in contrast to European cities, there was no mental or ideological distinction between "the rural" outside and "the urban" inside of those walls, but a rural–urban continuum (Mote 1977; Sit 1995). This, of course, changed under revolutionary rule, which fixed people in country versus city locations. As we saw in earlier chapters, during the Maoist period, danwei walls served as a means of control. They focused residents' attention inside where residences, workplaces, canteens, shops, and schools offered all the necessities for everyday life. And as politico-spatial cells, danwei completely merged the private with the public sphere. Today, in contrast, new commercial housing developments not only claim to form complete cities; these are physically secluded entities as well: by use of various technologies (walls, gates, surveillance cameras, and guards) nonresidents are effectively kept outside while residents enjoy the new and exclusive privacy inside. In tandem with the exclusive names, emerging socioeconomic differentiations embodied in residential complexes are thus magnified into spatially visible and clearly demarcated distinctions.

But the new housing complexes are supposed to offer even more than just exclusive living: they symbolize entire lifestyles, as promised by their advertising prospectuses, which claim, for example, "to choose a home means to choose a lifestyle" *(xuanze jia xuanze shenghuo fangshi)*.[13] Real estate companies produce large amounts of glossy brochures handed out for free and eagerly collected by visitors to frequently held housing fairs. These brochures create images of residents and their lives that include values and tastes, becoming

Figure 12. Advertising on a new residential complex promises "FUTURE." [2001]

manuals of lifestyles that teach potential residents about proper nutrition, exercise, community living, and so forth. This connection between a specific lifestyle and a residential complex is further underlined by the various architectural designs that projects offer, for example, "European Romantic" or "Modern International." The latter style, with its large living rooms, is aimed specifically at Chinese DINKS—white-collar working couples without children.

In Tatlow's analysis, the popularity of foreign-name and foreign-style luxury residences is an expression of the circumstance that, for China's new rich, living in Beijing today is all about pretending to be somewhere else. As a real estate agent said, "A lot of people who come to see these apartments say it's not like living in China, it's like living abroad" (2004). In contrast to Tatlow, I would maintain that the current "foreign craze" among newly affluent Chinese is not about pretending to be somewhere else but, on the contrary, it is exactly about being *in* China—being able to live a "modern, global" lifestyle in China. The "foreign craze" is less a blind copying of Western images and goods than an evocation of such "signs" suited for the Chinese context. In this evocation, architectural styles, images, and periods are mixed in an almost "postmodern" fashion, since their function is not to emulate but to symbolize and construct. Foreign names, foreign styles of architecture and construction are used in the national Chinese context for their symbolic and constituting values. Through them, consumers are marked as different, and of a higher status, since they not only have access to the symbols but also understand and manipulate them. Through them the consumers themselves feel elevated and empowered.

This point was supported by advertisements for new commercial housing complexes. Saint Angel Shengxin, for example, started its advertisement in the following way:

> Dance with Shengxin, and we will accompany each other in freedom. Shengxin's style, dedicated to old European flair, proud quality, and status of world rank, is filled with the spirit to be Wangjing's present and future.
>
> Faith in the finest artworks created the majestic outer appearance; knowledge, wealth, achievement, and passion is its character; Shengxin—eagerly looking forward to be a trendsetter; Shengxin earth—Wangjing's pride.[14]

As described in chapter 3 and indicated in this advertisement, the Saint Angel Shengxin complex combined various European architectural styles, topping the apartment towers with golden figurines. But this text also reflects the use of the "foreign" to assert a special and superior status and way of being. This claim became even more evident in the lifestyle booklet that the developer of the complex had published.

> Just getting out of the airplane, leaving the airport, I can immediately sense Wangjing's aroma; having thought of that soft and sweet name—Holy Fragrance (Shengxin), I impatiently long for being in her embrace. A very short fifteen-minute car drive later, I already have the kettle in hand and water the orchid below the window; having been away for a month on business, my wife has attended to it very well, and a newly developing leaf is faintly visible.[15]

We can see how this text adroitly invokes a whole array of imagery and messages, full of assumptions about gender and class: The wealthy male resident, owner of a private car, is returning from a month-long business trip. The airport here symbolizes the world beyond Beijing, which nonetheless is very close by. Wangjing's "smell" invokes images of "home," and a wife who is waiting patiently for her husband. The orchid that has grown during his absence conveys a rootedness of the resident in China, or more specifically in the Wangjing neighborhood. It also is a delicate treasure that needs care, thus symbolizing the modern lifestyle, cultivation, and exclusivity of the compound, and by extension, its inhabitants.

Other advertising brochures lure customers with the better environment in Beijing's north and the more ample space in the suburban location. In addition, the proximity to the airport, "the gateway to all China, and the world," is a selling point, as is the alleged convenient traffic connection. "It is as if the remotest corner of the world is the neighbor, but no matter from where you come back, Wangjing's convenient traffic network is awaiting you in every direction."[16]

While these examples of housing advertisements appear in glossy brochures that one would expect would reach only potential buyers, at a Beijing housing fair I observed urban residents indiscriminately gathering up this kind of print material, ensuring its wide circulation beyond the people who could really afford such development projects. Through the various messages that commercial housing developers put into their advertisements, they, therefore, actively participated in the reconfigurations of urban space. Importantly, the lifestyles described were based on private housing as the center of social interaction and consumption.

To conclude, the young, affluent residents of Wangjing embraced the various residential complexes and respective lifestyles as a means not only to underline their already evident social distinction as affluent suburbanites, but also to further set themselves apart by casting themselves as modern urbanites. They negotiated the "evaluative gaze of foreign capital" (Anagnost 1994, 279) to position themselves in the Chinese context. New commercial suburban housing complexes, with their mix of various European architectural referents and imbued with symbols of exclusive lifestyles, already signal on the outside that their residents are different, in fact, "a world apart."

The Hierarchy of the Market

The effects of global capital on rural migrants, and especially on women, have been primarily discussed in the context of mainland joint-venture factories (e.g., Lee 1998). But how are migrants in the cities, who work in shops and markets, affected by the growing integration of the Chinese economy and society into the global economic system?

As we saw in chapter 3, throughout Wangjing there are various markets, some of which are more established shoplike structures, while others are rather temporary affairs: a quickly put-up hall from corrugated iron, or even outdoor markets on a field. Among the more permanent places at the time of my research was a soccer-field-sized hall with shoplike partitions inside that specialized in housing decoration and refurbishing supplies. One could buy everything from bathroom appliances to curtains, carpets, and picture frames. Here salespeople were of varying ages, and many of them were Beijingers. Most were employees of small entrepreneurs who had various shops throughout the city or of the companies that produced the items on sale.

The majority of markets I witnessed around Wangjing were, however, more makeshift affairs. Some were set up on empty lots that were destined for development, and several different markets emerged and disappeared during my research. In some places, farmers from the rural hinterland offered their produce, and in others a mix of people—migrants, local Beijingers, and farmers—offered a variety of foods and goods. Several of these markets also offered clothes.

The salespeople in the market where I spent most of my time, which was located on the western side of the Capital Airport Highway, on the edge of the Wangjing neighborhood, were predominantly migrants from different provinces in China. Some of them had been laid off from their state job, while others had never been able to find employment; most of them had middle school education and had tried several jobs before settling on the sales business. When I asked the migrant market sellers why they did not work in any of the obviously better-located markets further into the city proper, where there was a higher customer frequency, they explained that they could not afford to do so:

> We work in this market because [in other, better-located markets with higher profit margins] we would need more money to start out, I mean, to rent a stall. We don't have that money. Our customers are people who live around here, not the people who have money. Those buy their things in nice places like the Lufthansa Center or at Wangfujing [in the city center].

In fact, there appeared to exist a hierarchy of informal markets within the city: generally, the further inside the city the market was located, the better the quality of items, the higher the prices, and the more expensive the rent for the stalls. Interestingly, the center of this hierarchy lay in, or close to, the area designated to be the new CBD, the area of foreign company headquarters and embassies. Correspondingly, the further inside the city, the more likely these markets were to have foreign customers. Salespeople therefore had to speak English if they wanted to be successful. The migrants from "my" markets considered these places out of their league. They assured me that the rent—about 2,000 yuan (US$250) per month—was unaffordable to them. But more importantly, they could not do so because they did not speak English. Physical closeness to the Western world, here in the form of foreign customers, in combination with the knowledge of a foreign language obviously put the salespeople in the more centrally located markets into a privileged position, giving them at least an economic advantage if not also a higher status than other salespeople.

Conclusion

Today migrants from the countryside can move widely throughout the country. Nonetheless, their access to certain "privileged" spaces remains limited. These spaces include public housing, but also more and more often the inner cities with their new high-tech development. City centers have in some cases been declared "beggar-free zones"

(Savadove 2003), and at the beginning of 2005, Beijing was even debating whether to completely curb the inflow of migrant workers (Agence France-Presse 2005). Less extreme, but equally symbolic, informal markets in the inner-city area are increasingly either destroyed or regulated, such as the Sanlitun street market and the Silk Market in Beijing, for example. Here makeshift stalls on the sidewalk were torn down, but after a couple of months the district government built malls close by and rented stalls to private entrepreneurs—at a rate that many of the former salespeople could not afford. But it is also the "privileged space" of equal citizenship that is limited through the public and official discourse on migrants' "otherness." Through this "technology," in Foucault's (1979) sense, which juxtaposes migrants as the inherent other to civilized, urban, and therefore modern residents, they are indeed kept out of the state project of modernization itself.

(Elderly) danwei residents, in contrast, while restricted in the consumption of physical space and commercial housing because of their limited financial means and perhaps their age, are nonetheless continuously granted access to certain "privileged spaces," such as state-provided housing and other public-sector social benefits. As a result of the growing marketization of society, today they remain more or less confined to the spatial orbit of the work-unit compound. At the same time, they also deliberately position themselves outside of present-day consumer society. They make sense of their different socialization by denying the imperative to continuously spend money and to receive instant gratification.

Finally, chuppies, Chinese urban professionals, travel city-, nation-, and worldwide. Growing wealth allows these urban Chinese to live "in the world," in contrast to their country's seclusion during the Mao years. "The world," by implication "the West," in turn, is also increasingly the scale by which they measure everything; or to put it differently, it is the imaginary modern world to which urban wealthy Chinese are aspiring. Their access to this highly privileged space in the state project of modernization is what most decisively differentiates young, affluent urban Chinese from the rest of the population.

China's growing integration into a global economic system, however, affects all Chinese citizens, from rural to urban, from poor to wealthy, from state-sector to private-sector employees. Especially since joining the WTO, and in Beijing since the successful bid to host the 2008 Olympic Games, China as a country and the people therein have to compete and compare with the global realm. It is in the face of this challenge that the state sector provides some citizens with a "padding" that softens the harshness of their "landing" in the market. Others, the vast millions who work in the burgeoning export industries of the coastal manufacturing zones and in the tragically neglected agricultural and mining sectors of the interior, as well as the growing numbers of those who have been laid off, are increasingly vulnerable to, and restive about, the harsh conditions they face.[17] Wangjing as a whole, although differentiated, is a space that is relatively insulated from these realities. At the same time, however, by promoting it as an upscale suburban neighborhood for the growing middle class, the government succeeds in glossing over the evident conflicts and contradictions that the ongoing negotiation between these divergent forces and actors entails. In this sense Wangjing is an epitome of the complex processes of present-day urban transformations in China.

CONCLUSION

Social Stratification, Consumption, and Housing

THE CITY OF BEIJING is made up of an intricate weaving of different layers and circuits that represent the various players and actors in the continuous production of urban space. These layers consist of the national, municipal, and district governments, politics, city planning, the economic system, the built environment, history, ideology, the international arena, and naturally the people living within these realms. The negotiation between these forces is a complex and dynamic process. Indeed, as I have shown in the previous chapters, young, affluent homeowners, old danwei residents, and migrant market sellers together inhabit, experience, and thus produce the suburban space of Wangjing. They reside and/or work in the area, organize their daily lives in this realm, and deal with the social, economic, political, and spatial challenges the suburb poses. At the same time, Wangjing residents weave on the social fabric of present-day Chinese society: they shape and are shaped by the distinctions and differentiations that are growing in the reform period. Yet, their power and agency is widely divergent in this process.

Old danwei residents are somewhat "left" in the suburb; they are "remnants" from a time past who somehow have to deal with the changes happening around them. They recede behind the walls of their compounds and claim a subject position "outside" or beyond the current consumption imperative. From this relatively protected place, they can support their children in the everyday challenges of urban life under market socialism. The old danwei residents' socialization as thrifty citizens, willing to sacrifice personal desires for the greater good of their children and the nation, thus importantly feeds the Chinese modernization project.

The young, educated, and wealthy, in turn, use or "consume" the suburb not only to realize their dreams and aspirations, but even more to raise their social standing—both in symbolic as well as in economic terms. Exclusive commercial suburban apartments fulfill their desire for private space, a safe and comfortable zone where they can express their individuality and escape from the frenzies of modern urban life. At the same time, the suburban space and the specific housing complex are means to claim and advance their status as wealthy modern urbanites. Buying, selling, and renting out their houses, the young and educated moreover actively shape the suburban space. They feel so firmly established and indeed entitled that they even challenge the authorities over housing disputes.[1]

Migrants, finally, also use the suburb, in the sense that they find a niche to work and live in it. But at the same time, they are "used" for the construction and economic development of the suburban space. Without them Wangjing would not exist, as migrants construct the new edifices and their rent fills the district coffers. Yet the consolidation of the suburb concomitantly means the displacement of the migrants when pingfang houses and makeshift markets are torn down. Nevertheless, for them too Wangjing is a means to realize dreams and aspirations, albeit of a more humble scale and born more from necessity than the young and educated residents' ambitions.

While their personal interaction was minimal, the three groups I have described in this study are intricately linked—to the suburban space and to one another. At the same time, as I have shown, Wangjing only grows and thrives through these residents and, indeed, through the differentiation processes that persist between them. It is this socioeconomic stratification process that is so intimately linked, in fact ingrained in (and built into) the suburban space, that I have called the social geography of space and status. Importantly, this new geography has a long trajectory. Present-day transformations did not happen overnight but are deeply embedded in social, economic, and spatial historical processes. Let us thus shortly revisit the historical process through which the Wangjing suburban space was produced.

The Urban Modernization Project

The economic policies and modes of social organization introduced by the Communist government after the 1949 revolution not only drew many of my older informants to the city but also, through the system of state-assigned jobs, placed them in the Wangjing locality. The establishment of the hukou system, in turn, gave these early migrants a new identity as urban residents and effectively segregated cities and countryside into separate realms. For the elderly, the experiences of war and violence before the revolution, and the zeal to create a new society during the early years of the People's Republic, had a deeply formative effect that continued to influence this generation in the reform period. Certain newly introduced forms of social organization, such as the danwei, and ideologies, such as the liberation of women through wage labor, for example, brought significant life improvements in people's subjective experience. Especially for many older women, the Communist transformation of society signified liberation and equality since they compared themselves to their mothers who had been confined by Confucian dogmas. Yet, the specificities of state-society relations during the Maoist era led to people's dependence on state services—they became "supplicants to the state" (D. Davis 1993). Moreover, the period was characterized by stratifications based on the rank and status of one's danwei, on one's class background, and on one's personal networks rather than on socioeconomic distinctions. The vertical relationship of obedience between subject-citizens and party or government officials corresponded to the extreme social supervision of citizens through the various institutions of control.

With the reform period, Chinese citizens' social and economic conditions, their daily lives, have been dramatically affected and transformed. State-sector employees have to accept layoffs, as well as significant cutbacks in social services and benefits, which are replaced by the market. At the same time, the growing private sector offers new employment opportunities and potential financial gains, although access to these is highly disparate. Chinese citizens confront the challenges of the reform period with various strategies. Urban residents either "moonlight," that is, work two or more jobs, or engage in the strategy of "one family, two systems," that is, one spouse stays in the state sector while the other one enters the private economy. Migrants, in turn, accept a semilegal or second-class existence in return for the chance to get their share of the new wealth in urban centers. In this manner, people negotiate—not always successfully—the advantages and disadvantages of safety and risk that come with the new opportunities to maximize their gains in the face of new hardships and challenges.

The land and housing reforms of the 1990s have significantly altered the urban landscape. In connection with the influx of foreign direct investment, space has been valorized in a center-periphery hierarchy of land and property prices. Downtown areas are rebuilt around the headquarters of multinational companies, high-value shopping and office complexes, and retail centers. Lower land prices in fringe areas, in turn, have attracted new residential developments. As a result, it is in the quickly developing suburban realm where the contradictions, conflicts, and problems of current transformations become visible, where they find a physical expression in everyday life. The suburb is, in fact, an arena of negotiation between the expanding restructured city and the receding prereform built environment, a zone of drastic and continuous transformation processes, which is shared by diverse groups of residents.

The Role of the State in Present-Day Transformations

As I have shown, Wangjing residents are set apart by the type of jobs they hold and their income levels. But the analysis has also shown that age, education, and residence status play an important role in social positioning—in people's access to resources, in the choices they have to design their lives, but also in their perspectives on life. All these factors, in turn, intertwine and reinforce each other. Born from individual trajectories, but influenced by shared experiences, the residents indeed showed group-specific attitudes, convictions, sentiments, and ideologies.

In comparing the three groups of Wangjing residents, we have also seen the growing impact of the economy's marketization on the social fabric. Wealth is undoubtedly beginning to generate social stratifications in the urban realm. While, at present, financial prowess cannot provide migrants with access to residency-connected rights, it can significantly improve their subjective living experience. For all Chinese citizens alike, today's greater financial means can provide access to better health services and education, but also the possibility to secure one's future through insurance and savings. In addition, money opens a whole new world of consumption of a previously unknown amount and variety of goods. In general, greater financial means, consumption, and the emerging socioeconomic differentiations increasingly blur Maoist-era social demarcations.[2]

Despite the growing influence of marketization, the preceding chapters have also demonstrated that the state continues to exert significant influence on Chinese society and people's lives. Indeed, as has been argued by Verdery (1996) in the case of Eastern Europe, and by Perry (1994), Oi (1989), Solinger (1999), and Zhang L. (2001), among others, in the case of China, today the state is not simply replaced by the market, but instead they intertwine in complex ways, differently influencing urban residents' daily lives. Based on the present investigation, I would suggest that in the present-day transformations of society and space in China, the state plays two specific roles.

First, the state's project of modernization is based on the idea of progress, of a linear development toward modernity, which now guides the plans to transform Beijing into an "international business center," "the Manhattan of Asia" (A. Cheng 2003a, 2003b), a city worthy of hosting the Olympic Games, among other things. In this vision, and its imposed realization, a modernist aesthetics, or a veneer of modernity, is applied especially to the center of social, economic, and global interaction—the inner city. Here, the old is mainly destroyed and replaced by glass-and-steel office towers, designed by internationally known architects. In addition, the government pushes the development and application of technology, such as broadband Internet access, and logistical features, such as a light-rail train, all of which have become markers of status and are implemented as tokens of "modernity." The emerging urban form, the new "global city," signifies and embodies what it means to be a modern urban Chinese citizen.

In this process of reconfiguration, *hutong* are razed, informal markets are either torn down or regulated and covered, inner cities are declared "beggar-free zones," and migrants are pushed further out of the central urban areas—out of the new, modern face of the city—to the lower visibility of the suburban fringes. In official and public discourse, migrants serve as the "other," against which the new state-project is defined and exemplified. "Uncultured," "uncivilized" migrants are blamed for disturbances of the new aesthetic of modernity.

The portrayal of migrants as "uncultured," "uneducated," the source of dirt and crime, the "floating population," with regional dialects and differing customs, who work in menial jobs, resembles remarkably the discourse on unwanted urban subjects by city reformers ranging from Baron Haussmann in Paris (see Harvey 2003) and Robert Moses in New York (see Caro 1974) to planners in Washington

D.C.'s nineteenth-century makeover (see Farrar 2002). In the frame-work of Kristeva's (1982) concept of "the abject," migrants to the city are "the other" that is needed to define modern citizenship and modern urbanity; they are a symbol of what is to be left behind on the path to the future of modern nationhood.[3] But with their "backwardness," poor peasants and uncultured migrants are also what threatens or endangers the modernization project in the eyes of the regime because they represent what the government wants to abolish. Therefore, while inherently necessary for the project—both for their labor power and for their symbolic "otherness"—migrants have to be kept under con-trol, pushed ever further out of the restructured urban landscape to the suburban fringe and beyond. It is against this social "othering" or "fringing" that the migrants in Wangjing have constructed their identities as honest, diligent, and modest salespeople, whose striving is for a better future for their children, derived through the ideal, indeed the trope, of education.

As Harvey has pointed out, Gramsci considered Americanism and Fordism the biggest collective effort to quickly and consciously create a new type of worker and a new type of man. He observed that the new methods of work were connected to a new mode of living, think-ing, and feeling. "Questions of sexuality, the family, forms of moral coercion, of consumerism, and of state action were, in Gramsci's view, all bound up with the search to forge a particular kind of worker 'suited to the new type of work and productive process'" (Harvey 1990, 126). Similarly, in the context of reform-period China, Anagnost (1997) observes that the readying of the Chinese population for partic-ipation in global capitalism has taken place through a state-initiated civilizing process that is aimed at remaking subjectivities into those appropriate for a disciplined, efficient workforce. The question is, what kind of citizen is "produced"?

It is in the process of creating new citizens that we can discern the second role of the state in present-day transformations: as part of the same project of modernization, the state is actively encouraging and facilitating consumption. Consumption is where the state project of modernization meets the growing force of "the market," and con-sumers are what the state wishes to "produce." The government aims to bring the economy to a Western level of living standard. Part of this project is to transform "supplicants" to the state into self-reliant indi-viduals. The regime needs Chinese citizens to consume in order to cut costs and to counter the extremely export-oriented economy, which is in turn an outcome of the off-shoring of production through foreign companies to special economic zones in the mainland and of foreign investment into companies producing export articles. Citizens who are willing and able to consume are, therefore, considered modern, valued citizens, while those who do not are obstacles in the way of development and of the bright, new future of modernity. At the same time, consumption is considered a "civilizing" force, one that can turn unruly protesters and discontent masses into submissive supporters of the regime. Thus, stimulating consumption is also a mechanism for legitimizing the state's continued claim to authority and power.

It is therefore not surprising that in many ways, the remaining state sector supports the emergence of "the market" in reform-period China. Government policies, in fact, have actively encouraged the rise of a middle class, largely made up from professionals in the public sector. But there are also more unofficial connections between the state and the market: As discussed in chapter 4, some of the market halls where migrants in Beijing worked, for example, were put up by district governments that filled the city coffers by renting out the sales stalls. In other cases, local officials just looked the other way when makeshift markets sprang up on empty lots.

One area where the continuous or renewed influence of the public sector becomes strongly evident is housing. Elderly Wangjing residents continue to receive certain benefits through their danwei, the most important of which are houses at significantly discounted prices. Similarly, many younger Wangjing residents have bought new housing through their work units, again providing them with relatively high-standard residences at prices substantially below the market price. Many couples who live in commercial housing can do so after they have profited for several years from danwei-discounted housing.

Where the state recedes, for example, as regards social services, either family or money has to substitute. The newly wealthy in my research increasingly relied on paid services, which in turn significantly altered family relations and dependencies. Many young adults, however, were actually financially and organizationally supported by their danwei-connected parents. Migrants, in contrast, unless they are married to urban residents, remain excluded from the multiple advantages of the state-sector and danwei-provided housing.

In many ways, the state sector thus provides a niche or a "padding" that softens the harshness of Chinese citizens' "landing" in the market. This "protection," however, only extends to a selected group. For them, the state sector can indeed become a stepping stone, enabling them to significantly advance their social and economic position. Citizens who remain outside this realm, especially the migrant population, must, in contrast, rely on their own efforts to secure a living. In the context of urban sociospatial reconfigurations, the state's involvement in these processes supports or even enforces growing neoliberal tendencies and the reemergence of class differentiations in the reform period. It is in this sense that I speak of the "citizenship of consumption," since citizens' rights, their social and economic position in society, are increasingly intertwined with their power to consume.

Social Differentiation and the Consumption of Housing

As we have seen in chapter 5, housing has turned into a special arena of consumption. Housing, in fact, serves as the subject of private and commercial discourse on space. It is an item on which Chinese citizens spend a great deal of thought, effort, and financial means. The reasons for the importance of housing in people's lives are manifold: new houses not only bring better living standards, but with the background of Maoist surveillance of public *and* private spheres—as embodied in the danwei compound—today housing also offers privacy, that is, personal space. This new space provides previously unknown intimacy, freedom, and individuality. Housing in the reform period is an "inside," a realm "outside" of the state's intrusion, a new private sphere. The time that young, affluent residents put into deliberations on *where* to live, however, points to an important and specific aspect of this new Chinese consumer society: people use housing as a social practice to distinguish themselves from others, and of constructing themselves as modern citizens.

Physical location within the urban landscape has assumed significance not only because of the reintroduced monetary value of land caused by China's integration into the global capitalist system, but also because of the newly produced ideational and symbolic imagery claimed and represented by new suburban commercial housing complexes. While the spatial valorization is part of the state project of modernization, exactly *where* people choose to live is less important to the government than to urban residents themselves. Assisted by advertising and promotion, they assign status to specific locations, perceive and claim advantages of certain parts of the city. After all, it is *residents* who justify their not always rationally based choices with the altered old saying about the preferable north of the city, which refers to the traditional, cosmologically inspired city structure. Residential communities are thus turned into "cultural milieus" (Fraser 2000; Zhang L. 2004) necessary for shaping subjectivity and for sustaining a distinct social group.

In various studies, Miller (1997, 1998) has shown consumption to be a political act. Writing about Trinidad, he observes that peanuts and soft drinks have "become fundamental to the daily lives of the mass population as consumers, who use such commodities and a vast rank of other goods in order to construct themselves in terms of historical projects of value and identity creation" (1997, 334). In an emerging consumer society such as China, after thirty years of anticonsumerism and anti-individual socialization, it may not be surprising to find conspicuous consumption breaking strongly to the fore in the present reform period. After all, as Borneman (1991, 81) aptly observed, "socialism had trained them to desire, capitalism stepped in to let them buy." The present study demonstrates, however, that we have to look at the time- and place-specific circumstances to understand *who* buys *what* and *why*. More than just functioning as a symbolic marker of stratification, the consumption of housing can be understood as a reflection and constitutive aspect of emerging social relationships and differentiations. In the current state project of modernization in China, aimed at producing consuming citizens through a mix of state and private economy, what emerges are socioeconomic differentiations that are importantly based on communities of consumers. Social status, identity, and habitus are formed in the context of local socialization patterns in residential neighborhoods at least as much as in the workplace. Over and above conspicuous consumption of goods, the consumption of lifestyle and space has become one of the foremost arenas of social differentiation processes in contemporary urban Chinese society.

Throughout the present-day process of transformation, while socioeconomic differentiations are only emerging and class is less structure than "structuration," consumption has become a practice to position oneself in contrast to others, a way to claim and derive greater social status. For their subjectively chosen new housing, residents are even willing to fight, facing authorities regarding what they perceive to be rightly theirs. In this manner, young, wealthy—consuming—citizens do not just follow blindly the "lure" of the market, but actively engage in the production of space. Consumption of the exclusive spaces that suburban housing complexes symbolize imbues consumers with higher status in the transforming social makeup, in the class structuration of Chinese society. It is in this sense that housing, and especially the consumption of exclusive suburban residential space, has become one of the prime arenas of the dynamic processes of social and spatial reconfiguration in contemporary urban Chinese society.

Wangjing Revisited

In the early spring of 2007, after five years of absence, I had the chance to revisit Wangjing. While housing construction was continuing on the far edges of the area, in the heart of the suburb the clouds of dust had settled. Trees and flower beds now lined the ample new roads; here and there a corner had been turned into a small park. With the imposing edifices and shiny apartment towers of the finished residential complexes, the area looked neat and tidy (Figure 13). Despite

Figure 13. Wangjing, January 2007: a fully established suburb with bus service, regulated roadways, and public green spaces.

its distinct Chinese form, in some ways it felt like an American suburb: roads were too wide and distances too large to invite pedestrian
strolling—at least outside the residential neighborhood compounds. In
sharp contrast to downtown Beijing, here only the occasional pedestrian was on the street. Modern public buses serviced the area, picking
up the few people who waited at the new bus stops. All along, in a sign
of suburban residents' growing affluence, a surprising number of new
cars zipped down the roads (Figure 14). Similarly symbolic, the fur-
nishing giant IKEA had relocated from its former location on the
north section of the Third Ring Road to a lot along the Capital Airport
Highway on the way to Wangjing. Middle-class homeowners can now
drive right by to shop at the increasingly popular retailer on their way
to or from work.

In the center of the suburb, a new shopping mall has opened with
high-end retail stores, Western-style cafes, and restaurants on the first
floor; a food court and fast-food joints in the basement; and a movie
theater and various entertainment facilities on the top floor (Figure
15). On my January visit, women in fur coats strolled through the

*Figure 14. Private car ownership is increasing, and some of the suburban roads
were already bogged down by traffic in 2007.*

expensive boutique-style stores, young couples in fashionable clothes snuggled in the cafés, and businessmen with suits and ties were deeply engaged in conversations with business partners or on their cell phones. Beyond the shopping mall, several restaurants offering an array of cuisines have opened around the Wangjing New City complex. In addition, now there are bookstores, coffee shops, and small boutiques selling fashionable apparel and popular knickknacks.

These new shopping facilities and structures have completely re-placed the migrant markets that I had visited during my fieldwork years before. Only one of them still existed, albeit in a refashioned form (Figure 16): now a proper building with large advertising on its front, inside the floor was neatly tiled and sales booths were put together from shiny metal frames and glass panels. The salespeople still seemed to be migrants, but the market was half empty and cus-tomers were few.

Despite my efforts, I was not able to locate the migrant salespeople I had talked to in 2001/2. The markets were gone and so were the houses where they had lived. Most dramatically, the village where I

Figure 15. By 2007 Wangjing had its own mall with exclusive designer stores, cafés, and entertainment facilities.

had visited Liang Jiehua had been razed to make space for a new road connecting to the Capital Airport Highway. The old danwei residents, in turn, mostly still lived in their compounds; for them nothing much had changed. The more dilapidated complexes, however, looked even worse. The structures that had been marked for teardown on the edge of Wangjing were gone, and their lots had already been filled with new commercial residences.

Among the young and affluent, several couples had moved into new, bigger, more expensive apartments—mostly within the Wangjing area. Some had actually moved two or three times already, renting out the old places while enjoying the luxuries of ever-new houses and compounds. Tellingly, affluent homeowners continue to be engaged in legal battles with housing developers. Recently they even challenged the district government over the design of individual compounds and the design of the suburb itself (e.g., Broudehoux 2004; *China Daily* 2008; see also Read 2003). Middle-class homeowners are increasingly aware of and willing to claim their growing power and agency in shaping the suburban space.

Figure 16. A rebuilt migrant market is now called Wangjing No. 1 Outlets Store. [2007]

ACKNOWLEDGMENTS

This book would not have been possible without the generous support of many individuals and institutions. My doctoral studies at the Graduate Center of the City University of New York were assisted by several small grants from the anthropology program. The writing of the dissertation on which this book is based was funded by the CUNY Graduate Center Alexander Naclerio Award and a Dissertation Writing Fellowship. Teachers and mentors at the Graduate Center provided critical intellectual support for the research and writing of the dissertation, but no one deserves more credit than my adviser, Jane Schneider. I greatly benefited from her high standards of scholarship and generous guidance throughout the years. Michael Blim challenged me to rethink and reorganize the arguments of my dissertation, for which I am extremely grateful. Neil Smith added his critical geographer's view. As external reader, Zhang Li, in the Department of Anthropology at the University of California, Davis, guided the dissertation writing process with valuable suggestions; her scholarship and work have been a great inspiration. My postdoctoral home institution, the Max Planck Institute for Social Anthropology in Germany, granted me the time and scholarly environment to finish the project. I thank Chris Hann, director of the Socialist and Postsocialist Eurasia Department at the Max Planck Institute, for encouraging me to pursue publication of this project.

In China, I am deeply indebted to the people of Wangjing who welcomed me into their lives and their houses. This study would not have been possible without their willingness to answer my questions and their incredible generosity to share with me their experiences. Yu Changjiang, from the anthropology department at Beijing University, and the researchers from the sociology department at the Chinese Academy of Social Sciences, where I was affiliated, provided practical help and scholarly advice whenever I needed it. The kind friendship and help of Wang Zhuning and Wei Kaiqiong were critical for the success of my research. Special thanks go to Li Ning Ning and her parents, who opened their home and their hearts for me many years ago.

Fellow scholars of China who supported and shaped this project at various stages include Wang Danning, Luigi Tomba, Sasha Welland, Kari Olson, Anru Lee, Maria Livia Iotti, Arianne Gaetano, Simone Schmidt, and Sabine Friedrich. I have also greatly profited from the critical minds and friendship of Laura Kaehler, Terese Lawinski, Pellegrino Luciano, Friederike Brockmann, Berit Fabricius, Elke Scheffelt, Veronica Hendrick, Maria Cristina Venditti, and Marcelo Bucheli.

I would like to thank Jason Weidemann, Danielle Kasprzak, and the rest of the team at the University of Minnesota Press for their careful guidance and useful suggestions throughout the publication process. Xin Liu, Wang Feng, and one anonymous reviewer of the manuscript provided invaluable comments; I greatly appreciate their contribution to the book.

Finally, I thank my parents, Rosemarie and Klaus Fleischer, for their unconditional encouragement and support to pursue my dreams. I deeply regret that my father passed away before I finished this book. My deepest appreciation goes to my husband, Andrés Páez, who contributed to this project in many ways. He not only accompanied me to China for part of my research but also tirelessly discussed the topic with me, as well as read, reread, and edited my work at every stage of the writing process. All this, however, pales in comparison to the support, inspiration, love, friendship, and happiness he has brought to my life.

APPENDIXES

Appendix A. Field Sites and Methods

I had several field sites within Wangjing. After some weeks during which I regularly visited local migrant markets, I eventually concentrated on two where I was able to establish contacts with some of the salespeople. One of these markets was a combined in- and outdoor affair that sold everything from daily necessities to clothes and knick-knacks, but also plants, pets, and fresh food products. In a corner behind the market hall, several food vendors had propped up their carts and arranged small folding tables and stools for customers to eat at. During several months, until the market was torn down, I regularly had my lunch here and used the occasion to talk to the migrant salespeople. The other market where I became friends with some of the migrant sellers was inside a corrugated iron hall. Salespeople rented makeshift stalls that were separated by mesh wire covered with bamboo mats. While there were also sellers of household wares and appliances, the greater part of this market, and the migrants I mostly interacted with, specialized in clothes. The majority of these sellers were women, who allegedly have a greater capability for selling clothes than men. I spent many afternoons "hanging out" at one or the other stall, sitting on a small stool in a corner, chatting with the salespeople, watching them interact with customers and one another. As they spent practically every day at the market, migrants' social life very much happened around the stalls: again and again, friends, husbands, family members came by to say "hello," and many times stayed for a while to chat. One of my key informants here was a woman from Shandong province who, because she was married to a Beijing resident, was in a more secure living situation than many of her colleagues in the market. During my conversations with the migrants I usually took short notes on which I expanded right afterwards. Quotations from these exchanges in the book are thus not verbatim, but close to the actual conversations.

Besides these markets, I also "hung out" in the different new and old residential compounds. As a foreigner it was not difficult to strike up casual conversations with residents. Many times, people actually approached me, curious about what I was doing "out there" in Wangjing. Yet, there was a markedly greater willingness to chat among the work-unit retirees who had enough time and probably also less opportunity for such an exchange. Apart from these informal exchanges with people I met by chance in the different compounds, detailed personal interviews in affluent residents' homes were only possible by introduction through a friend or acquaintance. Snowball sampling is certainly not statistically representative; nonetheless, by starting out with several initial contacts in different neighborhoods I was able to cover a spectrum of neighborhoods and informants. A group of friends of similar educational, professional, socioeconomic, and age background as my affluent Wangjing informants became a reference group for comparison. Contacts with danwei residents, in contrast, were initially established by the residents' organization of one of the old residential compounds around Wangjing. They generously introduced me to several elderly people, who in turn put me in touch with others, also from other danwei. While I had developed a catalog of questions for these appointed meetings, most of the time the structure was broken by the narratives of my interview partners, and more spontaneous and individually patterned conversations developed. The sessions lasted between one and two hours and were mostly tape-recorded.

Throughout the research I worked with two assistants who took turns in accompanying me to the interviews. Both women became extremely interested in my investigation, and during the interviews often began to ask their own questions, as I had urged them to do. The decision to work with the assistants was based on two considerations: First, while my Mandarin was good enough for conversations with Beijing people, I was worried that I would not understand some of the migrant salespeople in the markets around Wangjing who spoke in their local dialects. More important, local researchers advised me that it would be much easier to gain the confidence of residential neighborhood committees, which would help me to find interview partners in danwei compounds, if I was accompanied by a Chinese student. I would be regarded with much less suspicion of being a journalist looking for a sensationalist story.

In addition to this interaction with people in Wangjing, I met several times with different scholars at Beijing University and at CASS. In these encounters, I had the chance to discuss my impressions from the field and received some valuable background information and suggestions for my research. Throughout the research, I read and collected articles in English and Chinese newspapers and magazines that are now widely available in the city. My attention lay on discussions of lifestyle, public culture, housing, and social issues. This gave me an impression of what the government considered important issues and which messages it wanted to spread. A final contributor to the investigation was a Beijing journalist, specialized in the real estate market, who shared with me some of the facts, gossip, and rumors in the field.

Appendix B. Beijing Households and Population, Registered Statistics in 2000

Region	Total population in thousands	Households in thousands			Permanent residents in thousands			Temporary residents in thousands
		Total	Non-agricultural	Agricultural	Total	Non-agricultural	Agricultural	
City proper	2,663	877	877	–	2,382	2,382	–	281
Dongcheng	713	235	235	–	626	626	–	87
Xicheng	856	282	282	–	781	781	–	75
Chongwen	462	157	157	–	413	413	–	49
Xuanwu	632	203	203	–	562	562	–	70
Near suburbs	5,373	1,524	1,322	202	4,292	3,819	473	1,081
Chaoyang	1,897	569	487	82	1,522	1,335	187	375
Fengtai	1,103	314	253	61	822	675	147	281
Shijingshan	415	115	108	7	332	316	16	83
Haidian	1,958	526	474	52	1,616	1,493	123	342
Outer suburbs	2,778	919	359	560	2,539	912	1,627	239
Total	12,780	3,979	2,755	1,224	11,075	7,607	3,468	1,705

Source: Beijing tongjiju 2001

Appendix C. Annual Cash Income per Capita of 1,000 Beijing Urban Households in 2000

Income in yuan	Average	Low	Medium-low	Medium	Medium-high	High	As percentage of 1999 income
Cash	12,560.32	7,084.28	9,040.03	11,699.46	13,964.29	22,622.01	117.9
Real	10,416.39	5,824.60	7,972.40	9,685.31	11,932.44	17,931.36	112.7
Discretionary	10,349.69	5,774.64	7,916.37	9,624.04	11,861.15	17,831.19	112.7
Staff and workers	6,816.34	3,905.31	5,089.16	6,388.42	7,902.90	11,610.96	110.3
Individuals	119.40	49.20	49.74	154.70	121.31	241.30	181.9
Employment after retirement	252.74	108.70	171.17	236.62	318.10	467.72	106.4
Other employee	9.14	16.99	4.86	13.50	–	9.29	176.1
Other work	244.28	147.24	155.51	240.67	188.16	524.54	127.6
Property	112.25	17.07	64.97	81.29	72.71	356.36	122.1
Transfer	2,862.24	1,580.09	2,436.99	2,570.11	3,329.26	4,721.19	116.0
Pension	2,429.74	1,386.82	2,152.23	2,226.88	2,960.18	3,667.19	117.1

Source: Beijing tongjiju 2001

Appendix D. Sample Living Conditions of Fifteen Interviewees in the Hong Yuan Compound

	Age and sex (M or F)	Housing distributed to whom	Unit size	Year moved in	Year of purchase	Bought by whom	Price in yuan	Number of people; number of generations	Previous living condition
1	Over 60, M	Husband	40 m²	1987	1993	Children	Less than 10,000	5; 3 (until death of mother, then 4; 3)	Pingfang house
2	39, F	Husband	40 m²	–	–	Parents-in-law	Rented	3; 2	Pingfang house
3	62, F	Wife	50 m²	1983	1998	Husband and wife	40,000	3; 2	Pingfang house
4	67, M	Wife	40 m²	1986	2000	Husband and wife; loan	40,000	2; 1 (used to be 3; 2)	Pingfang house
5	54, M	Husband	40 m²	2000	2000	Daughter; loan	30,000	3; 2	Pingfang house
6	68, F	Husband	40 m²	1986	1997	Husband and wife	10,000	2; 1 (used to be 6; 2)	Danwei unit with shared bathroom
7	62, F	Wife	40 m²	1986	1998	–	30,000	3; 2 (granddaughter)	Pingfang house
8	61, F	Joint	40 m²	1988	1998	–	30,000	4; 2	Shared danwei unit (16 m²)
9	56, F	Husband	40 m²	1993	1993	–	10,000	6; 3 (husband and wife, son and daughter-in-law, grandchildren)	Danwei unit

10	60, M	Husband	42 m²	1990	1993	Husband and wife	20,000	3; 2 (grandson)	Danwei unit (17 m²)
11	62, F	Husband	40 m²	1986	1997	Husband and wife	20,000	3; 2	Danwei unit
12	63, F	Joint	40 m²	1986	1997	–	10,000	3; 2	Danwei unit
13	60, F	Husband	50 m²	1986	1997	Husband and wife	10,000	4; 2 (husband and wife, son and daughter-in-law)	–
14	33, F	Husband	30 m²	2001	2001	Husband and wife	40,000	2; 1	Danwei unit of parents-in-law
15	53, F	Joint	21.7 m²	1997	1997	Widow	10,000	2; 2 (widow and son)	Pingfang house

NOTES

Introduction

1. Beijing looks back upon more than two thousand years of history. Originally designed to represent ideas combining the cosmological order with rules of government and spatial form, key elements of the city epitomized the traditional Confucian worldview.

2. Hanser (2008) uses a similar tripartite comparison between a state-owned department store, an upscale private shopping center, and an "underground" migrant market to analyze different market settings and, through that, processes of stratification in China.

3. Acknowledging that modernity is a contested and multiply imagined term or reality, throughout the book I use the word "modernization" to describe the current state project of transformation and the concomitant endeavor to turn Beijing into a "truly global metropolis." This project is centered on reforming the economy by introducing market mechanisms, emphasizing efficiency and the generation of wealth, and improving living standards. It also involves a distinct ideology regarding the "quality" *(suzhi)* of people, which is linked to notions of self-improvement and self-cultivation.

4. In 2001/2, US$1 roughly converted to 7.5 yuan. The Chinese currency has since been revalued and in February of 2009 US$1 converted to 6.84 yuan. Throughout the book, however, I use the conversion rate at the time of my research.

5. During the Maoist period, inequalities derived, for example, from the government's occupational ranking system that produced a hierarchy of wealth, status, and opportunities. Other distinctions were based on one's class background. In the cities, individuals were stratified by the position of their work unit in the bureaucratic structure, their status within the unit, and the personal networks they were able to establish and maintain. See, for example, Bian 1994, 2002; Cheng and Seldon 1997; Hanser 2008; Tang and Parish 2000; Walder 1986.

6. The concept of *xiaokang* comes from the definition of an ideal society in the Confucian Book of Rites *(li ji)*. Its first appearance in the Communist era is attributed to a reference Deng made to a foreign guest in 1978, when he argued that

China's reform target was to reach a per capita GDP of US$1,000 by the end of the century. The concept's more recent revival is related to Jiang Zemin's use of the word in his report to the 16th Party Congress (see Anagnost 2008; Li Shouen 2003; Tomba 2004).

7. In the 1984 "Decision of the Central Committee of the Communist Party on Reform of the Economic Structure" the government explicitly denounced egalitarianism as "utterly incompatible with a scientific Marxist view on socialism" (Thelle 2004, 30).

8. One attempt to conceptualize the contemporary social structure is the published result of a ten-year study released by the Chinese Academy of Social Sciences (CASS) (Lu X. 2002). The report identified a total of ten classes that in turn were further subdivided into five rankings. The author of this study, Lu Xueyi, head of the Institute of Sociology at CASS, was criticized by conservative elements in the party for suggesting a much more complex stratification in China than the traditional "two classes and one stratum" and for pointing at bureaucrats and party officials as an independent upper class while workers and peasants lie at the bottom (Tomba 2004). A similar model of class structure in present-day China is elaborated by Li Chunling (2002). Neither study, however, takes continuing rural-urban distinctions as an aspect of social positioning into account. See also Su 2002.

9. Chinese Marxist rhetoric differentiated between "social role" *(chengfen)* and "social origin" *(chushen)*. Social role referred to a person's background or occupational status "before entering upon revolutionary work" *(geming gongzuo)*, that is, before being assigned to a job. A "social role" was not ascribed by birth and could thus change; it could also be different from that of other family members. "Social origin," in contrast, referred to a person's status based on her early experiences or her family's economic circumstances. It was the designation used to formally categorize most persons after the Communist revolution in 1949 (e.g., "textile worker," "landlord") and that determined their future under the new regime. Social origin is thus comparable to "class background"; it usually did not change even if one's social activities or consciousness changed (Watson 1984).

10. Bourdieu's (1990) study of the Kabyle household has shown this for the domestic realm.

11. The link between spatial organization and domination was already convincingly established in Foucault's (1979) writings on the prison. Similarly, Rabinow (1989), who built on Foucault's insights, showed how the French colonial state used architecture and urban planning as an expression of cultural superiority and thus as a means of domination. The way that state-sponsored architecture and urban planning become a form of domination that even invades the domains of daily life, in turn, is shown in Holsten's (1989) analysis of Brasilia. For China, in his genealogy of the *danwei* (work unit), D. Bray (2005) insightfully demonstrates how this specific style of urban planning was a means of "governmentality" and control in Communist China.

12. The *China Daily* reported on January 10, 2002, that the government planned to replace the hukou system over the following five years by an "employment

registration system," in which social security numbers would be issued to people as a way to guarantee benefits to help the unemployed find jobs (Jiang 2002). Yet in 2010, the hukou system is still in effect.

13. D. Bray (2005) similarly takes issue with Lefebvre's overly state-centered analysis: not all attempts to plan and program the production of space necessarily serve the interests of the capitalist state. Moreover, the implementation of governmental plans is rarely straightforward.

14. Lefebvre (1991), in fact, asserted that social groups, classes, or factions of classes cannot constitute themselves or recognize one another as subjects unless they generate or produce a space. See also Berking 2006.

15. See also Douglas and Isherwood (1979). Max Weber (1978), on the other hand, suggested that within the special domain of consumption style rather than position in the labor market stratifies and sustains social relationships.

16. Consumption is also implicated with nationalism as became evident in recent consumer boycotts. In 2005, for example, Japanese products were boycotted to protest Japan's denial of war crimes against the Chinese during World War II. In 2007 and 2008, in turn, French products and the retail chain Carrefour were targeted because of France's criticism of Chinese politics in Darfur and the president's reception of the Dalai Lama respectively.

17. See also Storper (2000) for a discussion of consumer culture, globalization, and inequality.

18. This "withdrawal" of the state is arguably more like a shift in the forms and ways that the state interferes with people's private sphere.

19. See Liu and Li (2006) for a similar survey-based analysis of stratification.

20. Latham (2002) similarly argues that it is through the rhetoric of progress and the discourse of transition that the Chinese government derives its legitimacy.

21. I derive the phrase "citizenship of consumption" from Zhang Zhen (2000), who talks of the "democracy of consumption" in her analysis of the gendered aspects of current economic and sociospatial transformations.

22. There existed, however, large state-regulated population transfers used by the Chinese government for achieving policy objectives. During the 1950s and 1960s, for example, millions of people were relocated inland to "Third Front" locations, and the 1960s–70s "rustification" *(xiafang)* campaign sent urban youth and intellectuals to the countryside. See Cheng C. 1991; Fan 1999; Li D. 1995; Naughton 1988.

23. Of these, forty-six cities reached a population of more than one million in 1992. Nationwide 102 cities have more than one million residents. Campanella 2008, 14.

24. Chinese statistics regarding "urban residents" are actually confusing. Some include all residents within a municipality, while others count only residents who do not work in agriculture. The number cited in the text above, 540 million urban residents, includes all registered urban residents.

25. In the United States, where suburbanization was almost emblematic of cities after World War II, the process has been explained by a complex mix of factors. A

simplified formula could describe it as improvement of transportation, growing affluence, rapid rate of urban growth, and growing dissatisfaction with the city itself. Supported by lower tax rates in the urban fringes and racial tensions, white Americans chose outer city locations over minority-dominated central city residences (Campanella 2008; Zhou and Logan 2005). Recent studies on suburbanization processes in Asian countries have stressed that here the continuing outward expansion of the big metropolitan regions has eroded the longstanding distinction between rural and urban (Yokohari et al. 2000). McGee (1989, 1991), for example, argues for a distinctive Asian variation of the usual pattern of suburbanization called *desakota*. These are former agricultural areas with an intense mix of settlement and economic activity, comprising agriculture, industry, housing development, and other land use. Rural economics and lifestyles in the *desakotas* become submerged under the expansion of urban economic activity and culture, but do not disappear altogether. See also Wu and Liu (2000) for a comparative study of suburbanization in China and abroad from a geographical point of view.

26. Norman Chance's (1991) study of a village on the outskirts of Beijing is somewhat of a forerunner to this project. At the time of his research, however, suburbanization in its present form had not yet set in.

27. Hanser (2008, 13) similarly argues for an ethnographic study of stratification processes that highlights relationships between people instead of the mechanics of differentiation.

28. During the Republican era, the Nationalist Government had moved the capital to Nanjing.

29. The Chinese saw the universe as a harmoniously functioning organism that consisted of innumerable objects, qualities, and forces. Despite their apparent heterogeneity these were integrated into a coherent pattern, as they all derived from one source. This source was the universe or *dao,* the "Great Unity." Translated into spatial form, this meant that the imperial city was to have a central position relative to its subjects and the natural environs. It was to be located on level lands and near water. It should be placed in precise alignment with the four directions and have a southward orientation. The general layout, finally, was to be square and orderly, expressing a need to conform with the orderliness of nature in order to avoid haphazard mishaps. See Mote 1977; Sit 1995.

30. In this, the concept resembles the traditional Chinese notion of the city as a nodal point for a rural hinterland, an integral part of the vast agricultural community rather than a distinctive, separate body. See Mote 1977; Sit 1995; Whyte and Parish 1984.

31. Part of this increase derives from migrants, who also concentrate in the suburban fringe. See Zhou and Logan 2008, 143.

32. See Appendix B for a table of Beijing households and population by districts.

33. In 2000, the "Number of Signed Agreements and Contracts of Foreign Capital to Be Utilized" was 188; the "Amount of Foreign Capital to Be Utilized through Agreements and Contracts" was US$115,757,000; and the "Amount of Foreign

Capital Annually Used" was US$134,796,000 (Beijing tongjiju 2001). During the first years of the reform period, foreign investors and businesses were still doubtful about China's course of development. For this reason, but also because of logistical considerations in expansive Beijing, many of them chose to set up offices close to their embassies in the eastern part of the city. This foreign quarter itself is a continuation of the historical layout of the city, begun in imperial times and continued under Communist planning. The reform-period conglomeration of foreign businesses, in turn, might have been the decisive influence for placing the new CBD in the eastern part of the city, despite the fact that various city districts attempted to win this prestigious and potentially lucrative project.

1. A History of Wangjing

1. In order to protect the interviewees' identities, throughout the book I use fictitious names for all persons and for all but the most prestigious residential compounds.

2. Chinese cities experienced dramatic transformations before that, especially in the treaty ports along the Chinese coast where foreign powers held extraterritorial privileges during the nineteenth century. Yet, the effect of these changes on people's lives remains contested (see Lu H. 1995). It would be wrong, however, to conceive of Chinese cities and the urbanization process as static unless inspired by the foreign powers during this time. Changes occurred before that, but probably at a different rate or pace. See, for example, Johnson (1995) for a study of earlier urban transformations in Shanghai.

3. See Dutton, Lu, and Wu (2008) for an illustrative description of the rebuilding efforts of Beijing by the new regime after 1949.

4. It is important to note that this was from the beginning more of a political slogan than an effective campaign to really change the imbalance between town and countryside. In reality, the gap between rural and urban areas widened to more dramatic dimensions than in other developing countries.

5. On the socialist urban planning principles, see also Tang Wing-shing (2006).

6. Fully 63 percent of the total state investment during this period went into capital construction, of which almost two-thirds went to the ministries of heavy industry, the fuel industry, and the machine-building industry (L. Ma 1979; Naughton 1995; Sit 1995; Whyte and Parish 1984).

7. In the countryside, with the aim of increasing agricultural output, people's communes were established where peasants worked and lived collectively. The urban equivalent was "scattered collectives," which meant that new factories were located in residential and educational areas to enhance convenience and a complementarity of functions. Extensive "greenbelts," in which farm crops were cultivated, separated the constellations so that the city would possess not only industrial but also agricultural functions. The scattered-collectives model for cities in Beijing had four objectives: (1) the city was to be extended into an urban region twenty-eight times bigger than the planned city but with the same population target; (2) the population of the inner city was to reduce from 5 million to 3.5 million;

(3) the city should be decentralized into "scattered collectives" that would be separated by agricultural land or green belts; and (4) parks and open space should be created on a large scale. While the plan was never fully realized, as a result of the planning principles Beijing became more dispersed and rural in character (Zhu and Kwok 1997; Sit 1995). In 1960, the party decided to also establish communes in urban areas with the intention to increase production. Moreover, they were designed to revolutionize the traditional social institution of the family and to liberate women from housework by offering communal services ranging from public canteens, nurseries, and kindergartens, to public homes for the aged. Beijing became an experimental site for this new project. Between 1958 and 1960 thirty-eight such communes were established in the capital. Yet, even though by April 1960 already twenty million people lived in such urban communes nationwide, they never became as widespread as their rural counterparts, on the one hand because work units gained growing importance in urban areas, and on the other, because the failing agricultural production quickly ended the movement. The only element that remained of this idea of integration and self-sufficiency was the principle of close association between work and home (Lu D. 2006; Li, Dray-Novey, and Kong 2008).

8. Nationwide the urban population rose from fifty-seven million in 1949 to eighty-nine million in 1957. Two-thirds, or more than twenty million, of this increase were rural migrants (Seldon 1979, 55).

9. Part of this increase resulted from the mobilization of women into neighborhood-run collective enterprises, the successors of the backyard steel furnaces (Tang and Parish 2000).

10. Spence (1990) points out that the number of victims of the Great Leap Forward is likely to be much higher because many more died from progressive malnutrition. In 1957 the average age of those dying was 17.6 years, while after the Great Leap in 1963 it had gone down to 9.7 years.

11. The hukou system was actually first set up in cities in 1951 and extended to rural areas in 1955. Initially, it served as a monitoring system of population migration and movements, not as a control mechanism. With the growing influx of peasants into cities, however, in 1958 the National People's Congress decided on legislation that gave way to an altered system of migration permits and recruitment and enrollment certificates, which in effect made rural–urban migration practically impossible (Chan and Zhang 1999).

12. Potter (1983) and Potter and Potter (1990) explain that the new hukou system of differentiation between population in the countryside and the cities connected to a long tradition of disregard for the peasantry. Already Confucian philosophy considered it immoral for officials to regard peasants' concerns with empathy. Socialism with its theoretical, not entirely sympathetic, understanding of peasants was superimposed on this negative attitude. Socialist theory questioned whether or not peasants could unite sufficiently to be useful subjects in a revolution. Socialist theory also predicted that peasants as a class would disappear after socialist revolution and industrial modernization, and that they would be replaced

by a rural proletariat. Nonetheless, in China peasants played a crucial role in the Communist revolution, and in the new socialist state the peasantry had not at all disappeared. Mao's thoughts reflected a conviction that peasants were not completely valid allies for workers and that only poor peasants with ideological purity could be relied on. In his opinion, most peasants would not understand their own class interests. As a result, even though Mao proclaimed that the antagonistic contradictions between peasants and workers had disappeared with the revolution, the differences in status and the overall rural-urban gap actually sharply increased. See also Cohen (1993) on the "cultural and political invention" of "peasants."

13. Some scholars have compared the hukou to the Indian caste system in which one cannot ever leave the caste into which one is born. See, for example, Gong 1998; Potter and Potter 1990. Indeed, even after the elimination of the communes in the early 1980s, the hukou system continued to control rural migration and exclude the rural majority from most government-subsidized goods and services (D. Davis 2000).

14. Hukou policies were also linked to the control of consumption. Those with agricultural registration had to grow their own food and were excluded from the subsidized state grain market. Thus, when agricultural production essentially collapsed after the Great Leap Forward, the overall living situation in the countryside deteriorated into unprecedented poverty (Cheng and Seldon 1997; Solinger 1999; Tang and Parish 2000).

15. Much of the rural–urban migration during the time was based on work-unit demand. At the end of the Great Leap Forward movement, millions of these migrants were sent back to the countryside, largely diminishing the previous population increase in urban centers.

16. This was a rather unusual case in that the wife decided to stay with her husband, despite not having a job any longer. Many families were actually separated during this time. This woman, however, became a housewife until several years later, when she found another job in the factory from which she eventually retired.

17. Focusing on the link between spatial forms and social organization, D. Bray (2005) offers a particularly illuminating "genealogical" account of the origins and development of the danwei to the present day. See also Lü and Perry (1997) for a historical and comparative analysis of the danwei.

18. The *dingti* policy was only effective for a limited time during the late 1970s and early 1980s.

19. Tang and Parish (2000, 27–29) explain that besides the danwei, the other important institution regulating citizens' lives was the neighborhood organization. In small cities, it was directly under the government's control, while in larger cities it was subject to the districts. Each neighborhood had a civilian neighborhood committee *(jiedao banshi shu)* that worked closely together with a local police office. Each neighborhood committee had a staff of around fifty people, who controlled a population of twenty thousand people, living in three to five thousand households. Most staff members were retired residents. The committee's functions

included the supervision of birth quotas, cleaning of the neighborhood, and mediating conflicts. In addition, the committee provided social services to the community and worked with the police unit in crime prevention. Even today, one can see retired elderly women with a red armband patrolling the streets in urban neighborhoods, who know everybody and everything going on in the neighborhood. Branch offices *(paichusuo)* of the public security bureau *(gonganju)* are located in every neighborhood, and one of its representatives is a member of the neighborhood committee. The *paichusuo* keeps the official household registration (hukou) of every resident.

20. The state had two roles. First, it provided funds to the work units, which developed housing for their employees. The amount of investment allocated depended on the importance of the work unit to the national economy, for example, whether it was a research institute for nuclear technology or a minor clothes factory. This was indicated by an administrative rank system. The higher the work unit ranked, the more housing investment it received. Second, the state also directly provided housing to households that could not access accommodation from their work units. This, however, applied only to households with a permanent urban hukou (see Huang and Clark 2002; Wu F. 1996).

21. At the same time, however, based on the politico-economic importance of the workplace, danwei had differential access to housing and benefits (in the form of government allocations). A family's standard of living was therefore more influenced by the resources of the workplace than by the wages earned by the household head. As a result, there was considerable competition to get into the best work units (Bian 1994; D. Davis 2000).

22. In this sense, danwei compounds were somewhat reminiscent of the walled wards of the historical Chinese city. The latter were, however, primarily residential in function (Gaubatz 1995).

23. Sit (1995, 205) lists the ratio of floor space constructed for production and for living as 1:1.12 for the years 1953–57. Between 1958 and 1976, however, it dropped to 1:0.9, and during the Great Leap Forward campaign it even went down to 1:0.64.

24. The Great Proletarian Cultural Revolution was Mao's last grand attempt to keep Chinese socialism on a populist track. In a backlash against the inevitable bureaucratization inherent in the Stalinist model of development, anything related to hierarchy and traditional authority was attacked. That is, not only bureaucratic leaders and their organizations became vulnerable, but also Confucian values, literature, and art, anything seen as impeding China's march toward a utopian revolutionary future (Logan 2002; Sit 1995; Tang and Parish 2000).

25. Anybody not conforming with the current party line could be called a "rightist," a designation that already emerged during the 1957 "Anti-Rightist Campaign" (see Andreas 2002).

26. For example, a person's "revolutionary background," that is, if one was born from peasant or landlord parents, significantly influenced a person's fate during the Cultural Revolution.

2. Reforming the State Sector, Opening the Private Sector

1. Tang and Parish (2000, 22) divide the post-Mao reform period into five different phases that started in 1978, when the Communist Party resolved to embark on a new campaign of economic modernization. After several years of changes in the agricultural sector, in the second period (1984–89) the party initiated urban reforms that included changes in enterprise structure, prices, finances, banking, housing, labor markets, welfare, pensions, and wages. During the same period, bureaucracy, polity, and mass media were also cautiously adjusted. In subsequent years unrestrained investments brought surplus demand and inflation; by early 1989 the economy was overheated while corruption was a widespread problem. After the urban demonstrations in Beijing's Tiananmen Square were violently suppressed, the state tightened its control, in both the economic as well as the political realm. This third phase of the reform (1989–92) was marked by a "freeze" of the reforms, underlined by the withdrawal of foreign direct investment and a society in shock. The fourth period of reforms (1992–97) began with Deng Xiaoping's visit to the south of China in which he emphasized a neoauthoritarian approach to reforms similar to Singapore and other east and southeast Asian countries. Deng's death in 1997 ushered in a fifth period of continued modernization. Since Tang and Parish's periodization, Jiang Zemin's resignation from the presidency and the appointment of Hu Jintao as his successor in 2002 has initiated a sixth phase of post-Mao reforms. One of the key concepts coined under the current leadership has been to "build a harmonious society," which is meant to ease growing socioeconomic differences in society and especially those between rural and urban areas. The effectiveness of this new policy remains to be seen.

2. The official age for retirement in China is fifty years for women workers, fifty-five for women cadres and staff, and sixty for men.

3. It took a number of gradual changes and massive layoffs from state-owned enterprises (especially after 1997) before this goal could be realized (D. Bray 2005).

4. Already during the Maoist era, women especially were encouraged to retire early and pass their jobs on to a child. This *dingti* system, however, was abolished in 1986.

5. Until the mid-1990s the rules regarding workers' pensions had remained largely unchanged since their establishment in the 1950s. To be entitled to retire, one had to work at least ten years, and one's pension was based on years of service and wages prior to retirement. If one began working before 1949 one received 100 percent salary. Those retiring after the required minimum work years got 60 percent of their previous wage; after fifteen years, 70 percent; and after twenty or more years, 75 percent. Pensions were based on the basic income, disregarding bonuses that greatly increased income. With the increasing life expectancy and an aging population (because of the one-child policy), however, pensions have become a growing burden for work units, which puts those with an older workforce at a disadvantage. Since individual enterprises became responsible for their retirees' pensions, they took on unequal burdens because of differences in the age composition of their workforces. Ikels (1996) gives the example of two factories: In 1980

a factory established in the mid-1950s was likely to have a middle-aged workforce, with most people in senior grades or retired, whereas a factory established in the late 1970s was likely to have a young workforce in the lowest pay grades and no retirees. The different wages and retirement burden of the two factories would have a major effect on their competitive position. In order to address this new inequality, in 1984 the central government began a new retirement fund. This measure was intended to shift the responsibility for financing retirement from the individual enterprise to employers and workers as a whole (Ikels 1996; Tang and Parish 2000). Under this system, enterprises contribute 15 to 18 percent of the wages they pay every month to a social labor insurance company, which pools the contributions from the province and redistributes them to retirees. Not all the money is reimbursed, however. A certain proportion is set aside each year to build up a retirement fund for the time when the ratio of workers to retirees is less favorable than now (Ikels 1996). Several recent scandals, in which the money of such funds was embezzled, however, show that the system is far from secure.

6. Informants reported pensions of 600–900 yuan per person per month; i.e., a married couple would receive a monthly income of 1200–1800 yuan. Average annual discretionary income of Beijing urban residents in 2000 was 10,349.7 yuan (US$1,293.75); average living expenditures were 8,493.5 yuan (US$1,061.75) (Beijing tongjiju 2001).

7. See also Thelle (2004) for an account of retirees whose pensions are not paid because of their danwei's economic problems.

8. Tang and Parish (2000, 41 n. 25) report that in 1992, administrators, managers, professionals, and retired state-firm workers received 88 percent medical coverage, manual workers 75 percent, service workers 62 percent, private-sector workers 4 percent, and farmers 5 percent.

9. While the measures have resulted in improved care, this applies only to a small number of hospitals in urban areas.

10. The average cost of a hospital stay, for example, increased by 11 percent over the past eight years, while urban incomes have risen by 8.9 percent. A nationwide survey in 2004 indicated that 48.9 percent of mainlanders did not go to the hospital when they needed medical care, and 29.6 percent of patients had cut short their stays in the hospital (I. Wang 2005). Indeed, the rising costs of health care and the lessening state subsidies have resulted in a stratification of health care access. One area that has been most affected by the commoditization of health care is medicine. Whereas the government upholds certain price restrictions on medical services, this does not apply to prescription drugs. Health providers, hospitals, and clinics today function as independent economic units that have to be profitable, and prescriptions are a sure way to increase income: The more expensive the medicine (i.e., imported drugs) the more revenue for the hospital. Wealth is thus the increasingly crucial determining factor in overall health maintenance (Chen 2001).

11. The right to dismiss workers and the five-year contracts already weakened public-sector job security in the 1980s. In the 1990s, however, pressure to reform

the state-owned enterprises stepped up considerably, with then Prime Minister Zhu Rongji announcing in 1998 that loss-making enterprises would be "turned around" within three years. Already in 1997, fifteen million workers had been made "redundant"; for 2000 official statistics registered a drop of twenty-six million state-owned-enterprise employees. This drop, however, is at least partly also due to changes in the way these numbers were recorded (Wang F. 2008, 145). Importantly, layoffs do not sever workers' relation with their danwei, which continues to support them at least for three years by paying a basic living allowance and providing the laid-off workers with some form of training. This arrangement is part of the "three lines of guarantees" *(san tiao baozhuangxian)* program developed to deal with the growing problem. According to these guarantees, if after three years a laid-off person has not been able to find alternative employment, their relationship with the danwei is terminated, and the responsibility for their support is transferred to the social security department of the local government. It is only at this stage that "redundant workers" officially become "unemployed" and are entitled to draw unemployment benefits from the government (and appear in official statistics). After two more years, if still unemployed, the worker ceases to receive unemployment benefits and their welfare is now put under the jurisdiction of the Ministry of Civil Affairs that will pay the individual a minimal living allowance (D. Bray 2005). The main problem with this system is the continuous reliance on the danwei. This sustained responsibility is based on the assumption that workers can be rapidly reemployed. In reality, however, as various scholars have pointed out (e.g., D. Bray 2005; Solinger 2002), the urban labor market has become very tight; redundant workers have to compete with the millions of migrant workers for few available positions. Thus, danwei find themselves in the paradoxical situation of having to support redundant workers whom they laid off in the first place because the company experienced financial difficulties. Not surprisingly, some sources report that up to half of all redundant workers receive little or no financial support from their danwei. Furthermore, a number of state-owned enterprises simply go bankrupt and close down, leaving their entire labor force out of work and with no source of even the most rudimentary support. This also affects retired workers who draw their pensions, health care, and other benefits from the danwei. Since efforts to establish a universal welfare system have lagged behind the pace of the state-sector reform, an ever larger number of people rely on family and wider social networks for support. One government response to the problems emerging from the state-sector reforms has been to promote "community building" *(shequ jianshe)* in an attempt to foster local solutions and local self-help to fill the void left by the demise of the danwei (D. Bray 2005).

12. Until 1978 practically every urban resident worked in state or collective work units, while the rural population was organized into production brigades and communes. The late 1970s, however, saw the legitimization of sideline activities and market trade in rural areas, and in 1981, the State Council issued a set of regulations for urban nonagricultural individual businesses. Initially, such businesses were considered a "private household" or *geti* and could hire not more than seven

employees, probably because of leaders' ideological discomfort with enterprises in which the workers were not clearly the owners. In 1987, however, the government allowed enterprises to hire eight or more employees, comprising the "private sector" *(siying)*.

13. For some time the government actually restricted business licenses to youths waiting for employment, to the unemployed, and to retirees with urban hukou. Only after 1988, when new regulations required private businesses to obtain insurance for their workers and comply with the requirements of all labor protection legislation, were people with state jobs willing to venture into the private sphere (Ikels 1996).

14. This includes collaborative investments from European, American, South Korean, and Japanese companies. But particularly companies from Hong Kong, Taiwan, and Macao, faced with labor shortages and rising labor costs, have been eager to move labor-intensive operations to special economic zones such as the ones in the Pearl River Delta in China's south. Here they have attracted especially rural migrants who work in their production facilities.

15. Especially since the early 1990s, both domestic and foreign private sectors have grown rapidly. Though the traditional state and collective sectors remain the dominant employers, these sectors are shrinking. By 1996, domestic private endeavors and joint ventures together employed nearly 17 percent of the urban labor force, compared to 3 percent in the beginning of urban reforms in 1984. The trend is even more obvious for new employees: in 1997, the private domestic and foreign sector hired 50 percent of newcomers, compared with only 6 percent in the 1980s (Tang and Parish 2000). The private sector, therefore, has offered new economic opportunities; for some it only eases the economic hardships that result from the reforms of the state sector, but for others it has indeed created unprecedented riches. Economic indicators paint a rosy picture. In 2000, the annual per capita income in Beijing was 15,000 yuan (US$2,000), while the annual disposable income of urban households reached 10,349.7 yuan (US$1,380). At the end of the same year, saving deposits of urban households in Beijing totaled 266.33 billion yuan (US$35.51 billion) (Beijing tongjiju 2001). For comparison, in 2006 the annual per capita income was 22,417 yuan (nationwide it was 12,719 yuan) and the annual disposable income of urban households in Beijing reached 19,978 yuan (Beijing tongjiju 2007). It is, however, important to note that at the same time that overall per capita income is rising in Beijing, income disparities are also growing. A survey of salaries in eighty-six occupations conducted by the Beijing Municipal Bureau of Statistics in 2001 showed that employees in some of Beijing's more lucrative occupations earned almost seven times as much as employees in low-end professions. The gap is, in fact, widening by 160 percent year by year. About four million people, that is, 39.4 percent of all workers in Beijing, earned more than the average, but 30 percent earned less than 15,000 yuan (US$2,000) annually. Workers' salaries were raised 72.5 percent in contrast to a 93.1 percent general average salary growth between 1995 and 2000, while 520,000 employees in the manufacturing sector were laid off during the same period (Beijing tongjiju 2001). Thus,

the new riches of some stand in stark contrast to the deteriorating situation of the working class. For a critical evaluation of the official statistics, see Khan and Riskin (2005).

16. With the reforms a number of new urban jobs have emerged, many of which carry distinctly gendered labels: women are predominantly recruited in the service sector while men work more often in technical and managerial positions (Wang Z. 2000). Other occupations have a distinctly "modern" aura. The figure of "the rice bowl of youth" *(qingchunfan),* which emerged in the early 1990s, describes a new urban trend in which a variety of well-paid jobs target exclusively young, beautiful women to work as bilingual secretaries, in public relations, or as fashion models. The attractive young women are sought out to represent a particularly shining image of "modernity" (Zhang Z. 2000). In fact, the one-child policy enacted since the late 1970s has led to a new generation of well-educated and strong-willed "only-daughters" who were brought up with high family expectations and who eagerly embrace new opportunities offered by the urban market economy, such as white-collar and managerial positions in foreign companies or "rice bowl of youth" occupations. The result is the rise of a new group of young, urban women with high incomes. Opportunities for these women emerged from specific gender norms. For example, command of a foreign language, especially English, was a requirement for these new positions. This was a qualification that women were more likely to fulfill since they predominated in the foreign language departments of universities based on their alleged special talent in that field. In addition, men often rejected clerical jobs that are frequently portrayed as "feminine" in society (Wang Z. 2000). The new "class" of wealthy young women, in turn, has already been discovered as a new market: in the south of China, new residential complexes are specifically fashioned to target young, urban, successful, and unmarried businesswomen (Xiao 2002a).

17. The economic background to the phenomenon is the rural reforms in the late 1970s that significantly improved agricultural efficiency. As a result, a large amount of rural labor became redundant and gave rise to increasing numbers of rural surplus workers. To address the problem, in 1983 the State Council issued a directive that allowed peasants to move to and settle in towns. Millions of surplus workers were absorbed in the growing rural industries that emerged after the abolition of the commune system. Millions of others, however, sought their fortunes in urban centers.

18. Before the reforms, it was virtually impossible to move between locations without an official permit because of surveillance, the rationing system, and the absence of markets. Since then, peasant markets have returned to cities, and rationing has been gradually abandoned. Moreover, realizing migrants' economic contribution, already early on officials either issued temporary work permits or ignored illegal transfers (Ma and Biao 1998; Tang and Parish 2000). In the mid-1990s, the central government introduced obligatory temporary residence permits *(zanzhu zheng)* for migrants at their destinations. Migrant women of child-bearing age are also required to carry a "marriage and fertility permit" *(hunyu zheng)*

issued by a body responsible for family planning in the place of temporary residence. The Ministry of Labor further stipulates that migrants must have an employment registration card *(waichu renyuan liudong jiuye dengji ka)* issued by the labor recruitment service in the county of the migrant's household registration. This is the basis for receiving an employment permit *(jiuye zheng)* at their destination. Some urban regulatory organs also require a certificate of good health before allowing migrants to register for other permits (Gaetano and Jacka 2004). As Zhang Li (2001, 35) points out, however, while the temporary registration gives migrants partial rights to work and live in the city, they remain excluded from access to state-subsidized services. Moreover, the costs for the temporary permits are so high that many migrants forgo the formalities (see also Jie and Taubmann 2002). According to the 1995 census, 13 percent of the city residents of Beijing, Tianjin, and Shanghai did not have temporary local registration, and more than three-quarters of these out-of-towners were from rural areas (Tang and Parish 2000).

19. Migrants work in (1) high-labor-intensity, low-income, but formal jobs, concentrated in secondary and tertiary industries, where they earn half the salary of urban residents or less, such as positions in chemical industries, some office services, public service in catering industries, and private services that urban residents don't like to take up, for example, professional typewriters, printing clerks, retailers, cashiers, and waitresses; (2) stable, contractual, but temporary jobs, such as manual labor in small firms, as family servants, house decorators, furniture repairers, deliverers, street cleaners, family electrical equipment cleaners, movers, and porters; (3) unstable, temporary, and insecure jobs such as supplying outdoor services, such as street stand owners, peddlers, rickshaw boys, shoe menders, bicycle mechanics, locksmiths, watch repairers, seal engravers, knife sharpeners, and trash collectors; or (4) as either employees or employers in small firms, such as the garment cottage industry set up by migrants from Zhejiang province (Gu and Liu 2002). Many employers actually recruit extensively in rural areas, hiring migrants as temporary contract workers and frequently providing dormitory housing for them. In sectors with labor shortages, often the process of labor recruitment is well organized and conducted by public agencies (Logan 2002).

20. For a detailed discussion of the various reforms, see, for example, Zhong and Hays (1996), Wu F. (2002), and Zhou and Logan (2002).

21. While in 1979 over 90 percent of urban housing was financed by funds channeled from the state to the danwei, by 1990 86 percent of capital for new public housing was being raised by individual danwei. As a result, the rate of housing construction was dramatically boosted: Between 1979 and 1992, the total area of urban housing increased more than four times, and average living space doubled from 3.6 square meters per capita to 7.1 square meters (D. Davis 2000). In Beijing, in the first quarter of 2002, 9.8 billion yuan (US$1.3 billion) were invested in the real estate industry, an increase of 46.5 percent over the same period in 2001. Investment in residential housing was up 32 percent, reaching 4.9 billion yuan (US$653 million). Housing areas under construction and reconstruction totaled 36.6 million square meters (*China Daily* 2002c).

22. Encouraging tenants to buy their apartments had already been unsuccessfully attempted in the 1980s. Low wages and the absence of a secondary property market made housing purchases unattractive, even at highly subsidized prices (D. Davis 2000).

23. The secondary market, although still small in comparison to more mature real-estate economies, corresponded to 85 percent of the new housing market in 2001 (Tomba 2004).

24. By 1992, five million urban households already held twelve-year mortgages from the Chinese Construction Bank, and by the end of 1994, 30.5 percent of urban households held some type of ownership rights (D. Davis 2000). There were basically three different ownership rights: ownership with the right to resell in the market, ownership with obligation to resell to the employer, and ownership of use rights with no right to resell. A limit of five years between the purchase of a public house and its possible sale was dropped in 2002.

25. In 2001, about 58 percent of Beijing's resident families had purchased properties from or through their work units (*China Daily* 2002a). Close to 90 percent of all residential units sold by Beijing work units to their employees cost less than 100,000 yuan (around US$13,333), considerably less than the average price of housing in the capital (Tomba 2004).

26. In 1997, the price for regular housing in Beijing's inner suburban areas was already more than 4,000 yuan (US$533) per square meter, while the average annual salary in the city amounted to 11,000 yuan (US$1,467). Among the factors that led to such high prices is the cost of land and high demolition fees per square meter. These costs account for nearly 30 to 40 percent of the total price of construction. All costs are paid by the developers who then pass them on to the apartment buyers. Although salaries have risen in recent years, property prices have increased more steeply. In 2002, the proportion of income to apartment prices in Beijing was 11:1, that is, much higher than the international average of 4.6:1, according to the State Bureau of Statistics (Wang and Wang 2002).

27. Discounted housing, however, includes only limited ownership. Buyers actually only own the equivalent of what they paid in relation to the full cost price; the rest belongs to the danwei (D. Bray 2005).

28. While the share of housing directly built by work units declined in the first part of the 1990s, public employers remained the engine of the real estate market, buying and constructing extensively to meet the needs of their employees (D. Bray 2005; Tomba 2004). The continuous role of the danwei is aptly illustrated by the practices surrounding the "housing provident fund" *(zhufang gongjijin)* that was instituted throughout the country in the later 1990s (in Beijing already in 1992); by the end of 1999 in Beijing most large state-owned organizations and enterprises were participating. This fund, which has been established in the public and private sectors, is intended to raise capital for the construction of housing. Each employee contributes a minimum of 5 percent of her or his wage while the employer contributes another 5 percent. While individual contributions theoretically remain the property of the contributor and may be withdrawn when he or she purchases

a home, in practice the fund has generally been used collectively by the danwei to fund large-scale housing development. Moreover, as D. Bray (2005) points out, if the housing fund is not sufficient for the planned development, the employer contributes the shortfall from retained profits or borrows the extra capital from one of the state banks. Thus, while the individual contributes to his or her own housing, property built in this way is still substantially subsidized, and the danwei continues to play a crucial role.

29. Several scholars actually consider these land reforms the crucial factor in the takeoff of the real estate sector. See, for example, Wu F. (1996); Wu and Yeh (1997); Yeh and Wu (1996).

30. In Beijing, the municipal government, for example, envisions the construction of edge areas and the development of the transportation system to draw more and more citizens to new houses in the suburbs. According to the general plan, 250,000 citizens are expected to have moved out of Beijing's downtown areas by 2010. By the middle of the twenty-first century, most people should live in suburbs, leaving a relatively small urban population. In the future, a Beijinger's morning is pictured to look like this: leave a forest-encircled apartment, jump into a light rail train, express public bus, or one's own car, and arrive at work downtown within an hour (Jin 2001; Tan R. 2002; Wang D. 2002a).

3. Daily Life in Wangjing

1. Overall, however, Beijing's real estate market is dominated by luxury apartments, many of which are located in the Asian Games Village and in the northwestern and northeastern areas of the city such as Wangjing (*China Daily* 1999). After the successful bid to host the Olympic Games 2008, Olympic fever further heated up Beijing's property market. Apartment projects mushroomed around the future Olympic site, and existing complexes jacked up their prices. Residential property near the proposed Olympic Village witnessed growing sales, for some time even mad purchases, with people queuing up for new projects (Gao 2001).

2. Zhang L. (2004) similarly reports that people in her Kunming research classified today's residential compounds into three broad categories: wealthy or luxury *(furen qu)*, mid-level *(zhongdang qu)*, and working-class neighborhood *(gongxin jieceng qu,* literally salary-class neighborhood).

3. See chapter 2, n. 28.

4. All prices and US$ conversion rates are for the year 2002. For comparison, in 2003 a new residential compound was planned in Jiuxianqiao for completion at the end of 2008 with units to be sold at 8,000 yuan per square meter.

5. The company has a total asset capitalization in excess of US$1.5 billion and is responsible for the construction of eleven million square meters of housing in the capital, or around 180,000 residential units (an estimated 660,000 Beijing people presently live in houses built by Chengkai). Information on the company's activity is available from its Web site (http://www.cbud.com.cn).

6. In 1996 the People's Bank of China lifted the limit of five years on mortgage lending, but only the 1998 housing reform regulations can be really taken as the beginning of a mortgage market in China.

7. There are also price differences within "economy" buildings depending on feng shui, views, floor space, and so on.

8. The similarity of the design and layout of new neighborhoods with the danwei compound is not accidental but derives from conscious urban planning policies that continue to favor the "integrated" lifestyle of the work unit. The construction of such residential compounds also makes for a marked difference to suburban development in other countries, especially the United States (D. Bray 2008; Campanella 2008; Huang and Low 2008).

9. The "graying" of the community would be even more striking if one considered all retirees, that is, all people over age fifty, since the official age for retirement in China is fifty years for women workers, fifty-five for women cadres and staff, and sixty for men.

10. The residents' committee (*jumin weiyuanhui*, short *juweihui*) is the representative of the state on the community level. It is in charge of implementing government policies, from the dissemination of information to the enforcement of regulations. The connection with the neighborhood residents and the quality of the services offered increasingly depend on the individuals working in the stations. In contrast to the prereform era, committee employees do not necessarily live in the community any longer, which significantly changes the relation between them. In the Hong Yuan neighborhood, however, the workers in the stations all lived in the community and apparently had a very personal relationship with residents. People dropped by to chat and were greeted by their names.

11. There existed two dilapidated danwei complexes on the Wangjing side of the suburban area which had been erected in the 1950s or 1960s. One of them was the already half-abandoned complex that was marked for tear-down, described in the introduction to this chapter. The other one remained occupied. My attempts to talk to residents, however, were met with unwillingness to answer any questions and a discouraging intervention by a representative of the local neighborhood organization. Apparently, the Chinese authorities did not want a foreign student to take a closer look at this destitution and eyesore to the state's vision of modernity. Even more so since there have been various protests by residents of such places against their resettlement and often insufficient compensation.

12. See Campanella (2008) for a comparison of U.S. and Chinese suburbanization processes.

13. Mortgages continue to be much easier to obtain for those with stable incomes and preexisting property. Other qualifications to access commercial bank loans are the ownership of assets or an employer's endorsement. All of these factors clearly limit the number of people who can obtain such monetary support (Tomba 2004).

14. See Appendix D for a table of sample living conditions of interviewees in one suburban danwei compound.

15. This is a common practice to address the growing unemployment problem especially of low-educated urbanites. It is also another example of the continuous importance of the state.

16. The fact that she worked in the local residents' committee might have helped her, even if she did not admit to this. As I was told, employees of the "work stations" should live within the neighborhood to enhance the community feeling and make them more accessible. Pan Suming thus might have been given preference over others in buying the available apartment.

17. See Ikels (2004) on the continued yet changing importance of filial piety in China and other Asian countries.

18. It has become a widespread fashion among young urban Chinese to adopt foreign names, many of which they first get in English courses they take. I usually asked my friends for their Chinese names. Several of them, such as Caroline, however, insisted on their English ones.

19. Other "fashionable," medium- to high-end residential areas at the time of the research were the Asian Games Village in the north of the city and the Zhongguancun Science and Technology Development Zone in Haidian District, in Beijing's northwest.

20. Newly developed suburban areas often lack in infrastructure and basic facilities, among them good schools (Campanella 2008). Besides sending a child to a school in a more central city location, boarding schools have thus also become increasingly more popular, especially among the new middle class.

21. The real estate market has "discovered" the rapidly growing retired population as a new target group for residential developments. Beijing has a population of 1.8 million aged sixty or more. However, most real estate projects in Beijing cater to the needs of young and middle-aged professionals. "Oriental Sun City," in contrast, is a new residential complex that aims at the elderly population and markets itself as "a multifunctional community aimed at senior citizens" and "a leader of a whole new retirement lifestyle." The construction of the buildings was supposed to take the needs of the elderly into account. Given the average incomes of senior citizens, however, they would have to rely on their children's support to be able to acquire property in a development such as Oriental Sun City, where apartments sold for a minimum of 3,500 yuan (US$467) per square meter in 2002 (Zhong 2002a).

22. In her research in Shanghai in 1987, D. Davis (1993) observed a predominance of coresidence with sons and a greater reliance on parents or employers of the husband. Indeed, comparing postmarital households of respondents who had married in the 1940s and early 1950s with the arrangements of their sons who had married in the 1970s and 1980s, Davis found a shift to greater virilocality. Davis relates these findings to changes in Chinese urban society since the reform period. First, since 1978 job assignments are increasingly rewarding credentials, but at the same time, there is an increase in discrimination against females. Parents could therefore expect more material gains by living jointly with a son than with a daughter. Nonetheless, preference of living with sons was not an entirely rational

choice but continued to be nourished by traditional preferences for male offspring, which produced such statements as "It is shameful for a man to move into his wife's house." The fact that I could not find this kind of gender bias in coresidence among my respondents might derive from the fact that the adult children in my investigation were a younger cohort, many of whom were educated, came of age, and began working during the reform era. Several of the women, actually, had higher-paying jobs than their husbands or brothers, which would make it more logical for elderly parents to live with them.

23. In 2002, a one-way taxi trip from Wangjing to the inner city would cost around 40 yuan (US$5.30), compared to 1 yuan (US$0.13) for the cheap bus and between 5 and 10 yuan (US$0.67 and 1.33) for a new, fast bus.

24. Feng shui, literally "wind" and "water," is often called the art of placement or the "art of flow." Feng shui is an ancient Chinese practice aimed at maximizing the beneficial movement of the *qi*—the universal life force present in all things—through an environment.

25. Since winds in the Beijing plain usually come from a northern direction, dust and industrial smoke is blown across the city toward its southern sections. In addition, the city is flanked in the northwest to northeast by extensions of the Taiheng Shan (Taiheng Mountains) that form an effective physical barrier in a horseshoe shape. According to feng shui teachings this is a favorable living environment (Sit 1995).

26. This is not supposed to imply that old danwei residents have become mere passive subjects. Indeed, there have been protests against urban transformation processes led by such state employees, the latest example actually arising around the destruction of one of the Jiuxianqiao residential complexes. Nonetheless, in contrast to younger, wealthier residents, in general terms the elderly danwei residents generally *live* their lives very much within, or in the direct vicinity of, their residential quarters.

4. Socioeconomic Differences

1. Hanser (2008) similarly examines the field of retail services as a locus where social differentiations are enacted and class formation is taking place.

2. The importance of community in class formation is aptly illustrated by E. P. Thompson's influential study, *The Making of the English Working Class* (1966). Similarly, Giddens (1973) highlights the influence of localized cultural factors in the process of class structuration. He argues that it takes place not only through relations of production but also outside of these, namely through the spheres of consumption, family, and community life. Although Weber differentiates classes from status groups in that the former is largely defined in production and the latter in consumption, he also emphasizes that the two modes of group formation are closely linked through property ownership that not only determines one's class situation but also serves as the primary basis for lifestyles (see Giddens 1981; see also Zhang L. 2004).

3. Thompson (1966), Bourdieu (1984), Giddens (1981), Miller (1998), and Zhang L. (2004) similarly highlight the cultural aspect of class-formation processes.

4. Clammer (2003) shows, for example, that in southeast Asia growing middle classes, created by economic changes in the past decade, have begun to develop new social patterns. The political visibility of the new middle classes in Asia is due in large part to their pushing for more public goods as the framework and guarantee of the security of private consumption.

5. Similarly, Harvey (1990) observed that each distinctive mode of production or social formation embodies a distinctive bundle of time and space practices and concepts.

6. This was a special middle school open to children of cadres. Since the reform period, educational fees have been reintroduced, and after 1991 Zhu's second daughter had to pay tuition. These fees, however, were still low in comparison to the present.

7. Author translation from Chinese.

8. William Hinton (1966; cited in Anagnost 1997, 28) wrote in *Fanshen,* "Every revolution creates new words. The Chinese revolution created a whole new vocabulary."

9. Erwin (2000) explains, "to *eat* bitterness" *(chi ku)* is a Chinese expression, taken from a Buddhist poem, that represents the hardship of life through a bodily metaphor. Linked to notions in Chinese medicine according to which eating bitter herbs is necessary for good health, "to eat bitterness" means to bear adversities that spring from one's gender and class position, and that were one's fate in the rigid Confucian social hierarchy.

10. "Speaking bitterness," of course, evokes Louis Althusser's theory of the interpellation function of ideology through the spoken word. Anagnost (1997, 31) explains the wider importance of this interpellation: "Giving 'voice' to the subaltern class subject, the party engaged in a myth of presence, one that authenticated its leadership as representing the constituencies its own discourse had constituted. Thus speaking bitterness was not simply an imposition of a narrative structure on the speaking subject. It represented for the party the process of merging the consciousness of the party with that of 'the people,' which legitimated its claims to represent the voice of the masses."

11. "Lao wai" literally means "*old* foreigner." The "lao" in this context, however, is a respectful address. Nonetheless, there has been considerable discussion—among scholars in and outside China, as well as among my friends—whether the term is indeed a positive or negative one. I always had an ambiguous feeling about being called "lao wai," and several of my friends insisted on talking about their *deguo pengyou* (German friend) instead of using the phrase, even correcting others who referred to me in that way.

12. When I lived in Beijing in the summer of 1993, the recently opened McDonald's flagship at the corner of the traditional main shopping street of Wangfujing drew crowds of people. They stood in a line over a hundred meters long that wound down the street in front of the restaurant. Observing that various people

tried only a few bites of the coveted, but at that time disproportionately expensive, fast-food items and left most of it to be thrown away, a friend conducted a small investigation interviewing the manager of the franchise as well as several customers about what attracted them to come to visit. Several reasons were mentioned; the most important was, of course, curiosity. But apart from that, a major incentive to visit the restaurant was that this was considered the kind of food "big, strong foreigners" ate, and the Chinese visitors hoped to gain some of that strength. Another factor was that it had become a kind of "status symbol" or, better, proof of affluence to be able to visit McDonald's restaurants. It was considered "chic" and an appropriate place to bring a "date," to celebrate a child's birthday, or even to take out the family on a special occasion. Last, but not least, another "pull factor" was the desire to change the diet, to have some variation in cuisine, to find a different, new taste. McDonald's in Beijing has since become a focus of scholarly attention. For a discussion of the consumption of Americana, see, for example, Yan Y. (1997).

13. According to the Beijing Statistics Bureau (2001), in 2000 high-income households had an average yearly cash income of 22,622.01 yuan (US$3,016.27), medium high–income households had 13,964.29 yuan (US$1,861.90), and medium-income households 11,699.46 yuan (US$1,559.93) per annum (see Appendix C for complete data). The Chinese Academy of Science reported that in 2004, 19 percent of Chinese people (49 percent of urban Chinese) belonged to the "middle class," defined as families with assets of 150,000 to 300,000 yuan (US$20,000 to 40,000), up from 15 percent in 1999 (Wan 2004). Other studies, however, find that only 5.04 percent of the Chinese population can be considered "middle class" as defined by earning a minimum of 80,000 yuan (US$10,667) per annum. These kinds of statistics, however, are questionable and likely to be politically influenced. In January 2004, Communist Party leaders decided that 5,000 yuan income per month should qualify a household to be considered "middle class." This figure is needed to achieve the party's set target that by 2020 a "considerable portion" of the population will be categorized as "middle income" earners. Keeping the minimum income for middle-class status at 80,000 yuan per annum would prevent the fulfillment of the plan (see SCMP 2005). The background for lowering the minimum income definition of "middle class" is that income inequalities in China are actually rising. One measure of inequality, the Gini coefficient, has risen sharply in the last years. Between 1988 and 1997, the Gini coefficient rose from 0.35 to 0.4 (Wang, Hu, and Ding 2002). In Beijing in 2000, the average annual per capita salary for employees and workers was 15,600 yuan (US$2,080), up 13.2 percent from the previous years. The annual per capita disposable income of urban households reached 10,349 yuan (US$1,379.87), up 12.7 percent from 1999 (Beijing tongjiju 2001). In order to meet the 60,000 yuan (US$8,000) per annum target, salaries will have to continue rising at least at the current rate.

14. The growing social pressure to achieve and/or perform certain lifestyles in urban China could certainly also be seen as a new form of constraint after the political and ideological demands of the Maoist period.

15. After I left China, newspaper reports about similar disputes in the research area soared. In July of 2003, for example, there was a series of scuffles between homeowners and construction workers in one complex. Several people were injured and many cars destroyed. Clashes broke out after developers and city planners altered the original layout of the complexes. Three days later, homeowners drove along Chang'an Avenue in a forty-eight-car convoy, equipped with banners and slogans, to protest outside the city construction commission (see J. Ma 2003a, 2003b).

16. See Tomba (2004) for a study of homeowner protests in Wangjing. Read (2003) has made similar observations among affluent homeowners in Guangzhou.

17. The focus on Liang springs from the fact that she volunteered the most comprehensive and encompassing information among the migrants in the suburban markets, possibly because her marriage to an urban resident put her into a somewhat safer situation than other migrants. Nonetheless, interviews with other migrants revealed many similarities with Liang's account. Furthermore, while I hung out in the markets even the more hesitant migrants chipped in to the conversations, and shared bits and pieces of their lives with me, thus adding to Liang's account, contrasting or complementing her information, as will become apparent in the following.

18. Fan (1999), for example, shows that there are actually a multitude of migration types ranging from legal job transfers to marriage migration—both aspects that either have been overlooked so far or are indeed new developments. Similarly, Roberts et al. (2004) have recently challenged the notion that women do not migrate after marriage. Their study shows that since the late 1990s married women from Anhui and Sichuan province migrate, both with and without their children.

19. At the same time, however, there is growing concern over the rise of illiteracy among Chinese, and especially among migrants, mainly due to dropping out of school and lack of practice (see R. Li 2007a). Both observations are not necessarily contradictory, but just another proof that broad generalizations about the migrant population fail to capture the—presumably growing—differences among them.

20. The preference for sons is related to various issues. Among them is the continued idea that the family line is carried through the male descendants and that women upon marriage cease to be members of the natal family. This latter point in turn produces further economically based considerations: if the labor power of a daughter is lost by her natal family upon marriage, then there is no economic reason to invest in a daughter's education or training. See also Tan S. (1997) for a discussion of gender differences among rural migrants.

21. In fact, there are more connections between gender and migration. As Jacka (2005) elaborates, women's contribution to the rural household economy is often considered secondary since older or male family members can take care of farm work. Moreover, chores such as child care and domestic work are generally not valued in rural China because they do not generate income; they are thus not considered "work." Therefore, if women say there is "nothing to do" in the countryside,

this connotes not just inactivity and the boredom that goes with it but also a sense of worthlessness. Finally, single women might also resort to migration to "change their fate"; i.e., they reject that the only important thing in their lives is marriage, which, due to continuous patrilocal, exogamous marriage patterns, also means departure from the natal family and from their villages. In certain ways, therefore, gender ideologies facilitated migration decisions of women.

22. Shi (1999) similarly argues that the migrant women she studied in Guangdong province could find a niche in the domestic service sector into which they were predominantly channeled. Even though this is the lowest sector of the urban labor market, the women could pursue jobs considered appropriate for their sex and successfully confront the patriarchal structures to which they were subjected.

23. This observation reverberates with Glick-Schiller's recent (2005) call for migration studies to examine the impact of *locality* on migration and migrants themselves.

24. Given migrants' unstable living conditions, migrants' parents almost always remained in their home places. Other reasons why parents stayed in the countryside were a continued claim to their rural land and the older generation's frequent reluctance to move to the city.

25. This stands in sharp contrast to migrant enclaves or villages such as described by Zhang Li (2001), for example. See also Ma and Biao (1998).

26. Zhang Li (2001, 142) compares the Chinese notion of suzhi to Bourdieu's concept of habitus. She points out that suzhi, like habitus, refers to a person's "disposition, ability, and way of acting," characteristics that are conditioned by a person's upbringing and are therefore hard to change. Zhang's point in the context of her study of the Wenzhou migrant community in Beijing is that suzhi is a fluid and vague concept that is manipulated by people to serve their own interests. The concept gains specific importance in the process of stereotyping migrants as a homogeneous low-suzhi group that is inherently different and eternally juxtaposed to the modern Beijing citizen.

27. Zhang Li (2001, 25) explains that until the introduction of the hukou, rural–urban migrants were not treated as distinct groups in need of special control and regulations. Moreover, they were referred to in neutral terms such as *yimin* "migrants" or *ximin* "migrating or relocating people." The official Chinese designation of present-day migrants as *liudong* (floating), in turn, sharply contrasts them to a long historical emphasis on rootedness and spatial immobility in China.

5. Consumption and the Geography of Space and Social Status

1. If state consumption is subtracted, the rate falls to 47.1 percent (while the world average is 60.0 percent) (Tomba 2004).

2. Jiang Zemin's Report to the 16th Party Congress. Author translation from Chinese.

3. Employees in the health-care sector, for example, saw a pay raise of 168 percent between 1995 and 2000. Their median income is thus about 40 percent

above the urban average. Salaries in tertiary education and in scientific institutions increased by 158 percent over the same period; they are now 31 percent above the average. Shortages in specific areas of expertise have also contributed to the competitiveness of professionals' salaries. Moreover, skills now often provide higher remuneration than administrative responsibility. Highly demanded occupations, such as telecommunication technicians, software engineers, and bank clerks, today earn higher salaries than a state factory director. In addition, forty-five million public servants in administrative positions are likely to profit from the policy of paying a "high salary to foster honesty" *(gaoxin yanglian)* (Xie 2002). Some especially sensitive categories such as judges could see a fourfold increase in salary by the end of this decade (Pan 2001). Finally, already in 1995, with the aim to increase consumer spending, the government introduced the five-day working week; major national holidays were turned into week-long vacation periods. Urban employees now have 115 days a year off work (Tomba 2004).

4. Rofel (1999, 8) similarly states: "The ruptures of China's successive imaginaries of modernity mark a desire, begun within a history of semicolonialism and repeatedly deferred, to position China as a nation-state that has fully arrived in the selfsame identity as former Western colonizers. Indeed, the answer to why the project of modernity presents itself as so compelling in China, why it has been pursued so persistently, lies in the specter of China's exclusion, which serves to construct a Eurocentric universalist modernity. The strength of socialism in China derived, in part, from this history of semicolonialism and the search to make China a vigorous nation-state. This deferred desire lives on, now motivating postsocialist pursuits of wealth and power."

5. Similarly, Yan Y. (1997) shows how young couples in the countryside today consider it more *"fangbian"* to live in the nuclear family households. He argues that *"fangbian,"* usually translated as "convenient," refers to the notion of family privacy, especially a little accessible space for conjugal intimacy.

6. A survey of 7,817 migrant workers' children under eighteen years of age, conducted by the National Working Committee on Children and Women under the State Council in the fall of 2003 in China's major cities, found that 9.3 percent of the children interviewed had either dropped out of school or had never gone to school (Yu 2003).

7. Jacka (2005) makes a similar point.

8. My argument here draws on various studies of the relationship between spatial and social organization that frequently refer to Bourdieu (1977), who suggests that spatial and temporal experiences are primary vehicles for the coding and reproduction of social relations. Symbolic orderings of space and time provide a framework for experience through which we learn who and what we are in society. In his study of the Kabyle house, Bourdieu (1990) shows how social relationships and people's conceptions of the world are shaped by and inscribed in the spatial organization of the domestic realm. It is, suggests Bourdieu, through the dialectical relationship between the body and a structural organization of space and time that common practices and representations are determined. Precisely out of such

experiences (particularly in the home) enduring schemes of perception, thought, and action became inscribed. Harvey (1990), however, alerts us that Bourdieu's conceptualization is too static. Instead, he stresses that value and meaning are not inherent in any spatial order but must be produced. Similarly, in the context of women's subordinate position in society, Henrietta Moore (1988) has pointed out that it is not work per se but what is conceived as "work" and the social value assigned to it in a given cultural context that shapes women's domestic and societal status. Zhang Li (2001) extends this idea to argue that gender domination and the value of women's work are closely linked to the construction of gendered spaces (household, workshop, marketplace, bar and hotel, etc.) and to the cultural perceptions of what is proper or improper, domestic or wild, pure or dangerous, productive or unproductive. See also F. Bray 1997.

9. Wang and Li (2004, 2006) make a similar point for Beijing and Guangzhou based on survey data.

10. Jansson (2003) similarly argues for a connection between consumption and space, or "place-making," in Göteborg.

11. This point reverberates Liu X.'s (1997) findings in his study of strategies of Shaanxi peasants and overseas scholars in the "geographic production of social relations" (Massey 1993, 60–61). Liu argues that mobility and imagination of new social-spatial hierarchies have become important sources in the negotiation of power in everyday life in China since the reform period.

12. The most exclusive residential developments, in contrast, often used the word "garden" *(yuan)* in their names, suggesting even more spacious layout with more greenery.

13. Another suggestive slogan was "Buy a house, live a free life" (see Xiao 2002a).

14. Shengxin Real Estate Development 2000a. Author translation from Chinese.

15. Shengxin Real Estate Development 2000b. Author translation from Chinese.

16. Beijing City Xinxing Real Estate Developing Head Office 2000. Author translation from Chinese.

17. This circumstance has been dramatically reconfirmed since the 2008 global economic downturn when export-dependent factories in southern China were closed overnight and migrant workers not only lost their workplaces but often also lost significant amounts of money they were owed in back pay.

Conclusion

1. In contrast to legal battles over resettlement and compensation when entire neighborhoods in Beijing (and other cities) are marked for redevelopment, the housing disputes of middle-class homeowners with development companies not only have a more conciliatory tone but are also more likely to be resolved in favor of the claimants (Jacobs 2008; R. Li 2007b; J. Ma 2003b, 2003c).

2. A survey of seven hundred citizens in Beijing, Shanghai, and Guangzhou conducted by the China Economic Monitoring Center analyzed Chinese urbanites'

attitudes toward the division of society into different social classes. Over 78 percent of the surveyed admitted there was an inequality among people in different social classes, but they believed that people should not use these to maximize their individual benefits. However, nearly 25 percent highlighted the negative effects of such inequalities and wished that the government would solve the conflicts they saw as inevitably arising from them. Meanwhile, 70 percent of the surveyed said that there was nothing wrong for people in different social classes to have diverging social status and wealth. But 31 percent of the surveyed insisted that people should have equal resources. They believed a disparity in the division of social resources would endanger the basis of a socialist society. The survey also found that nearly 63 percent believed that wealth was the most effective resource in terms of dividing social classes, followed by 60 percent who considered education and personal capability as the most important distinguishing factors. In contrast, slightly over 50 percent said the nature of employment was more important and thought power was embodied in money and social status. Of those surveyed, 44 percent said that the division into social classes was a matter of personal trust. They pointed out that in present-day China more people emphasized social relationships and were concerned with their reputation (*Beijing Today* 2002). See also Liu X. (2002), who offers a study of strata consciousness in present-day China.

3. The "othering" of present-day migrants has an interesting parallel to the state and identity construction during the early decades of the twentieth century. As Cohen (1993) argues, in order to facilitate change in the country, China's intellectuals, Communists and non-Communists, created an image of the old society that had to be rejected. Key to this image was the redefinition of traditional Chinese culture and of the vast majority of people who still adhered to it, especially in the countryside. China's elite came to regard the rural population as "backward" and as a major obstacle to national development. Rural China was considered a "feudal society" of "peasants" who were intellectually and culturally held back by "superstition." "Farmers" were transformed into "peasants," "tradition" into "feudalism," and "customs" or "religion" into "superstition." This was the invention of the "old society" that had to be overcome. The new ideology, however, also created the basic negative criteria that designated a new status group, peasants, who by definition were considered to be incapable of participating in China's reconstruction.

BIBLIOGRAPHY

Agence France-Presse. 2003. "Man Sets Himself on Fire in Beijing Protest Over Real Estate Project." http://www.china.scmp.com (accessed September 25, 2003).

———. 2005. "Beijing Debates Barring Migrants from Rest of China." http://www.china.scmp.com (accessed January 26, 2005).

Anagnost, Ann. 1994. "Who Is Speaking Here? Discursive Boundaries and Representation in Post-Mao China." In *Boundaries in China*, ed. John Hay, 257–79. London: Reaktion.

———. 1997. *National Past-Times: Narrative, Representation, and Power in Modern China*. Durham, N.C.: Duke University Press.

———. 2008. "From 'Class' to 'Social Strata': Grasping the Social Totality in Reform-Era China." *Third World Quarterly* 29(3): 497–519.

Andreas, Joel. 2002. "Battling over Political and Cultural Power during the Chinese Cultural Revolution." *Theory and Society* 31:462–519.

Ballew, Tad. 2001. "Xiaxiang for the '90s: The Shanghai TV Rural Channel and Post-Mao Urbanity amid Global Swirl." In *ChinaUrban: Ethnographies of Contemporary Culture*, ed. Nancy N. Chen, Constance D. Clark, Suzanne Z. Gottschang, and Lyn Jeffrey, 242–73. Durham, N.C.: Duke University Press.

Barlow, Tani. 1994. "Theorizing Women: Funü, Guojia, Jiating (Chinese Woman, Chinese State, Chinese Family)." In *Body, Subject, and Power in China*, ed. Angela Zito and Tani Barlow, 253–89. Chicago: University of Chicago Press.

———. 1995. "Politics and Protocols of Funü: (Un)Making National Woman." In *Engendering China: Women, Culture, and the State*, ed. Christina Gilmartin, Gail Hershatter, Lisa Rofel, and Tyrene White, 339–59. Cambridge, Mass.: Harvard University Press.

Baudrillard, Jean. 1981 [1972]. *For a Critique of the Political Economy of the Sign*. Trans. Charles Levin. St. Louis: Telos Press.

Beijing City Xinxing Real Estate Developing Head Office. 2000. *Xinghai Mingzhu* [Star-Sea Jewel]. Beijing: Beijingshi Xinxing Fangdichan Kaifa Zonggongsi.

Beijing Today. 2002. "Variety of Interpretations of 'Social Class.'" April 26, 7.

Beijing tongjiju [Beijing Statistical Bureau]. 1996. *Beijing Shi Shehui Jingji Tongji Nianjian 1996* [Beijing city social, economic, and statistical yearbook 1996]. Beijing: Beijing Tongji Chubanshi [Beijing Statistics Press].

———. 1999. *Beijing Wushi Nian* [Beijing's fifty years]. Beijing: Zhongguo Tongji Chubanshi [Chinese Statistics Press].

———. 2001. *Beijing Shi Shehui Jingji Tongji Nianjian 2001* [Beijing city social, economic, and statistical yearbook 2001]. Beijing: Beijing Tongji Chubanshi [Beijing Statistics Press].

———. 2007. *Beijing Shi Shehui Jingji Tongji Nianjian 2007* [Beijing city social, economic, and statistical yearbook 2007]. Beijing: Beijing Tongji Chubanshi [Beijing Statistics Press].

Berking, Helmuth. 2006. "Contested Places and the Politics of Space." In *Negotiating Urban Conflicts: Interaction, Space, and Control,* ed. Hermuth Berking, Sybille Frank, Lars Frers, Martina Löw, Lars Meier, Silke Steets, and Sergej Stoetzer, 29–39. Bielefeld: Transcript.

Beynon, Louise. 2004. "Dilemmas of the Heart: Rural Working Women and Their Hopes for the Future." In *On the Move: Women and Rural-to-Urban Migration in Contemporary China,* ed. Arianne M. Gaetano and Tamara Jacka, 131–50. New York: Columbia University Press.

Bian Yanjie. 1994. *Work and Inequality in Urban China.* Albany: State University of New York Press.

———. 2002. "Chinese Social Stratification and Social Mobility." *Annual Review of Sociology* 28:91–116.

Bian, Yanjie, Ronald Breiger, Deborah Davis, and Joseph Galaskiewicz. 2005. "Occupation, Class, and Social Networks in Urban China." *Social Forces* 83(4): 1443–68.

Borneman, John. 1991. *After the Wall: East Meets West in the New Berlin.* New York: Basic.

———. 1997. "State, Territory, and National Identity Formation in the Two Berlins, 1945–1995." In *Culture, Power, Place: Explorations in Critical Anthropology,* ed. Akhil Gupta and James Ferguson, 93–117. Durham, N.C.: Duke University Press.

Bourdieu, Pierre. 1977. *Outline of a Theory of Practice.* Cambridge: Cambridge University Press.

———. 1984. *Distinction: A Social Critique of the Judgment of Taste.* Trans. Richard Nice. Cambridge, Mass.: Harvard University Press.

———. 1990. "The Kabyle House or the World Reversed." In *The Logic of Practice,* trans. Richard Nice, 271–83. Stanford, Calif.: Stanford University Press.

———. 1991. *Language and Symbolic Power.* Cambridge, Mass.: Harvard University Press.

Bray, David. 2005. *Social Space and Governance in Urban China: The Danwei System from Origins to Reform.* Stanford, Calif.: Stanford University Press.

———. 2008. "Master Plans and Model Communities: Rationalities of Planning in Contemporary Urban China." Paper presented at the 107th Annual Meeting of the American Anthropological Association, San Francisco.

Bray, Francesca. 1997. "Women's Work: Weaving Patterns in the Social Fabric." In *Technology and Gender: Fabrics of Power in Late Imperial China*, ed. Francesca Bray, 173–272. Berkeley: University of California Press.

Broudehoux, Anne-Marie. 2004. *The Making and Selling of Post-Mao Beijing.* London: Routledge.

Brownell, Susan. 1995. *Training the Body for China: Sports in the Moral Order of the People's Republic.* Chicago: University of Chicago Press.

Bruegmann, Robert. 2005. *Sprawl: A Compact History.* Chicago: University of Chicago Press.

Brugger, Bill, and Stephen Reglar. 1994. *Politics, Economy and Society in China.* Stanford, Calif.: Stanford University Press.

Business Beijing. 2002. "Survey Shows Widening of Beijing's Income Gap." April, 6.

Campanella, Thomas J. 2008. *The Concrete Dragon: China's Urban Revolution and What It Means for the World.* New York: Princeton Architectural Press.

Carmel, Alan. 2001. "Cultural Auto Suggestion." *Beijing This Month*, October, 14–17.

Caro, Robert A. 1974. *The Power Broker: Robert Moses and the Fall of New York.* New York: Alfred A. Knopf.

Castles, Stephen. 2000. "Migration as a Factor in Social Transformation in East Asia." Paper presented at the Conference on Migration and Development, Princeton University, 4–6 May 2000, session on "Asian Migration: Characterizing an Emerging System." http://www.theglobalsite.ac.uk.

Chan Kam Wing and Zhang Li. 1999. "The Hukou System and Rural-Urban Migration in China: Processes and Changes." *China Quarterly* 160:818–55.

Chance, Norman A. 1991. *China's Urban Villagers: Changing Life in a Beijing Suburb.* Fort Worth, Texas: Harcourt Brace College.

Chaoyang Tourism Administration, ed. N.d. *A Shining Spot of Beijing Tourism – Golden Chaoyang.* Information brochure. Beijing: Chaoyang Tourism Administration.

Chen, Nancy N. 2001. "Health, Wealth, and the Good Life." In *ChinaUrban: Ethnographies of Contemporary Culture,* ed. Nancy N. Chen, Constance D. Clark, Suzanne Z. Gottschang, and Lyn Jeffrey, 165–82. Durham, N.C.: Duke University Press.

Chen, Nancy N., Constance D. Clark, Suzanne Z. Gottschang, and Lyn Jeffery, eds. 2001. *ChinaUrban: Ethnographies of Contemporary Culture.* Durham, N.C.: Duke University Press.

Cheng, Allen T. 2003a. "Beijing Is Aiming to Be the Next Manhattan." http://www.china.scmp.com (accessed October 10, 2003).

———. 2003b. "Pie in the Sky." http://www.china.scmp.com (accessed October 13, 2003).

———. 2004. "Concrete Jungle." http://www.china.scmp.com (accessed April 19, 2004).

Cheng Chaoze. 1991. "Internal Migration in Mainland China: The Impact of Government Policies." *Issues and Studies* 27(8): 47–70.

Cheng Tiejun and Mark Seldon. 1997. "The Construction of Spatial Hierarchies: China's Hukou and Danwei System." In *New Perspectives on State Socialism in China,* ed. Timothy Cheek and Tony Saich, 23–50. Armonk, N.Y.: M. E. Sharpe.

China Daily. 1999. "Wangjing Accounted for 13 Percent of Total Housing Construction." http://www.chinadaily.com.cn (accessed January 31, 2002).

———. 2002a. "58 Percent of Resident Families Purchased Properties from Work-Units." http://www.chinadaily.com.cn (accessed January 4, 2002).

———. 2002b. "Beijingers' Income to Increase." May 21, 3.

———. 2002c. "Real Estate Industry Grows." *China Daily, Real Estate Supplement,* May 24, 1.

———. 2008. "China's Newly Emerging Middle Class." http://www.chinadaily.com.cn (accessed October 6, 2008).

ChinaToday.com. 2007. "General Statistics about Chinese Cities." http://www.chinatoday.com/city (accessed July 15, 2007).

Clammer, John. 2003. "Globalisation, Class, Consumption and Civil Society in South-east Asian Cities." *Urban Studies* 40(2): 403–19.

Cohen, Myron L. 1993. "Cultural and Political Inventions in Modern China: The Case of the Chinese 'Peasant.'" *Daedalus* 122(2): 151–70.

Collier, Andres K. 2004. "High-End Goods Fuel Boom in Retail Sales." http://www.china.scmp.com (accessed March 16, 2004).

Davis, Deborah S. 1993. "Urban Households: Supplicants to the Socialist State." In *Chinese Families in the Post-Mao Era,* ed. Deborah S. Davis and Stevan Harrell, 50–76. Berkeley: University of California Press.

———. 1995. "Introduction: Urban China." In *Urban Spaces in Contemporary China: The Potential for Autonomy and Community in Post-Mao China,* ed. Deborah S. Davis, Richard Kraus, Barry Naughton, and Elizabeth J. Perry, 1–22. Cambridge: Cambridge University Press.

———, ed. 2000. *The Consumer Revolution in Urban China.* Berkeley: University of California Press.

Davis, Deborah S., and Stevan Harrell, eds. 1993. *Chinese Families in the Post-Mao Era.* Berkeley: University of California Press.

Davis, Deborah S., Richard Kraus, Barry Naughton, and Elizabeth J. Perry, eds. 1995. *Urban Spaces in Contemporary China: The Potential for Autonomy and Community in Post-Mao China.* Cambridge: Cambridge University Press.

Davis, Mike. 1990. *City of Quartz.* London: Verso.

de Certeau, Michel. 1984. *The Practice of Everyday Life.* Trans. Steven Rendall. Berkeley: University of California Press.

Douglas, Mary, and Baron Isherwood. 1979. *The World of Goods.* New York: Basic Books.

Dutton, Michael, ed. 1998. *Streetlife China.* Cambridge: Cambridge University Press.

Dutton, Michael, Hsiu-ju Stacy Lu, and Dong Dong Wu. 2008. *Beijing Time.* Cambridge, Mass.: Harvard University Press.

Erwin, Kathleen. 2000. "Heart-to-Heart, Phone-to-Phone: Family Values, Sexuality, and the Politics of Shanghai's Advice Hotlines." In *The Consumer Revolution in Urban China,* ed. Deborah S. Davis, 145–70. Berkeley: University of California Press.

Fan, Cindy C. 1999. "Migration in a Socialist Transitional Economy: Heterogeneity, Socioeconomic and Spatial Characteristics of Migrants in China and Guangdong Province." *International Migration Review* 33(4): 954–87.

Fang, David. 2003. "Breakdown in Communal Life Is the Heavy Price of Progress." http://www.china.scmp.com (accessed September 22, 2003).

Farrar, Margaret E. 2002. "Making the City Beautiful: Aesthetic Reform and the (Dis)placement of Bodies." In *Embodied Utopias: Gender, Social Change and the Modern Metropolis,* ed. Amy Bingaman, Lise Sanders, and Rebecca Zorach, 37–54. New York: Routledge.

Feng J. et al. 2004. "1990 niandai Beijing jiaoqu huade zuixin fazhan qushi jiqi duice" [The development of suburbanization of Beijing and its countermeasures in the 1990s]. *Chengshi Guihua* [City Planning Review] 28(3): 13–29.

Feng Wang. 2003. "Housing Improvement and Distribution in Urban China: Initial Evidence from China's 2000 Census." *China Review* 3(2): 121–43.

Fleischer, Friederike. 2006. "Speaking Bitter-Sweetness: China's Urban Elderly in the Reform Period." *Asian Anthropology* 5:31–55.

———. 2007a. "'To Choose a House Means to Choose a Lifestyle': The Consumption of Housing and Class-Structuration in Urban China." *City & Society* 19(2): 287–311.

———. 2007b. "Settling into Uncertainty: Migrants in Beijing's Suburban Transformations." Max Planck Institute for Social Anthropology Working Paper 96.

Flyvbjerg, B., and T. Richardson. 1998. "In Search of the Dark Side of Planning Theory." Paper presented at the Third Oxford Conference on Planning Theory, Oxford Brookes University, April 2–4.

Foucault, Michel. 1972. *Power/Knowledge.* New York: Pantheon.

———. 1979. *Discipline and Punish: The Birth of the Prison.* New York: Vintage.

Fraser, David. 2000. "Inventing Oasis: Luxury Housing Advertisements and Reconfiguring Domestic Space in Shanghai." In *The Consumer Revolution in Urban China,* ed. Deborah S. Davis, 25–53. Berkeley: University of California Press.

Friedmann, John. 2005. *China's Urban Transition.* Minneapolis: University of Minnesota Press.

Gaetano, Arianne M., and Tamara Jacka, eds. 2004. *On the Move: Women in Rural-to-Urban Migration in Contemporary China.* New York: Columbia University Press.

Gao Haiping. 2001. "Olympic Bubble to Burst Over Your Apartment?" *MetroZine Beijing,* September 2, 56–57.

Gaubatz, Piper Rae. 1995. "Urban Transformation in Post-Mao China: Impacts of the Reform Era on China's Urban Form." In *Urban Spaces in Contemporary China: The Potential for Autonomy and Community in Post-Mao China,* ed.

Deborah S. David, Richard Kraus, Barry Naughton, and Elizabeth J. Perry, 28–60. Cambridge: Cambridge University Press.

———. 1999. "China's Urban Transformation: Patterns and Processes of Morphological Change in Beijing, Shanghai, and Guangzhou." *Urban Studies* 36(9): 1495–1522.

Giddens, Anthony. 1973. *The Class Structure of the Advanced Societies.* London: Hutchinson.

———. 1981. *The Class Structure of the Advanced Societies.* London: Hutchinson.

———. 1990. *The Consequences of Modernity.* Stanford, Calif.: Stanford University Press.

Gilmartin, Christina. 1993. "Gender in the Formation of a Communist Body Politic." *Modern China* 19(3): 299–329.

Gilmartin, Christina, Gail Hershatter, Lisa Rofel, and Tyrene White, eds. 1994. *Engendering China: Women, Culture, and the State.* Cambridge, Mass.: Harvard University Press.

Glick-Schiller, Nina. 2005. "Transnational Urbanism as a Way of Life: A Research Topic Not a Metaphor." *City & Society* 17(1): 49–64.

Gong Xikui. 1998. "Household Registration and the Caste-Like Quality of Peasant Life." In *Streetlife China,* ed. Michael Dutton, 81–85. Cambridge: Cambridge University Press.

Gu Chaolin and Liu Haiyong. 2002. "Social Polarization and Segregation in Beijing." In *The New Chinese City: Globalization and Market Reform,* ed. John R. Logan, 198–211. Malden, Mass.: Blackwell.

Gu C. and Shen J. 2003. "Tranformation of Urban Socio-spatial Structure in Socialist Market Economies: The Case of Beijing." *Habitat International* 27(1): 107–22.

Guojia tongjiju [China Statistics Bureau]. 2007. *Zhongguo Tongji Nianjian 2007* [China statistical yearbook 2007]. Beijing: Beijing Tongji Chubanshi [Beijing Statistics Press].

Guojia tongjiju shehui tongjisi [National Statistics Bureau Social Statistics Department], ed. 1994. *Zhongguo Shehui Tongji Ziliao* [Statistical material on Chinese society]. Beijing: Zhongguo Tongji Chubanshi [China Statistics Press].

Hanser, Amy. 2008. *Service Encounters: Class, Gender, and the Market for Social Distinction in Urban China.* Stanford, Calif.: Stanford University Press.

Harvey, David. 1989. *The Urban Experience.* Baltimore, Md.: Johns Hopkins University Press.

———. 1990. *The Condition of Postmodernity.* Malden, Mass.: Blackwell.

———. 2003. *Paris, Capital of Modernity.* New York: Routledge.

He Xinghan. 1998. "People of the Work Unit." In *Streetlife China,* ed. Michael Dutton, 42–52. Cambridge: Cambridge University Press.

Hinton, William. 1966. *Fanshen: A Documentary of Revolution in a Chinese Village.* New York: Monthly Review Press.

Holsten, James. 1989. *The Modernist City: An Anthropological Critique of Brasilia.* Chicago: University of Chicago Press.

Holt, Douglas B. 1998. "Does Cultural Capital Structure American Consumption?" *Journal of Consumer Research* 25:1–25.

Hsu, Caroline. 2007. *Creating Market Socialism: How Ordinary People Are Shaping Class and Status in China.* Durham, N.C.: Duke University Press.

Hu Xiuhong and David H. Kaplan. 2001. "The Emergence of Affluence in Beijing: Residential Social Stratification in China's Capital City." *Urban Geography* 22(1): 54–77.

Huang Youqin and William A. V. Clark. 2002. "Housing Tenure Choice in Transitional Urban China: A Multilevel Analysis." *Urban Studies* 39(1): 7–32.

Huang Youqin and Setha M. Low. 2008. "Is Gating Always Exclusionary? A Comparative Analysis of Gated Communities in American and Chinese Cities." In *Urban China in Transition,* ed. John R. Logan, 182–202. Malden, Mass.: Blackwell.

Ikels, Charlotte. 1996. *The Return of the God of Wealth: The Transition to a Market Economy in Urban China.* Stanford, Calif.: Stanford University Press.

———, ed. 2004. *Filial Piety: Practice and Discourse in Contemporary East Asia.* Stanford, Calif.: Stanford University Press.

Jacka, Tamara. 2005. "Finding a Place: Negotiations of Modernization and Globalization among Rural Women in Beijing." *Critical Asian Studies* 37(1): 51–74.

Jacobs, Andrew. 2008. "Two Women Sentenced to 'Re-education' in China." http://www.scmp.com (accessed August 21, 2008).

Jansson, André. 2003. "The Negotiated City Image: Symbolic Reproduction and Change through Urban Consumption." *Urban Studies* 40(3): 463–79.

Jeffrey, Lyn. 2001. "Placing Practices: Transnational Network Marketing in Mainland China." In *ChinaUrban: Ethnographies of Contemporary Culture,* ed. Nancy N. Chen, Constance D. Clark, Suzanne Z. Gottschang, and Lyn Jeffrey, 23–42. Durham, N.C.: Duke University Press.

Jiang Zhuqing. 2002. "Decades-old Residence System Being Replaced." *China Daily,* January 10, 5.

Jie Fan and Wolfgang Taubmann. 2002. "Migrant Enclaves in Large Chinese Cities." In *The New Chinese City: Globalization and Market Reform,* ed. John R. Logan, 184–97. Malden, Mass.: Blackwell.

Jin Liming. 2001. "Qianlun xin chengshi wenhua yi xin chengshi kongjian guihua linian" [Discussion of the new urban culture and new urban spatial planning]. *Chengshi Guihua* [City Planning Review] 25(4): 14–20.

Johnson, Linda Cook. 1995. *Shanghai: From Market Town to Treaty Port, 1074–1858.* Stanford, Calif.: Stanford University Press.

Kaneff, Deema. 2002. "Why People Don't Die 'Naturally' Any More: Changing Relations between 'The Individual' and 'The State' in Post-Socialist Bulgaria." *Journal of the Royal Anthropological Institute* 8:89–105.

Kellner, Douglas. 1994. *Baudrillard: A Critical Reader.* Cambridge, Mass.: Wiley-Blackwell.

Khan, Azizur Rahman, and Carl Riskin. 2005. "China's Household Income and Its Distribution, 1995 and 2002." *China Quarterly* 182:356–84.

Kristeva, Julia. 1982. *Powers of Horrors: An Essay on Abjection.* Trans. L. S. Roudiez. New York: Columbia University Press.

Latham, Kevin. 2002. "Den Kosum Überdenken: Soziale Palliative und Rhetorik der Transition im postsozialistischen China." In *Postsozialismus: Transformationsprozess in Europa and Asien aus ethnologischer Perspektive,* ed. Chris Hann, 317–44. Frankfurt/Main: Campus.

Lechte, John. 1994. *Fifty Key Contemporary Thinkers: From Structuralism to Postmodernity.* London: Routledge.

Lee Ching Kwan. 1998. *Gender and the South China Miracle: Two Worlds of Factory Women.* Berkeley: University of California Press.

Lefebvre, Henri. 1991. *The Production of Space.* Trans. D. Nicholson-Smith. Malden, Mass.: Blackwell.

Li Bin. 2002. "Zhongguo zhufang gaige zhidu de fenge xing" [The unequal nature of China's housing reform]. *Shehuixue Yanjiu* [Research in the Social Sciences], 2:80–87.

Li Chunling. 2002. "The Class Structure of China's Urban Society during the Transitional Period." *Social Sciences in China* 23(1): 91–99.

Li D. 1995. "Dangdai Zhonguo Yimin Jiben Jingyan" [Basic experiences of the contemporary migration in China]. *Renkou Yanjiu* [Population Research] 2:57–60.

Li Jian and Niu Xiaohan. 2001. "New Middle Class in Beijing: A Case Study." Unpublished paper, Lund University, Centre for East and Southeast Asian Studies.

Li, Lillian M., Alison J. Dray-Novey, and Kong Haili. 2008. *Beijing: From Imperial City to Olympic City.* New York: Palgrave Macmillan.

Li Lulu, Yang Xiao, and Wang Fengyu. 1991. "The Structure of Social Stratification and the Modernisation Process in Contemporary China." *International Sociology* 6(1): 25–36.

Li Qiang. 2001. *Shehui Fenceng Yu Pinfu Chabie* [Social stratification and inequality]. Xiamen: Lujiang Chubanshi [Lujiang Press].

Li, Raymond. 2007a. "Can't Read, Can't Write, No Job: Rural Poor Struggle in Big Cities." http://www.china.scmp.com (accessed May 4, 2007).

———. 2007b. "Property Owners Plant Seed of Democracy." http://www.scmp.com (accessed May 6, 2007).

Li Shouen. 2003. "Lun quanmian jianshe xiaokang shehui" [On building a well-off society in an all around way]. *Shishi Qiushi* [Seek Truth from Facts] 1:13–16.

Li Si-ming. 2003. "Housing Tenure and Residential Mobility in Urban China: A Study of Commodity Housing Development in Beijing and Guangzhou." *Urban Affairs Review* 38(4): 510–34.

Li Si-ming and Siu Yat-ming. 2001. "Residential Mobility and Urban Restructuring Under Market Transition: A Study of Guangzhou, China." *Professional Geographer* 53(2): 219–29.

Li Xin. 2001. "2008 Beijing Olympics . . . Unique Legacy, Historic Opportunity." *Business Beijing,* August, 14–17.

————. 2002. "Party Chief's Pledge to 'Elevate' People's Lives." *Business Beijing,* June, 38–39.

Liechty, Mark. 2003. *Suitably Modern: Making Middle-Class Culture in a New Consumer Society.* Princeton, N.J.: Princeton University Press.

Lietsch, Jutta. 1995. "Baomu: Domestic Workers." In *China for Women: Travel and Culture,* ed. Feminist Press, 153–60. New York: Feminist Press at City University of New York.

Lim, Louisa. 2004. "Beijing's Building Revolution." http://news.bbc.co.uk (accessed March 9, 2004).

Lin Nan and Bian Yanjie. 1991. "Getting Ahead in Urban China." *American Journal of Sociology* 97:657–88.

Liu Guoguang. 2002. "Tigao xiaofeilü shi kuoda neixu de biyou zhi lu" [Increasing the consumption rate is the road we have to follow to raise domestic demand]. *Zhongguo Jingmao Daokan* [Journal of Chinese Economy and Trade] 8:9–11.

Liu Jingming and Li Lulu. 2006. "Stratification: Residential Space, Lifestyle, Social Interaction, and Stratum Identification." *Chinese Sociology and Anthropology* 38(4): 55–90.

Liu Xin. 1997. "Space, Mobility, and Flexibility: Chinese Villagers and Scholars Negotiate Power at Home and Abroad." In *Ungrounded Empires: The Cultural Politics of Modern Chinese Transnationalism,* ed. Aiwah Ong and Donald Nonini, 91–114. New York: Routledge.

————. 2002. "Strata Consciousness in Transformation-Era Urban China." *Social Sciences in China* 23(1): 81–89.

Logan, John R., ed. 2002. *The New Chinese City: Globalization and Market Reform.* Malden, Mass.: Blackwell.

Logan, John R., and Bian Yanjie. 1993. "Inequalities in Access to Community Resources in a Chinese City." *Social Forces* 72(2): 555–76.

Logan, John R., Bian Yanjie, and Bian Fuqin. 1999. "Housing Inequality in Urban China in the 1990s." *International Journal of Urban and Regional Research* 23:7–25.

Low, Setha M. 1996. "The Anthropology of Cities: Imagining and Theorizing the City." *Annual Review of Anthropology* 25:383–409.

Lu Duanfang. 2006. *Remaking Chinese Urban Form: Modernity, Scarcity and Space, 1949-2005.* London: Routledge.

Lu Hanchao. 1995. "Away from Nanking Road: Small Stores and Neighborhood Life in Modern Shanghai." *Journal of Asian Studies* 54(1): 92–123.

Lü Xiaobo and Elizabeth Perry, eds. 1997. *Danwei: The Changing Chinese Workplace in Historical and Comparative Perspective.* Armonk, N.Y.: M. E. Sharpe.

Lu Xueyi, ed. 2002. *Dangdai Zhongguo Shehui Jieceng Yanjiu Baogao.* [Research report on contemporary China's social stratification] Beijing: Shehui kexue wenxian chubanshe [Social Sciences Document Press].

Ma, Josephine. 2002. "Holidaying Rural Migrants Leave Vacuum in Cities." http://www.china.scmp.com (accessed February 18, 2002).

———. 2003a. "Parents Assail Kindergarten Contract." http://www.china.scmp.com (accessed July 30, 2003).

———. 2003b. "Middle-Class Homeowners Stand Up for Their Rights." http://www.china.scmp.com (accessed August 6, 2003).

———. 2003c. "Beijing Flat-Owners in Police Standoff." http://www.china.scmp.com (accessed September 24, 2003).

Ma, Laurence J. C. 1979. "The Chinese Approach to City Planning: Policy, Administration, and Action." *Asian Survey* 19(9): 838–55.

———. 1981. "Urban Housing Supply in the People's Republic of China." In *Urban Development in China,* ed. Laurence J. C. Ma and Edward W. Hanten, 222–59. Boulder, Colo.: Westview Press.

Ma, Laurence J. C., and Biao Xiang. 1998. "Native Place, Migration and the Emergence of Peasant Enclaves in Beijing." *China Quarterly* 155:546–81.

Massey, Doreen. 1992. "Politics and Space/Time." *New Left Review* 196:65–84.

———. 1993. "Power-Geometry and a Progressive Sense of Place." In *Mapping the Future: Local Cultures, Global Change,* ed. J. Bird, Barry Curtis, Tim Putnam, and George Robertson, 59–69. New York: Routledge.

———. 1994. *Space, Place, and Gender.* Minneapolis: University of Minnesota Press.

McGee T. 1989. "Urbanisasi or Kotadesasi? Evolving Patterns of Urbanization in Asia." In *Urbanization in Asia,* ed. F. J. Costa, A. K. Dutt. L. C. J. Ma, and A. G. Noble, 93–108. Honolulu: University of Hawaii Press.

———. 1991. "The Emergence of Desakota Regions in Asia: Expanding a Hypothesis." In *The Extended Metropolis: Settlement Transition in Asia,* ed. N. B. Ginsburg, B. Koppel, and T. McGee, 3–25. Honolulu: University of Hawaii Press.

Meng Yanchun. 2000. "Jincheng gaizao guochengzhongde zhongchan jiecenghua xianjia" [Gentrification in the process of urban renewal]. *Chengshi Guihua Huikan* [City Planning Forum] 1:48–51.

Miller, Daniel. 1997. *Capitalism: An Ethnographic Approach.* Oxford: Berg.

———. 1998. *A Theory of Shopping.* Ithaca, N.Y.: Cornell University Press.

Modan, Gabriella G. 2006. *Turf-Wars: Discourse, Diversity, and the Politics of Place.* Malden, Mass.: Blackwell.

Moore, Henrietta L. 1988. *Feminism and Anthropology.* Minneapolis: University of Minnesota Press.

Mote, F. W. 1977. "The Transformation of Nanking, 1350–1400." In *The City in Late Imperial Times,* ed. G. William Skinner, 101–53. Stanford, Calif.: Stanford University Press.

Naughton, Barry. 1988. "The Third Front: Defense Industrialization in the Chinese Interior." *China Quarterly* 115:315–86.

———. 1995. "Cities in the Chinese Economic System: Changing Roles and Conditions for Autonomy." In *Urban Spaces in Contemporary China: The Potential for Autonomy and Community in Post-Mao China,* ed. Deborah S. David, Richard Kraus, Barry Naughton, and Elizabeth J. Perry, 61–89. Cambridge: Cambridge University Press.

Ning Deng. 2000. "21 shijie zhongguo chengshihua jizhi yanjin" [Study on China's urbanization mechanism in the twenty-first century]. *Chengshi Guihua Huikan* [City Planning Forum] 3:41–46.

Oi, Jean C. 1989. *State and Peasant in Contemporary China: The Political Economy of Village Government.* Berkeley: University of California Press.

Painter, Joe. 2000. "Pierre Bourdieu." In *Thinking Space,* ed. Mike Crang and Nigel Thrift, 239–59. London: Routledge.

Pan Jianfeng. 2001. "Gaoxin zhi: shenpan gongzhen, lianjie he faguan gao suzhi de jiben baozhang" [High salaries system: the basic guarantee of fair trials and honest and high-quality judges]. *Zhengfa Luntan* [Legal Forum] 6:15–21.

Patico, Jennifer. 2008. *Consumption and Social Change in a Post-Soviet Middle Class.* Stanford, Calif.: Stanford University Press.

People's Daily Online. 2001. "Premier Reports on Outline of Five-year Plan." http://www.peoplesdaily.com.cn (accessed March 6, 2001).

Perry, Elizabeth. 1994. "Trends in the Study of Chinese Politics: State–Society Relations." *China Quarterly* 139:704–13.

Pine, Frances. 2006. "Lost Generations and the Problem of Reproduction: Emerging Inequalities in Kinship in Poland." Paper presented at Global Inequalities Workshop, Max Planck Institute for Social Anthropology, Halle, Germany.

Potter, Sulamith Heins. 1983. "The Position of Peasants in Modern China's Social Order." *Modern China* 9(4): 465–99.

Potter, Sulamith Heins, and Jack Potter. 1990. *China's Peasants: The Anthropology of a Revolution.* Cambridge: Cambridge University Press.

Rabinow, Paul. 1989. *French Modern: Norms and Forms of the Social Environment.* Cambridge, Mass.: MIT Press.

Read, Benjamin. 2003. "Democratizing the Neighbourhood? New Private Housing and Home-Owner Self-Organization in Urban China." *China Journal* 49:31–59.

Richardson, Tim, and Ole Jensen. 2003. "Linking Discourse and Space: Towards a Cultural Sociology of Space in Analysing Spatial Policy Discourse." *Urban Studies* 40(1): 7–22.

Roberts, Kenneth, Rachel Connelly, Xie Zhenming, and Zheng Zhenzhen. 2004. "Patterns of Temporary Labor Migration of Rural Women from Anhui and Sichuan." *China Journal* 52:49–70.

Robinson, Jean. 1985. "Of Women and Washing Machines: Employment, Housework, and the Reproduction of Motherhood in Socialist China." *China Quarterly* 101:32–57.

Rofel, Lisa. 1997. "Rethinking Modernity: Space and Factory Discipline in China." In *Culture, Power, Place: Explorations in Critical Anthropology,* ed. Akhil Gupta and James Ferguson, 155–78. Durham, N.C.: Duke University Press.

———. 1999. *Other Modernities: Gendered Yearnings in China after Socialism.* Berkeley: University of California Press.

Sack, Robert David. 1992. *Place, Modernity, and the Consumer's World.* Baltimore, Md.: Johns Hopkins University Press.

Samuels, Marwyn S., and Carmencita M. Samuels. 1989. "Beijing and the Power of Place in Modern China." In *The Power of Place*, ed. J. A. Agnew and J. S. Duncan, 202–27. Boston: Unwin Hyman.

Savadove, Bill. 2003. "Shanghai May Bring in Beggar-Free Zones." http://www .china.scmp.com (accessed November 20, 2003).

Schein, Louisa. 2001. "Urbanity, Cosmopolitanism, Consumption." In *ChinaUrban: Ethnographies of Contemporary Culture*, ed. Nancy N. Chen, Constance D. Clark, Suzanne Z. Gottschang, and Lyn Jeffrey, 225–41. Durham, N.C.: Duke University Press.

SCMP (Staff Reporter). 2005. "5,000 Yuan a Month puts Families in Middle Class." http://www.china.scmp.com (accessed January 20, 2005).

Seldon, Mark, ed. 1979. *The People's Republic of China: A Documentary History of Revolutionary Change*. New York: Monthly Review Press.

Shengxin Real Estate Development. 2000a. "Saint Angel wanshi ju cheng" [Saint Angel everything together development]. Beijing: Beijing Shengxin Fangdichan Kaifa Youxian [Beijing Shengxin Real Estate Development].

———. 2000b. "Shengxin dadi jiayuan . . ." [Shengxin mother earth homeland . . .]. Beijing: Beijing Shengxin Fangdichan Kaifa Youxian [Beijing Shengxin Real Estate Development].

Shevchenko, Olga. 2002. "'Between the Holes': Emerging Identities and Hybrid Patterns of Consumption in Post-Socialist Russia." *Europe-Asia Studies* 54(6): 841–66.

Shi Nianwen. 1999. "Survival and Mobility in Urban Labor Markets: A Case Study of Migrant Domestic Workers in Guangzhou City, People's Republic of China." Unpublished Ph.D. diss., Northeastern University, Chicago.

Sit, Victor F. S. 1995. *Beijing: The Nature and Planning of a Chinese Capital City*. New York: John Wiley and Sons.

Soja, Edward D. 1989. *Postmodern Geographies: The Reassertion of Space in Critical Social Theory*. London: Verso.

———. 1996. *Thirdspace: Journeys to Los Angeles and Other Real-and-Imagined Places*. Malden, Mass.: Blackwell.

Solinger, Dorothy J. 1995. "China's Urban Transients in the Transition from Socialism and the Collapse of the Communist 'Urban Public Goods Regime.'" *Comparative Politics* 7:127–46.

———. 1999. *Contesting Citizenship in Urban China: Peasant Migrants, the State, and the Logic of the Market*. Berkeley: University of California Press.

———. 2002. "Labour Market Reform and the Plight of the Laid-off Proletariat." *China Quarterly* 170:304–26.

Spence, Jonathan D. 1990. *The Search for Modern China*. New York: W. W. Norton.

Storey, John. 1993. *An Introductory Guide to Cultural Theory and Popular Culture*. Athens: University of Georgia Press.

Storper, Michael. 2000. "Lived Effects of the Contemporary Economy: Globalization, Inequality, and Consumer Society." *Public Culture* 12(2): 375–409.

Strand, David. 1995. "Conclusion: Historical Perspectives." In *Urban Spaces in Contemporary China: The Potential for Autonomy and Community in Post-Mao China*, ed. Deborah S. Davis, Richard Kraus, Barry Naughton, and Elizabeth J. Perry, 394–426. Cambridge: Cambridge University Press.

Su Wei. 2002. "Workers and Farmers No Longer Backbone of Society." *Beijing Today*, March 1, 7.

Tan Rui. 2002. "Growing Pains." *Beijing Weekend*, April 19–21, 5.

Tan Shen. 1997. "Nongcun laodongli liudongde xingbie chayi" [Gender difference among rural migrants]. *Shehuixue Yanjiu* [Research in the Social Sciences] 6(1): 42–48.

Tang Wenfang, and William L. Parish. 2000. *Chinese Urban Life Under Reform: The Changing Social Contract*. New York: Cambridge University Press.

Tang Wing-Shing. 2006. "Planning Beijing Strategically: 'One World, One Dream.'" *Town Planning Review* 77(3): 257–82.

Tang Xiaobing. 1998. "Decorating Culture: Notes on Interior Design, Interiority, and Interiorization." *Public Culture* 10(3): 530–48.

Tatlow, Didi Kirsten. 2004. "The 'Burbs of Beijing." http://www.china.scmp.com (accessed March 14, 2004).

Thelle, Hatla. 2004. *Better to Rely on Ourselves: Changing Social Rights in Urban China since 1979*. Copenhagen: NIAS Press.

Thompson, E. P. 1966. *The Making of the English Working Class*. New York: Vintage.

Tomba, Luigi. 2004. "Creating an Urban Middle Class: Social Engineering in Beijing." *China Journal* 51:1–26.

Treas, Judith, and Chen Jieming. 2000. "Living Arrangements, Income Pooling, and the Life Course in Urban Chinese Families." *Research on Aging* 22(3): 238–61.

Unger, Jonathan. 1993. "Urban Families in the Eighties: An Analysis of Chinese Surveys." In *Chinese Families in the Post-Mao Era*, ed. Deborah S. Davis and Stevan Harrell, 25–49. Berkeley: University of California Press.

Veeck, Ann. 2000. "The Revitalization of the Marketplace: Food Markets in Nanjing." In *The Consumer Revolution in Urban China*, ed. Deborah S. Davis, 107–23. Berkeley: University of California Press.

Verdery, Katherine. 1991. "Theorizing Socialism: A Prologue to the 'Transition.'" *American Ethnologist* 18(3): 419–39.

———. 1996. *What Was Socialism, and What Comes Next?* Princeton, N.J.: Princeton University Press.

Walder, Andrew G. 1986. *Communist Neo-Traditionalism: Work and Authority in Chinese Industry*. Berkeley: University of California Press.

Wan, Freda. 2004. "19pc Now Belong to the Middle Class." http://www.china.scmp.com (accessed March 31, 2004).

Wang Dandan. 2002a. "City Plan Depicts Life in Suburbs, Work Downtown." *Beijing Today*, May 31, 14.

———. 2002b. "Rent in Beijing Defies the Odds." *Beijing Today*, June 21, 14.

Wang Dandan and Wang Yang. 2002. "Five Factors behind High Apartment Prices in Beijing." *Beijing Today,* March 1, 14.

Wang Donggen and Li Si-ming. 2004. "Housing Preferences in a Transitional Housing System: The Case of Beijing, China." *Environment and Planning A* 36(1): 69–87.

———. 2006. "Socio-economic Differentials and Stated Housing Preferences in Guangzhou, China." *Habitat International* 30(2): 305–26.

Wang Fahui and Zhou Yixing. 1999. "Modeling Urban Population Densities in Beijing 1982–90: Suburbanisation and Its Causes." *Urban Studies* 36(2): 271–87.

Wang Feng. 2008. *Boundaries and Categories: Rising Inequality in Post-Socialist Urban China.* Stanford, Calif.: Stanford University Press.

Wang, Irene. 2005. "Only Half of the Nation Able to See Doctors." http://www .china.scmp.com (accessed January 11, 2005).

Wang Shaoguang, Hu Angang, and Ding Yuanzhu. 2002. "Behind China's Wealth Gap." http://www.china.scmp.com (accessed October 31, 2002).

Wang Ya-ping. 2001. "Urban Housing Reform and Finance in China: A Case Study of Beijing." *Urban Affairs Review* 36(5): 620–45.

Wang Ya-ping and Alan Murie. 1996. "The Process of Commercialization of Urban Housing in China." *Urban Studies* 33(6): 971–89.

Wang Zheng. 2000. "Gender, Employment and Women's Resistance." In *Chinese Society: Change, Conflict and Resistance,* ed. Elizabeth J. Perry and Mark Selden, 62–83. New York: Routledge.

Watson, James L., ed. 1984. *Class and Social Stratification in Post-Revolution China.* Cambridge: Cambridge University Press.

Weber, Max. 1978. *Economy and Society: An Outline of Interpretive Sociology.* Berkeley: University of California Press.

Whyte, Martin King. 2003. *China's Revolutions and Intergenerational Relations.* Ann Arbor: University of Michigan Center for Chinese Studies Press.

———. 2004. "Filial Obligations in Chinese Families: Paradoxes of Modernization." In *Filial Piety: Practice and Discourse in Contemporary East Asia,* ed. Charlotte Ikels, 106–27. Stanford, Calif.: Stanford University Press.

———. 2005. "Continuity and Change in Urban Chinese Family Life." *China Journal* 53:9–33.

Whyte, Martin King, and William L. Parish. 1984. *Urban Life in Contemporary China.* Chicago: University of Chicago Press.

Worldwatch Institute. 2006. "Rapid Growth of China's Cities Challenges Urban Planners." http://www.worldwatch.org/node/4148 (accessed July 23, 2007).

Wu Fulong. 1996. "Changes in the Structure of Public Housing Provision in Urban China." *Urban Studies* 33(9): 1601–28.

———. 1998. "The New Structure of Building Provision and the Transformation of the Urban Landscape in Metropolitan Guangzhou, China." *Urban Studies* 35(2): 259–84.

———. 2002. "Real Estate Development and the Transformation of Urban Space in China's Transitional Economy, with Special Reference to Shanghai." In *The*

New Chinese City: Globalization and Market Reform, ed. John R. Logan, 153–66. Malden, Mass.: Blackwell.

Wu Fulong and Anthony Gar-On Yeh. 1997. "Changing Spatial Distribution and Determinant of Land Development in Chinese Cities in the Transition from a Centrally Planned Economy to a Socialist Market Economy: A Case Study of Guangzhou." *Urban Studies* 34(11): 1851–80.

Wu Guobing and Liu Junyu. 2000. "Zhongwai chengshi jiaoquhuade bijiao" [Comparative study of suburbanization in China and abroad]. *Chengshi Guihua* [City Planning Review] 24(8): 36–39.

Wu Weiping. 2002. "Migrant Housing in Urban China: Choices and Constraints." *Urban Affairs Review* 38(1): 90–119.

Xiao Yin. 2002a. "Buy a Home, Live a Free Life." *China Daily, Real Estate Supplement,* June 20, 1.

———. 2002b. "More Economical Houses Demanded in Beijing." *China Daily, Real Estate Supplement,* August 1, 1.

Xie Ming. 2002. "Lun 'gaoxin yanglian'" [On "high salaries to foster honesty"]. *Beijing Xingzheng Xueyuan Xuebao* [Journal of the Beijing Institute of Public Administration] 3:14–19.

Xie Qingshu, A. R. Ghanbari Parsa, and Barry Redding. 2002. "The Emergence of the Urban Land Market in China: Evolution, Structure, Constraints and Perspectives." *Urban Studies* 39(8): 1375–98.

Xing Quan Zhang. 2002. "Governing Housing in China: State, Market, and Work-Units." *Journal of Housing and the Built Environment* 17(1): 7–20.

Yan Hairong. 2003. "Spectralization of the Rural: Reinterpreting the Labor Migration of Rural Young Women in Post-Mao China." *American Ethnologist* 30(4): 578–96.

Yan Xiaopei, Li Jia, Li Jianping, and Weng Jizhuan. 2002. "The Development of the Chinese Metropolis in the Period of Transition." In *The New Chinese City: Globalization and Market Reform,* ed. John R. Logan, 37–55. Malden, Mass.: Blackwell.

Yan Yunxiang. 1997. "McDonald's in Beijing: The Localization of Americana." In *Golden Arches East: McDonald's in East Asia,* ed. James Watson, 39–76. Stanford, Calif.: Stanford University Press.

Yan Zhimin, ed. 2002. *Zhongguo Xian Jieduan Jieji Jieceng Yanjiu* [Research on the classes and strata in China during the initial phase]. Beijing: Zhonggong Zhongyang Dangxiao Chubanshe [Central Chinese Communist Party School Press].

Yanagisako, Sylvia J. 2002. *Producing Culture and Capital: Family Firms in Italy.* Princeton, N.J.: Princeton University Press.

Yang, Mayfair Mei-hui. 1994. *Gifts, Favors, and Banquets: The Art of Social Relationships in China.* Ithaca, N.Y.: Cornell University Press.

———. 1997. "Mass-Media and Transnational Subjectivity in Shanghai: Notes on (Re)Cosmopolitanism in a Chinese Metropolis." In *Ungrounded Empires: The Cultural Politics of Modern Chinese Transnationalism,* ed. Aiwah Ong and Donald Nonini, 287–319. New York: Routledge.

————, ed. 1999. *Spaces of Their Own: Women's Public Sphere in Transitional China.* Minneapolis: University of Minnesota Press.

Ye Jun. 2002a. "In the Driving Seat." *Beijing Weekend,* May 31–June 2, 6.

————. 2002b. "Going Nowhere Fast." *Beijing Weekend,* June 7–9, 6.

Ye Shunzan. 1987. "Urban Policies and Urban Housing Programs in China." In *Urbanization and Urban Policies in Pacific Asia,* ed. Roland J. Fuchs, Gavin W. Jones, and Ernesto M. Pernia, 301–16. Boulder, Colo.: Westview.

Yeh, Anthony Gar-On, and Wu Fulong. 1995. "Internal Structure of Chinese Cities in the Midst of Economic Reform." *Urban Geography* 16(6): 521–54.

————. 1996. "The New Land Development Process and Urban Development in Chinese Cities." *International Journal of Urban and Regional Research* 20:330–53.

Yi Shijie. 2002. "Tigao xiaofeilü ladong jingji cengzhang" [Increase the consumption rate, stimulate economic growth]. *Jingjixue Dongtai* [Trends in Economics] 10:14–17.

Yokohari, M., K. Takeuchi, T. Watanabe, and S. Yokota. 2000. "Beyond Greenbelts and Zoning: A New Planning Concept for the Environment of Asian Mega-Cities." *Landscape and Urban Planning* 47:159–71.

Yu, Verna. 2003. "Misery of Migrant Children Exposed." http://www.china.scmp .com (accessed November 7, 2003).

Zhang Li. 2001. *Strangers in the City: Reconfigurations of Space, Power, and Social Networks within China's Floating Population.* Stanford, Calif.: Stanford University Press.

————. 2002. "Spatiality and Urban Citizenship in Late Socialist China." *Public Culture* 14(2): 311–34.

————. 2004. "Intersecting Space, Class, and Consumption: A Cultural Inquiry of a New Jieceng Formation in the Neoliberalizing China." Paper prepared for the workshop "The Social, Cultural, and Political Implications of Privatization in the People's Republic of China," Shanghai, China, June 28–29.

Zhang T. 2000. "Land Market Forces and Government's Role in Sprawl." *Cities* 17:123–35.

————. 2001. "1990 niandai zhongguo chengshi kongjian jiegoude bianhua ji qi dongli jizhi" [The urban restructuring of Chinese cities in the 1990s: its dynamic mechanism]. *Chengshi Guihua* [City Planning Review] 25(7): 7–14.

Zhang Zhen. 2000. "Mediating Time: The 'Rice Bowl of Youth' in Fin de Siècle Urban China." *Public Culture* 12(1): 93–113.

Zhong Rong. 2002a. "Retirement Complex to Care for Aged." *China Daily, Real Estate Supplement,* May 24, 1.

————. 2002b. "Xiangshan Area to Become Real Estate Hot Spot." *China Daily, Real Estate Supplement,* August 1, 1.

Zhong Yi Tong and R. Allen Hays. 1996. "The Transformation of the Urban Housing System in China." *Urban Affairs Review* 31(5): 625–58.

Zhou Changcheng, ed. 2001. *Shehui fazhan yu shenghuo zhiliang* [Social development and the quality of life]. Beijing: Shehui Kexue Wenxian Chubanshi [Social Sciences Document Press].

Zhou Min and John R. Logan. 2002. "Market Transition and the Commodification of Housing in Urban China." In *The New Chinese City: Globalization and Market Reform,* ed. John R. Logan, 137–52. Malden, Mass.: Blackwell.

Zhou Yixing and John R. Logan. 2005. "Suburbanization of Urban China: A Conceptual Framework." http://www.albany.edu/chinanet/neworleans/Zhou-Logan .doc.

———. 2008. "Growth on the Edge: The New Chinese Metropolis." In *Urban China in Transition,* ed. John R. Logan, 140–60. Malden, Mass.: Blackwell.

Zhou Yixing and Laurence J. C. Ma. 2000. "Economic Restructuring and Suburbanization in China." *Urban Geography* 21(3): 205–36.

Zhu Jieming. 2000. "The Changing Mode of Housing Provision in Transitional China." *Urban Affairs Review* 35(4): 502–19.

Zhu Zixuan and Reginald Yin-Wang Kwok. 1997. "Beijing: The Expression of National Political Ideology." In *Culture and the City in East Asia,* ed. W. B. Kim, M. Douglas, S.-C. Choe, K. C. Ho, 125–50. New York: Oxford University Press.

INDEX

advertising: environment and, xxiii, 37, 132; new housing complexes and, 37–39, 129–32. *See also* status

affluence: consumption and, 182n12; suburbanization and, 49, 165n25; young, educated couples and, 94, 147. *See also* class; consumption; home-ownership; income; lifestyle; middle class; modernity; state sector; structuration; Wangjing

agency: consumption and, xxi–xxii; diverging, 137; middle class and, 149; migrants and, 122; place making and, xxxiv, 49, 109, 145

agents, social, xi, xiii, 67, 137–38, 149, 165n13

airport, x; advertisement and, 33, 132; Capital Airport Highway, xiv, 33

Anagnost, Ann, xxiii, 105, 124, 127, 133, 142, 182n10

anonymity: middle-level complexes and, 41, 60, 66. *See also* housing; neighborhood; new residential compounds

apartments, 36; cohabitation and space, 22, 52; danwei compounds and, 9, 22, 45, 51–54, 58, 92; decoration of, 34, 40, 113–14, 116;

individualism and, 115–16; low-level commodity housing and, 64; mid-level commodity housing and, 37–39, 40–41, 93; mid-level economy housing and, 42, 90; prices, xv, 37, 40, 43, 45, 50–51, 55, 59, 177n26, 178n1, 180n21; purchase, 30, 45, 91, 177n22. *See also* cohabitation; consumption; housing; neighborhood

architecture (design), xv, 164n11; as distinction, 131; low-level commodity complexes and, 43–44, 64; mid-level commodity complexes and, ix, xv, 34, 36–41, 117, 131, 179n8; mid-level economy complexes and, 42–43; old danwei compounds and, 9, 44–47; pingfang houses and, 47–49, 65–66. *See also* neighborhood; Wangjing

Atlantic Place, xv, 94, 129

Beijing, ix, xxviii–xxxi, 123, 163n1; communist make-over and, 2–4, 167n7; districts, xxix; reform period and, 17, 31, 34, 59, 82, 88–90, 111, 124, 128, 135, 137, 141, 163n3, 178n30; after the revolution, 3. *See also* city structure; urban development

complexes and, 36–37, 39, 131, 173n11. *See also* housing
commute: socialism and, 4–5, 11; reforms and, xvi, 24, 48, 55, 93. *See also* city structure; housing; urban development
compound. *See* neighborhood
construction, x, xiii, xxvi, 33, 48, 124, 131; companies, 39, 178n5; housing and, 4, 5, 9, 14, 29–30, 31–32, 36, 53, 146, 176n21, 177n28, 178n30; migrants and, ix, 100, 138; socialism and, 3–4, 5, 21, 167n6. *See also* city structure; housing; real estate; urban development
consumption, xix–xxii, 109, 112, 169n14; belonging and, xxi; citizenship and, xxiv, 143–44; class formation and, xii, xvii, xix–xxii, xxxiv, 71, 109–10, 111–12, 118–19, 181n2; conspicuous, xx, 110, 118, 145; consumer culture, xxi, 114, 124; as creative act, xxi, 119, 128, 145; distinction and, 109, 111–12, 117–19, 131, 145–46; economic development and, xx, 142; emotions and, 115; frugality, thrift, 113–14; generations and, 84, 112–14; global scale and, xx, 124–25, 128, 135, 182n12; government and, xxxiv, 78, 110, 142–43, 185n3; housing and, xii, 36, 109–10, 114–19, 132, 144–45; ideology of, xx; indirect spending, xxi, 119–22; lifestyle and, 118, 133, 145; as message, xxi, 109, 112, 118–19, 131; Miller on, xxi–xxii, 114–15, 145; modernity and, xx, xxxiv, 112, 114, 124–25, 142–43; modes of, xii; nationalism and, 165n16; place creation and, 109–10; socialism and, xx–xxi, 11, 17, 169n14; space and, 109, 118–19, 124, 138, 144–45; spending and, xx, 142–44; status and, 117–18, 124, 131, 145–46;

stratification and, xix–xxii, 36, 71, 124; structuration and, xxii, 109–10, 117, 145–46, 165n15; as telos, xx; Tomba on, 111. *See also* affluence; citizenship; class; habitus, housing; middle class; structuration; young and educated couples
control: built environment and, xix; danwei and, 9, 13, 93, 129, 164n11; migrants and, 142, 169n13, 185n27; modernity and, xxiii, 105; space and, 66, 125; state and, xxiv, 15, 26, 139. *See also* discourse; modernity; state
countryside, xv, 2, 5, 7, 26, 79–81, 96–100, 184n21; modernity and, xxii, 105–6. *See also* migrants; peasants; rural hinterland; work
cultural capital, xxiii, 121, 128; lack of, 98
Cultural Revolution, 13–14, 84, 170n24; city structure and, 14. *See also* city structure; urban development

daily life, xxi, 77, 88; organization of, xxv, 55; urban structure and, 58, 66. *See also* elderly; migrants; young and educated couples; young people
danwei (work-unit), xxv, 8–11, 20, 139, 164n11, 179n11; Bray on, 164n11, 169n17; class and, 80; community and, 12, 46–47, 60, 72; compound, 9–10, 44–47, 57, 60, 72, 129, 144, 179n11; continued importance, xxvii, 29, 31, 35, 55, 58, 63, 71, 111, 143, 172n11, 177n28; economic difficulties and, 64; health and, 21; housing and, 9–11, 29–30, 32, 35–36, 41–43, 44–47, 50–52, 56, 58, 60–63, 72, 86–87, 92–93, 143, 170n20, 170n21, 176n21, 177n27; privacy and, 92–93; reforms and, 19–22;

FRIEDERIKE FLEISCHER is assistant professor of anthropology at the Universidad de los Andes, Bogotá, Colombia, and an associate at the Max Planck Institute for Social Anthropology in Germany.